THEOLOGY WITHOUT
FOUNDATIONS

THEOLOGY WITHOUT FOUNDATIONS

RELIGIOUS PRACTICE AND THE FUTURE OF THEOLOGICAL TRUTH

Edited by

Stanley Hauerwas

Nancey Murphy

Mark Nation

ABINGDON PRESS
Nashville

THEOLOGY WITHOUT FOUNDATIONS:
RELIGIOUS PRACTICE AND THE FUTURE OF THEOLOGICAL TRUTH

Copyright © 1994 by Abingdon Press

94 95 96 97 98 99 00 01 02 03—10 9 8 7 6 5 4 3 2 1

Library of Congress Cataloging-in-Publication Data

Theology without foundations: religious practice and the future of theological
truth. / edited by Stanley Hauerwas, Nancey Murphy, and Mark Nation.
    p.   cm.
    ISBN 0-687-00280X
    1. Philosophical theology.   2. Truth (Christian theology).   I. Hauerwas, Stanley.
II. Murphy, Nancey.   III. Nation, Mark.
BT40.T438   1994   94-31027
230'.01--dc20   CIP

Scripture quotations, unless otherwise noted, are from the New Revised Standard Version
Bible, Copyright 1989 by the Division of Christian Education of the National Council of
Churches of Christ in the USA. Used by permission.

Printed in the United States of America on recycled, acid-free paper.

CONTENTS

NON-FOUNDATIONALISM
WITHOUT RELATIVISM

EDUCATION WITHOUT FOUNDATIONS

ACKNOWLEDGMENTS

Though we may believe that theology does not have the philo-sophical foundations many wish it had, that does not mean we do not receive support in a variety of ways in our doing of theology. Quite the contrary. In fact, it is partly because of friends that we do not need such foundations. The friends who have contributed essays to this book—friends of ours and friends of Jim McClen-don—were generous in offering their contributions and we thank them.

Though theology does not need philosophical foundations, it does need institutional support. We are grateful for the Divinity School at Duke University, Fuller Theological Seminary, and Abingdon Press for their support of this project. And, of course, it is the human faces of institutions that make them not only bearable but, at times, a joy to be affiliated with. In this regard, we want to thank Bob Ratcliff, editor at Abingdon, for his support and wise guidance in shaping the book, and Wanda Dunn, at Duke, whose willing spirit and graciousness have made the mechanics of putting the essays into the form of a book much more pleasant.

And, finally, we are grateful to Jim McClendon whose gener-ous spirit has enriched our lives and theologies in a variety of ways. We hope that spirit is evident throughout these essays and that they bring honor to this fine theologian.

With or Without Foundations?

This collection of essays came into being at the suggestion of Stanley Hauerwas, a long-time friend of James Wm. McClendon, Jr., and Mark Nation, one of McClendon's doctoral students. It was planned as a *Festschrift* to honor McClendon in the 70th year of his life, and his 40th year of teaching. Bob Ratcliff at Abingdon Press impressed upon us the need for the book to have a clear focus. Thus, "theology without foundations" was chosen as the organizing theme, in line with Hauerwas's recognition that one important characteristic of McClendon's work, across the several disciplines it spans, is its non- or anti-foundational character. In this regard it is akin to that of Hauerwas himself, as well as John Howard Yoder, and others, many of whom are contributors. It is the purpose of this introduction to orient the reader to the current discussion of foundationalism, and indicate briefly how the essays herein relate to that theme.

Foundationalism

Foundationalism is a theory about knowledge. More specifically, it is a theory about how claims to know can be justified. When we seek to justify a belief, we do so by relating it to (basing it upon, deriving it from) other beliefs. If these other beliefs are called into question, then they too must be justified. Foundationalists insist that this chain of justifications must stop somewhere: it must not be circular nor must it constitute an infinite regress. Thus, the regress must end in a "foundation" of beliefs that cannot themselves be called into question.[1]

The plausibility of the foundationalist theory of knowledge comes from a metaphor: knowledge as a building. Upper stories are built upon lower stories, but the whole thing comes tumbling down if it has no solid foundation. This metaphor has so thoroughly imbued our thinking that we can scarcely talk about knowledge without hints of it: good arguments are well-grounded and solidly constructed; suspicions are unfounded or baseless; disciplines that explore presuppositions are called foundational.

Some historians (Richard Rorty, for example) trace foundationalism all the way back to Plato, but more commonly it is identified with modern philosophy, beginning with René Descartes (1596–1650). It was a fateful day when Descartes, forced by cold weather to spend a day in a warm room in Germany, examined his "ideas," while meditating on the architecture visible through his window. "It is true," he said,

> that we never tear down all the houses in a city just to rebuild them in a different way and to make the streets more beautiful; but we do see that individual owners often have theirs torn down and rebuilt, and even that they may be forced to do so when the building is crumbling with age, or when the foundation is not firm and it is in danger of collapsing. By this example I was convinced that . . . as far as the opinions which I had been receiving since my birth were concerned, I could not do better than to reject them completely for once in my lifetime, and to resume them afterwards, or perhaps accept better ones in their place, when I had determined how they fitted into a rational scheme.
>
> And I firmly believed that by this means I would succeed in conducting my life much better than if I built only upon the old foundations and gave credence to the principles which I had acquired in my childhood without even having examined them to see whether they were true or not.[2]

Modern philosophy from then on has been captivated by the architectural picture.

Why the anxiety? Why the perceived need to justify all received knowledge? We are so much the children of the modern world view that this question may not even arise. Yet there is an historical explanation. Stephen Toulmin offers plausible speculations regarding the cultural climate that gave foundationalism its appeal. Descartes lived through the Thirty Years' War (1618–1648). The bloodshed and chaos that followed upon differences of belief lent urgency to the quest for universal agreement; the epistemologist could render a service to humanity by finding a way to produce such agreement. Science and religion stood for two paths to knowledge: pure reason versus tradition. If human reason was a faculty shared universally, then a new structure built on the deliverances of human reason must garner universal assent. So, from Descartes's time, the ideal of human knowledge focused on the general, the universal, the timeless, the theoretical—in contrast to the local, the particular, the timely, the practical.[3]

One can do a tidy job of summing up the main currents in epistemology since Descartes by answering two questions: What is the nature or source of foundational beliefs—clear and distinct ideas, or impressions, or sense-data? and What kind of reasoning is to be used for the construction—deductive, inductive, constructive, hypothetico-deductive?

But if the story of modern philosophy has been that of a quest for certain and universal knowledge it is a sad story, for it has been a series of disappointments. Ideas that were clear and distinct to Descartes appear to others hopelessly vague or just plain false— for example, the premise in his argument for the existence of God, stating that "there must be at least as much reality in the efficient and total cause as in the effect."[4] Empirical foundations have proven to be less troublesome in themselves, but here the problem of construction looms large. David Hume showed that from a foundation in immediate experience, no solid (deductive) conclusions could be drawn regarding anything but immediate experiences. So there appears to be an epistemological corollary of Murphy's law at work: whenever the foundations are suitably indubitable, they will turn out to be useless for justifying any interesting claims; when we do find beliefs that are useful for justifying the rest of the structure, they always turn out to be questionable.

Two other problems undermine (note the metaphor!) the foundationalist project. One is that beliefs that are in fact usable for purposes of justification often turn out to presuppose beliefs that belong to the higher stories. For example, my belief that I am now seeing a blue book depends on background knowledge that I am viewing it under normal lighting conditions. Thus the foundationalist picture of linear reasoning (bottom to top) is an oversimplification; and if one of the rationales for having a foundation was to avoid circular reasoning, this is a devastating criticism.

Finally, Descartes's supposition that it was possible to begin philosophy with a clean slate turns out to have been mistaken.

One thing he failed to doubt was language,[5] and the wealth of knowledge (or error) enshrined therein (recall the connection between 'causation' and 'reality' in the premise quoted above). Also, *reasonably* to call a belief into question requires *reasons*, and those reasons must be unquestioned, at least for the time. For instance, one of Descartes's most powerful arguments against the reliability of sensory knowledge was based on the supposition that he might be dreaming—but this presupposes that there are such things as dreams. Only one beguiled by a picture could imagine that the whole had been called into question by means of such arguments.

Holism

Philosopher of science Karl Popper makes an interesting transition figure. Popper is still imagining knowledge to be structured as a building, but there is no longer a foundation:

> The empirical basis of objective science has thus nothing 'absolute' about it. Science does not rest upon solid bedrock. The bold structure of its theories rises, as it were, above a swamp. It is like a building erected on piles. The piles are driven down from above into the swamp, but not down to any natural or 'given' base; and if we stop driving the piles deeper, it is not because we have reached firm ground. We simply stop when we are satisfied that the piles are firm enough to carry the structure, at least for the time being.[6]

The decisive break with foundationalism came with the works of Willard V. O. Quine. In "Two Dogmas of Empiricism" he argued against the empiricist 'dogma' that each meaningful statement is equivalent to or can be reduced to terms that refer to immediate experience. The other 'dogma' was the analytic-synthetic distinction, which provided justification for a sharp differentiation between the sciences as empirical disciplines and philosophy as purely conceptual.

Quine's most important contribution, however, was a new picture or metaphor for knowledge: knowledge as a web or net:

> The totality of our so-called knowledge or beliefs, from the most casual matters of geography and history to the profoundest laws of atomic physics or even of pure mathematics and logic, is a man-made fabric which impinges on experience only along the

edges. Or, to change the figure, total science is like a field of force whose boundary conditions are experience. A conflict with experience at the periphery occasions re-adjustments in the interior of the field. Truth values have to be redistributed over some of our statements. Re-evaluation of some statements entails re-evaluation of others, because of their logical interconnections—the logical laws being in turn simply certain further statements of the system . . . . But the total field is so underdetermined by its boundary conditions, experience, that there is much latitude of choice as to what statements to re-evaluate in the light of any single contrary experience. No particular experiences are linked with any particular statements in the interior of the field, except indirectly through considerations of equilibrium affecting the field as a whole.[7]

Apart from the picture, Quine's "holist" theory of knowledge differs in several important respects from foundationalism. First, there are no indubitable (unrevisable) beliefs; nor are there any *sharp* distinctions among types of belief, only degrees of differences in how far a belief is from the experiential boundary.

Second, for foundationalists, reasoning (construction) goes in only one direction—up from the foundation. For holists there is no preferred direction, and the kinds of connections among beliefs in the web are many: strict logical implication, weaker probabilistic arguments, arguments 'forward' to further conclusions; arguments 'backwards' to presuppositions. In general, what 'holism' means is that each belief is supported by its ties to its neighboring beliefs, and ultimately, to the whole; the criterion of truth is coherence.

Quine's concern with justification, however, reached only to the question of how one justifies individual beliefs given the rest of the web. A second and more difficult question arises: given the actual (or even imagined) existence of more than one web, how is one to justify the whole? This may be the most pressing philosophical question for our day. Many argue it is not possible to justify an entire web; some say that it is not needed; and a few have proposed methods for such justification. One of these is Imre Lakatos in philosophy of science;[8] another is Alasdair MacIntyre.[9] Both have argued that justification of an entire "research program" or "tradition" requires attention to the way it has changed over time, taking account of new data or responding to new intellectual crises. Thus, narrative enters at a meta-level: justification of a tradition involves telling the story of the problems it has encountered and how it has overcome them.

An interesting development in recent epistemology from the point of view of theology and philosophy of religion has been the recognition of the role of formative texts—for Thomas Kuhn, classics such as Newton's *Principia*; for MacIntyre, literary or scriptural texts that create a world view. Thus, when we look at knowledge on a large enough scale, it all turns out to be the result of the interplay of texts and experience.

Relating Theories of Knowledge and Theories of Language

The standard theory of language in the modern world (at least in Anglo-American thought) has been referential and representative. That is, language has been thought to get its *meaning* by referring to objects or states of affairs in the world; its primary *function* has been taken to represent or mirror that reality.

Another characteristic of modern thought in general has been its atomistic and reductionistic tendencies. Thus, it is not surprising that philosophers of language have assumed that the proper way to understand language is to analyze it into its most basic components.

The referential theory of meaning in philosophy of language is the equivalent of foundationalism in epistemology: If we are to have a solid basis for attaching meaning to terms, one that is not subject to timely, local, particular uses and connotations, then reference is the only way to go.

Referentialism, however, is not merely a parallel to foundationalism; it is an integral part of the modern epistemological project itself. This fact shows up most clearly in the alliance between the logical positivists and the logical atomists: atomic sentences were to represent (refer to) atomic facts, which were to provide the foundation for all knowledge.

For language that did not fit this materialist model, some added expressivist theories; for example, moral language is significant because, while it does not describe facts in the world, it serves to express the emotions, attitudes, intentions of the speaker.

Because of the intimate connection between foundationalism and a referential theory of language, we should expect the rejection of foundationalism to be accompanied by equally significant changes in understandings of the nature of language. Compatible linguistic theories are also *holist*, but in a somewhat different sense. In the works of J. L. Austin and Ludwig Wittgenstein, attention shifts from concern to give a single theory of meaning for all language, to a concern to understand the multiple functions of language.[10] The focus on *use* leads to a concern with the relation of language to its context, both to the system of linguistic conventions that govern its use, and to the social context that makes it meaningful. The connection with non-foundational epistemology shows up in Wittgenstein's claim that there is no more basic foundation for language than the conventions of the community that uses it.

Theological Consequences of Foundationalism and Allied Theories of Language

Theologians in the modern period attempted to meet the foundationalist requirement for an indubitable starting point in several ways. Conservative theologians turned to Scripture, and here we can see the appeal of an inerrantist doctrine of Scripture—it is the only way to satisfy the demand for an unquestionable foundation.[11]

When the results of historical critical treatment of the Scriptures seemed to yield too meager a foundation for Christian doctrine, other theologians turned to religious experience for a foundation, and the liberal tradition was born. But foundationalism required a special kind of experience—not perceived miracles, or answered prayers, or even conversion experiences—but rather an inward experience that was *sui generis* and self-authenticating; an experience such that the one who had it could not doubt it.

Some would say that both the liberal and conservative strategies have failed. For the liberals, the problem is one of construction: how to get from an inward, subjective awareness to knowledge of a real God, external to the believer? In Karl Barth's terms, a Schleiermacher will lead inevitably to a Feuerbach. For the conservatives, the foundation turns out not to be a foundation at all, but the first floor of the construction, since the prior question always arises: how do you know that these books are in fact revelation? The grounds that can be given here always turn out to be less secure than foundationalist theories of knowledge require.

The impossibility of fitting theological method to the demands of foundationalist epistemology has resulted, in Jeffrey Stout's terms, in "endless methodological foreplay."[12] If this is an over-statement, we can at least make the more guarded claim that it has provided a key element of the standard shape of modern systematic theologies: most begin with a lengthy philosophical prolegomenon intended to lay out the foundation for the doctrinal work to follow.[13] It has ordinarily been assumed, as well, that doctrine is foundational for theological ethics.

George Lindbeck has explored modern theories of religious language. Two types of approach to the nature of religion and doctrine are the propositional and the experiential-expressivist. Again, philosophical theories help make clear the differences dividing liberals and conservatives. Conservatives hold to a propositional view of doctrine: religious language refers to and describes transcendent realities. Liberals take religious language, in the first instance, at least, to be descriptive of the believer's inner awareness—it expresses the experiences that are foundational for Christian theology.

The Role of James Wm. McClendon

The fact that this Introduction is written by McClendon's wife precludes the usual flowery and lavish praise. He will have to be content with the following sober and objective assessment of his place in recent scholarship.[14]

If philosophical foundationalism and allied theories of language, with the limited options they presented for theological method, have done so much to shape modern theology, we should expect dramatic repercussions to follow from the rejection of those long-entrenched philosophical positions. The essays in this volume will begin to display and describe these changes. However, great strides in this direction have already been made in the assorted writings of James McClendon.

In *Understanding Religious Convictions*, McClendon and James M. Smith used Austin's theory of language as "speech acts" to analyze religious language. Austin's non-reductionist account of language asks how an utterance fits into the broader context of human activity. Here the philosopher's concern is not with the meaning (alone), but with the broader category of success—in

Austin's terms, felicity or happiness. McClendon and Smith used Austin's theory of language to understand religious convictions—those deeply held beliefs that form our identities. The felicity or happiness of a *confession* of one's convictions depends not only upon the relevant linguistic and social conventions, and upon the confessor having the proper attitudes, but also upon how the confessed belief relates to "whatever else there is." Thus, the question of the happiness of religious language leads directly to a problem in the philosophy of religion: how are religious beliefs (convictions) to be justified, especially in a world of multiple convictional communities?

The non-foundational character of McClendon's and Smith's approach to the justification of convictions shows up most clearly in their claim that there is no conviction-free place to stand from which to evaluate religious convictions—the value-free study of religion is a fiction. In other words, there is no foundation (scientific, philosophical, or otherwise) from which to work toward consensus. However, this does not mean the rational debate of interconvictional issues is impossible.

Understanding Religious Convictions[15] may have been a book delivered prematurely from the press,[16] since it did not provoke much discussion at the time. Today, however, it would provide a voice in several lively debates, such as the discussion of Lindbeck's "cultural-linguistic" theory of religion and doctrine, and of MacIntyre's theory of tradition-constituted rationality and the justification of traditions. There are especially interesting parallels between McClendon's and Smith's approach to the justification of convictions and William Werpehowski's theory of "ad hoc apologetics";[17] for both, rational debate between convictional communities can proceed by finding, on an ad hoc basis, points of agreement about what is true, or just, or contributory to human flourishing, and from these shared starting points seek to enlarge the areas of agreement.

McClendon's earlier book, *Biography as Theology*,[18] had already explored the relations between professions of belief and their lived context—picking up the Wittgensteinian point that we do not really know what language (here, doctrines) means unless we can see how it is enfleshed in human life. Furthermore, doctrinal claims fail the test if they cannot be lived out. To put it in philo-

17

sophical terms, both meaning and justification require exemplification in life.[19]

But how does one describe a life (and the doctrines it exemplifies) apart from narrative? Here we see in germinal form the rationale for "narrative theology."

Is God GOD,[20] a collection of essays co-edited with Axel Steuer, displays the non-foundational trajectory of McClendon's thought in its assumption that arguments for the existence of God are secondary to discovery of a community's actual concept of God; that is, one approaches such apologetic questions not by finding (foundational) resources outside of Christian forms of life, but rather by displaying the rationality *and morality* of those forms of life themselves. In this case, the question is whether there is or can be a suitable coherence between the Christian concept of God and the one true GOD, as we come to know that one in trust, worship, and obedience.[21]

McClendon has completed two volumes of a projected three-volume systematic theology. The first volume, *Ethics: Systematic Theology,* Volume 1 appeared in 1986; *Doctrine:Systematic Theology,* Volume 2 in 1994; the third volume, *Vision*, is yet to be written.[22]

A persistent but mistaken criticism of *Ethics* is that it is an attempt to base doctrine on ethics. This mistake can be readily understood if those who make it are assuming a foundationalist model: the two subdisciplines of theology must be related as one 'story' to another, and the lower story must be constructed first. In fact, McClendon claims that the church's teachings and practices cannot be separated; the descriptive and normative task of displaying and reforming the shared life and convictions of the church can just as well begin with norms for living as with normative teachings.

The central aim of McClendon's systematics is to provide a theological exposition of the convictions and way of being Christian that he labels "baptist" (translation of the German *Täufer*). This broad and diverse stream of Christian life includes some contemporary Baptists, but also Mennonites, Brethren, Disciples of Christ, Pentecostals, Christian base communities, and others. There is no (foundational) justification for taking this particular starting point; its justification, if there is any, will be in the displayed coherence, fidelity to Scripture, and apt response to the experiences of human life that this way represents.

McClendon adopts a narrative methodology for the project, pursuant to his earlier recognition that convictions are not fully intelligible until we see how they are lived out, and also in line with current claims that the Scriptures can best be understood if we recognize their narrative shape,[23] and do not move immediately to reduce that storied content to doctrinal propositions, principles, and values.

The third volume, *Vision*, will not be a foundationalist prolegomenon simply moved to the end—a postlegomenon. Rather, it will take a broad look at the context in which the two earlier volumes do their work—the philosophical context, and the context of the many convictional communities that inhabit our globe.

The Present Volume

Contributions to this book were solicited in the four areas in which McClendon has done significant work: philosophy of religion, theological ethics, doctrinal theology, and narrative. However, we have arranged the essays into somewhat different categories, as the following overview makes clear.

Philosophy of Religion without Foundations

The rejection of foundationalism, and its allied theory of language-as-representation, has significant consequences for philosophy of religion, as we have already seen in *Understanding Religious Convictions*.

In "Worship and Autonomy," **James M. Smith**, extends the work done in *Understanding Religious Convictions*. He begins with reflections on the change from foundational to non-foundational philosophy of religion. The philosophy of religion up through the 1950s and 1960s assumed that one goal of philosophy of religion was to make religious belief appealing by deriving it from non-problematic, non-theological beliefs. But if theology is without foundations, in this sense, then the appeal must come from other sources.

One criterion that plays an especially important role in non-foundational treatments of religious belief is coherence. It is exactly this coherence that has been called into question by James

19

Rachels, who charges that worship is incompatible with human moral autonomy.[24] Smith answers by pointing out that the very meanings of 'moral autonomy' and 'worship' are matters of conviction. When we understand these terms within their proper religious settings, the incoherence disappears: for the happy *worshiper*, it is exactly in knowing and obeying God that one finds what conscience truly requires, and can thus take clear-eyed (*autonomous*) responsibility for one's behavior.

David B. Burrell, C.S.C, in "Convictions and Operative Warrant," tackles the problem of justifying a community's religious beliefs within a religiously pluralist world. He, too, turns to *Understanding Religious Convictions* for resources, pointing out that the relevant question, in this light, is the question whether *I* can truly profess the faith I do. However, Burrell is happier with unresolved questions of justification than McClendon and Smith, who hope that their work can help to discover what Wordsworth calls the "dark inscrutable workmanship" that can make even discordant elements one.[25] Here Burrell advocates what he calls an attitude of Socratic unknowing, which recognizes that I am not in a position to make an assessment of the truth of professions of other faiths, nor to dismiss them. In addition, Burrell emphasizes what might be called a Matthean pragmatism (see Mt. 7:16): the signs of authenticity of others' faith lie in their manner of living it out; it is the fruits that are telling.

Burrell compares McClendon's and Smiths's theory of convictions to Bernard Lonergan's understanding of the *activity* of making judgments as "virtually unconditioned." That is, one holds the object of that judgment to be true, while recognizing that problems may arise in the future that will overturn it. Similarly, McClendon and Smith recognize that our convictions must be held with *conviction* if we are to be people of character, despite the fact that this commitment goes beyond our capacities for 'rational' (in the Enlightenment sense) assessment of their worth.

Terrence W. Tilley, in his contribution, "In Favor of a 'Practical Theory of Religion': Montaigne and Pascal," further develops the "practical" theory of religion espoused by McClendon in *Doctrine*. According to McClendon, religions ought to be understood as sets of powerful practices, which embody the life-forming convictions of their practitioners. Tilley notes that this move distances

McClendon from the dominant strand of modern philosophy of religion, which focuses attention on religious belief abstracted from religious practice, and thus on issues of pure rationality suitable for the academic mind alone, to the exclusion of the more important question of the reasonableness or wisdom of participation in religious life. A practical approach to philosophy of religion must consider doxastic *practices*, the social location of the knower (which might induce "positional defects" in one's ability to know), and other non-cognitive ingredients, such as emotion, in the knowing process.

Michel de Montaigne anticipated current debates in philosophy of religion in his recognition of two patterns for justifying religious belief: the externalist and the internalist. The former seeks a solid external foundation for religious knowledge; the latter, often labeled fideist, presumes that whatever reasonableness can be found for religion will be found within, not before or under, religious commitment—and foreshadows positions such as those of Kierkegaard and D. Z. Phillips.

Montaigne's own position, which Tilley endorses, is that neither approach rightly understands the *practical* problem of choosing a *way of life*. His practical prescription is a form of dialogue that is truth-seeking, and anticipates the proposals of Jürgen Habermas and Richard Rorty in that it does not pretend to be uncommitted.

Tilley construes the problem that Pascal's wager was intended to solve as a practical one. Blaise Pascal recommends to unbelievers that they take up the practice of religion, since that set of practices will change them and enable them to believe what reason (by means of the wager) tells them it is in their best interests to believe. That is, unbelief is not a problem of the intellect, but of the passions; it is cured by practicing the faith, not by further arguments.

However, this solution fails to solve a further (practical) problem: which religious practices to take up? It is a mistake to assume that all religions are a live option, and the practical maxim is to choose among the available traditions the one that encourages devotion to that than which a greater cannot be conceived. This judgment is provisional, however, and subject to refinement through conversations with practitioners of other traditions.

So, what do we learn from these essays about philosophy of religion without foundations? All three essays assume points made in *Understanding Religious Convictions*: religious beliefs cannot be understood or evaluated in abstraction from the practices of the various religions; there is no universal, conviction-free place to stand from which convictional disputes can be adjudicated; however, this does not mean that rational assessment is impossible.

The three essays pursue the nature of that rational assessment, and make it clear that there are at least two strands of thought within post-foundationalist philosophy of religion. There is the strand Tilley identifies with Montaigne's internalists, nicely illustrated by Smith's work on the coherence of biblical traditions; there is also the practical or pragmatic strand, represented by Montaigne, Tilley, and Burrell. However, the line between these strands is not sharp if one takes internalists to be seeking coherence and consistency not only among beliefs but also with practices. One is obviously unreasonable to adhere to practices that are not practical. Thus, concern with practice versus coherence is more a difference of emphasis than a stark disagreement.

Theology Without Foundations

The branch of theology that deals with theological method and the justification of theological claims has often been called theological foundations. As already mentioned, systematic theologians influenced by foundationalism have generally begun theology with a prolegomenon—a philosophical justification for the doctrinal work to follow, and ultimately for ethics. All of this must be rethought in a post-foundationalist era, as the following essays make clear.

In "Walk and Word: The Alternatives to Methodologism," **John H. Yoder** criticizes the tendency of academic discussions of moral reasoning to begin with 'meta-ethics'—debates about the correct first principles for the discipline. He points out that this is in fact a foundationalist move—to find a level of thought that is somehow 'before' or 'beneath' the consideration of moral issues themselves.[26]

Yoder claims, instead, that meta-ethical issues properly arise only after a community has established moral guidelines and laws, usually when different and conflicting systems come into contact. Here such debates are useful.

It is not necessary, Yoder claims, to settle upon one moral idiom ('virtue' versus 'duty' versus 'rights') in order to carry on intelligible and effective discussions of moral issues. Rather, the focus should be on acquiring *skill* in matching linguistic resources to the shape of particular debates. The Bible's own pattern is to use a variety of ethical styles; the continued faithfulness of the community to the God of the Bible requires that the community's discourse be no narrower than the biblical story itself.

Ched Myers addresses the issue of theological method in "'I Will Ask *You* a Question': Interrogatory Theology." His goal is to follow McClendon's lead in doing theology from the more modest but authentic perspective of a determinate convictional community. He provides guidelines for a theology that is 'baptist,' but also non-Constantinian, post-modern, and biblical. Such a theology, he claims, will be just the opposite of a sectarian, 'withdrawn' stance; it will be an interrogatory or problematizing theology, which will engage the Powers whenever anyone is marginalized or oppressed.

Clues for how to do theology in this mode come from Mark's Jesus, whose questions to his interlocutors lay bare their inner conflicts—"I will ask *you* a question. . . . Did the baptism of John come from Heaven. . . ?" (Mk. 11:29–30).

Additional resources can be found in critical theory, with its tools for deconstructing society's foundational myths, but also from a set of practices developed by the Society of Friends, called testimonies, advices, and queries. These practices provide a vehicle for community self-assessment—a means of asking the hard questions about the community's own faithfulness. This method, says Myers, has three characteristics that reflect the concerns of post-modern theology: it puts the concrete before the theoretical; it puts the communal before the private; and it is open to constant rearticulation.

In "Ethnography-as-Theology: Inscribing the African American Sacred Story," **Theophus Smith** takes his departure from McClendon's work in *Biography as Theology*, wherein McClendon treated lives, such as Martin Luther King's, as performances of strategically selected biblical stories and images. However, Smith is interested in the way *communities* of African American Christians have lived out the biblical stories.

Scripture interprets itself typologically, and Christian communities interpret their lives in light of its figures. Smith highlights some of the types and figures that have given shape to African-American Christianity in his section on ethnography and biblical narrative.

David Kelsey has pointed out that the manner in which a community will take Scripture as authority depends on a prior metaphorical judgment regarding what Christianity is basically all about. Smith claims that the central metaphor that organizes black experiences of transformative cure, of healing and wholeness, is the Bible as "pharmacopeia." This image incorporates and transforms African experiences such as spiritual healing, as well as motifs such as the "trickster."

What do we learn from these essays about the direction for theology without foundations? The Enlightenment distinction between fact and value (theology and ethics) does not hold up. All three essayists, whether writing as theologians or ethicists, are asking how we find ways of living *and* thinking that are faithful to the biblical story. All three are attentive to the communal nature of life and thought. Smith, in particular, recognizes the contextual character of faithfulness—how must this particular people in this situation perform the biblical stories?

While all three authors take the Scriptures as normative for theology or ethics, all recognize that *how* a community uses and interprets the texts depends on prior judgments about the nature of the texts and how they figure into the community's ongoing practices—in short, they all espouse, in one way or another, a non-foundational use of Scripture.

Despite a great deal of agreement and overlap in these papers, they also illustrate an ongoing debate in post-foundational thought about the role and value of methodology—the study and exposition of methods of reasoning.

Non-foundational Theology and Narrative

The preceding section has already prepared the way for narrative approaches to theology and ethics. We have seen an emphasis on the Scriptures as narratives, and on the shaping of the ongoing life of the community in the light of these stories. We have also seen that stories of communal faithfulness provide sources for systematic reflection. The following essays illustrate some of the varied ways in which the turn from theories and propositions to stories is reshaping theology in this post-foundationalist era.

Stanley Hauerwas, in "The Church's One Foundation is Jesus Christ Her Lord; Or, In a World without Foundations: All We Have is the Church," includes three sermons, each intended to display one of the three "strands" that constitute McClendon's ethics. The body strand attends to our condition as a part of the material creation; Hauerwas's first sermon is on the Eucharist and the way in which its very materiality highlights the fact that Christianity is not against the body, sex, or pleasure. McClendon's second strand is the communal; Hauerwas's sermon celebrates the 100th anniversary of the Broadway United Methodist Church of South Bend by recognizing how scarce are communities such as that one, which manifest the unity Christ desired for his followers. That unity is expressed in the Eucharist (not only food for the body but remembrance of the story of how we became God's people); the unity is constituted by the fact that members are unable to tell their own stories without also telling one another's stories.

McClendon's third strand is the resurrection strand. Hauerwas's third sermon was preached at his own father's funeral, and tells his father's life story as a man whose character was shaped not only by the (harsh) communities in which he lived and worked (a bricklayer in Texas), but also by the in-breaking of God, whose gentle character produced a gentleness in him, preparing him ahead of time to gather with the other saints around God's throne.

McClendon, and now Ronald Thiemann and George Lindbeck as well, have stressed that theology is a second order discourse that describes and sometimes helps reform the first-order language of religion—its praying, preaching, confessing. Yet the first-order language is primary, and a theology that does not enrich preaching is of no value. Thus, Hauerwas's three sermons go some distance toward showing the legitimacy of McClendon's ethics.

Hauerwas would probably not appreciate our drawing methodological conclusions from this fact for testing theological and ethical claims. He echoes Yoder's judgment that there can be no formal method for theology in a world without foundations.

There is instead only the church and its practices, one of which is the practice or skill of doing theology.

Richard Steele, in "Narrative Theology and the Religious Affections," argues that *emotions* are a central component of human life in general, and of Christian faithfulness in particular. He claims that it is the stories of the communities to which we belong that shape our emotions, since those stories shape our view of reality and thus the *judgments* that are integral to emotion.

This paper extends and confirms McClendon's thesis that emotions, as one of the resources of our *embodied* selves, are an important focus of Christian ethics, as well as McClendon's claim that while certain sorts of emotions may be common to all cultures, the community in which one lives will form and re-form one's emotions.[27]

Steele contrasts his understanding of religious affections with that of Lindbeck's "experiential-expressivist" type. The latter understands the various religions to be cultural expressions of a universal human religious awareness. Steele sees this understanding of religion as a species of foundationalism, in that its proponents seek a universal origin for all religions that is more basic than the things that give a particular religion its distinctive character, such as its scriptures, liturgical customs, ascetic disciplines, and creeds.

In "Community, Narrative, and an Ecological Doctrine of Creation: Creation and Ecology Beyond Modern Atheism," **Elizabeth Barnes** contrasts McClendon's doctrine of creation, and its value for ecological ethics, with proposals by Rosemary Radford Ruether, and Herman Daly and John Cobb. Barnes argues that the success of McClendon's ecological doctrine of creation is due to his non-foundational methodology, which keeps his work closely tied to the biblical narratives wherein we find an account of the true purpose, the final end, of all creation.

In contrast, Ruether uses Christian and Hebrew stories and language merely as a means toward the end of enticing Christians toward an ecological consciousness. Furthermore, Ruether's project is bound to fail if foundationalism in general fails, since she seeks to produce a story of "the total biotic community." In this attempt to tell everyone's story, she ends up being committed to no one's. Similarly, Daly and Cobb, seeking an all-encompassing community, fail to appreciate and exploit the resources of particular existing communities, the "indispensable context for knowledge about God and God's story with us."

Barnes's paper calls us to make careful distinctions when we speak of the role of narratives in theology. It is not the case that all humankind forms one community—in Hauerwas's terms, it *is* possible for us to tell our story without mentioning them. So communities' stories are particular. This may suggest a crass relativism: our stories are true for us, theirs for them. However, this reaction overlooks the fact that the stories of (belonging to) some particular communities nonetheless have universal scope or applicability. The Christian Scriptures, while the Scriptures of a particular community, intend to give a true account of the origin, character, and final end of all people and of all creation as well.

So Barnes's critique of Ruether's search for universal foundations for an ecological ethic should not be read as a critique of all attempts to speak about the whole of creation, the whole of the human race, but merely of her failure to recognize that our *access* to such knowledge comes through the stories of particular communities, and must be tested according to their ability to be lived out fully and fruitfully in actual, particular communities. One can make claims whose content is universal, even though the epistemological warrant is particular. In fact, **Glen H. Stassen** shows how it is possible to begin with particular, narratively dependent understandings of justice and then work toward universal applications. In "Narrative Justice as Reiteration," he asks why narrative ethicists generally fail to pay attention to criteria of justice and injustice. He fears that it may be due, in part, to an over-zealous rejection of Enlightenment thought. While he agrees with narrative ethicists in rejecting "thin" theories of justice, putatively derived from universally accepted foundations, he argues that a solid theory of justice is necessary as a basis for social criticism.

Stassen strongly endorses Michael Waltzer's contextual theory of justice. A key feature of Waltzer's approach is the way he works from particular to general, rather than the reverse. That is, beginning from our particular, historically-conditioned sense of rights and justice, we find ever broadening applications by means of "reiteration." Martin Buber has written: "We understand others by reiterating our self-understanding." This is not the same as stepping back from our particular perspectives—it is stepping into another community's experience to confirm truths we have come to know on our own. So, for instance, countless stories reiterate the Exodus story of deliverance from suffering and oppression.

Waltzer's "Babbette's feast" of rich narratives can help all narrative ethicists to do what they intended all along—to return from abstract speculation to concreteness, particularity, and practical applicability.

Non-foundationalism Without Relativism?

Many criticize non-foundational approaches in general, and narrative methods in particular, because they see them as relativistic. In contrast to a propositional approach to Scripture, narrative methods lack rigor and logical control. And there is the greater worry, mentioned above, about the particularity of appeal to *this* community's narrative, rather than to some other. It may well be that the battle against relativism will be as long and hard as was the battle against the peculiar form of skepticism that foundationalism engendered. While they do not answer all of the relativist worries, two essays address particular aspects of the problem.

In "Living in Another World as One Response to Relativism," **Mark Nation** recognizes that while there are serious philosophical issues at stake, much of what counts as relativism today is not a philosophical position, but is rather more akin to a feeling—the "vertigo of relativity"—that comes from the recognition of a plurality of convictional options. Insofar as this problem is *not* one that arises from a reasoned philosophical position, its proper antidote is practical, not philosophical. The antidote to relativism, for Christians, is more determined and self-conscious participation in the life of the community, for it is this participation that keeps the "plausibility structures" in place.

To confirm this point, Nation recounts the story of the French village of Le Chambon, wherein several thousand Jews were sheltered during World War II. The people of this village found no difficulty in maintaining the Christian world view that justified their actions, despite the fact that they were surrounded by a culture imbued with anti-Semitism, because of their previous formation through Bible study and worship, but also because each small act of faithfulness led to others, and finally to a pattern that has testified to millions of the truth of their convictions.

The point is that when one is faced with a variety of conviction sets, a better response than succumbing to relativism is to count these sets as rival truth claims, whose validity can only be known in the success or failure of the attempt to live them out.

In "Textual Relativism, Philosophy of Language, and the baptist Vision," **Nancey Murphy** considers the problem of relativism with regard to textual interpretation, a problem that has arisen as a result of the rejection of modern 'foundationalist' approaches to textual interpretation by contemporary literary critics. She claims that the way to argue for the stability of textual meaning is to pay more attention than do the deconstructionists and many reader-response critics to the *community* as the repository of the linguistic and social conventions that establish the meaning of the text.

Furthermore, the best strategy for overcoming the problem of the historical distance between the contemporary Christian community and the communities for whom the texts were originally written is by means of McClendon's baptist vision, which is both a hermeneutic strategy—take the text as addressed to the church now—and also an ecclesiology—the church now is to be as much like the primitive church as possible.

So both Nation and Murphy adopt practical responses to relativism, consonant with proposals by Burrell and Tilley with regard to the problem of religious pluralism.

Education without Foundations

The rejection of foundationalism is nothing less than a revolution in our culture's understanding of knowledge, truth, justification, and language. We have seen already the extent to which it re-orders the theological disciplines with regard to their own methodologies, to one another, and to the living of the Christian life. It would be surprising, then, if there were no consequences for education. The following two essays address this issue.

Charles Scriven, in "Schooling for the Tournament of Narratives: Postmodernism and the Idea of the Christian College," asks what shape Christian higher education should take amid sweeping pluralism. After reviewing the history of modern Enlightenment liberalism and its effects on education—and noting that the

Enlightenment itself is a story lived and told—Scriven concludes that the question is not *whether* but *how* to be partisan.

Institutions of Christian higher education should aim for a kind of partisanship that is unapologetic and countercultural; it must avoid the self-deception involved in claiming only to teach *how* to think, without teaching *what*; it must involve the whole person and a whole way of life. In short, Christian schools must be training grounds whose goal is the formation of lives that will honor and reflect the church's narratives. However, this is not to say that the church's convictions need no justification; that justification will be found in living and in dialogue with others formed according to other narratives.

In "Discipleship: Basing One life on Another—It's not What You Know, It's Who You Know," **Michael Goldberg** contrasts the Weberian notion of being educated into a discipline with the Jewish (and Christian) notion of discipleship. Weber's view of education relied on the supposition that the inculcation of a method would result in each individual acquiring the objectivity and universality so prized by Enlightenment culture.

In contrast, the Jewish tradition has seen the educational task to be the formation of rabbinic character such that the Torah was not only known, but enacted in the Rabbi's life. This learning comes primarily from following the lives of others.

Goldberg makes the contrast concrete by describing his own seminary experience—all too much affected by the Weberian ideal—with his years of "sitting at the feet" of James McClendon, who, he says, has taught him "more about practicing the ministry of the sacred service between master and disciple than anyone else." So both of these essays reject the idea that one can educate the intellect alone. Both call for institutions formed after an earlier model of character formation and inculcation of a community's entire way of life.

Conclusions

This reader is struck by the extent to which the essays included in this volume represent a recovery of the past, as well as a pressing forward into a new era. There is the recovery of older models of education, just mentioned. There is a recovery of the significance of narrative for understanding both the Scriptures and our own lives. This is in contrast to the modern attempts to reduce Scripture's content to propositions or history or religious meanings, and to the Enlightenment project of attempting to know all things 'objectively' and 'from the standpoint of eternity.'

There is the recovery of the importance of the community, epistemologically, linguistically, ethically. This is in contrast to modern individualist notions wherein the solitary knower (speaker, actor) was the paradigm. This is not to say that post-foundationalists deny the existence of the role of individuals; only that they recognize certain functions of the community to be irreducible.

There is a return, as well, to a view of human reason that Stephen Toulmin sees as characteristic of the Renaissance. In contrast to the Enlightenment ideal of certitude and universality, Renaissance reason was tolerant of diversity and ambiguity, modest about its own powers, and concerned with the practical. The essays in this volume, I believe, exemplify this softer, more modest sort of reasonableness. Yet it would be a mistake to see these positions merely as reversion to earlier ways of thought. There was a naiveté that can never be regained. Our appropriation of the past must from now on be critical, for the historicist turn in modern thought can never be undone.

This peculiar combination of recovered tradition and new philosophical insights provides rich resources for theology and allied disciplines. The way forward, as must be the case, remains uncharted. However, we at least have the example of James William McClendon to guide our way, for it was the baptist McClendon, stripped of Constantinian pretensions, but clothed with the courage and wisdom of the Gospel, who has led us into this wonderful new land of theology without foundations.

Nancey Murphy (McClendon)

PHILOSOPHY OF RELIGION
WITHOUT FOUNDATIONS

CHAPTER 1

Worship and Autonomy

James M. Smith

Twenty years ago, when Jim McClendon and I were finishing *Understanding Religious Convictions*[1] (*URC*), the eponymous task had a rather different shape than it does now. Verificationism, while moribund in its philosophical home of epistemology and philosophy of language, still exercised considerable influence in philosophy of religion (and in the social sciences as well). To ask how religious convictions should be understood seemed to those under this influence to beg a prior question: was there anything there to be understood? Moreover, the fact that religious or theological disputes were so intractable and interminable seemed to confirm, or at least support, the verificationists' view; perhaps such disputes couldn't be settled because nothing *could* settle them. Clearly, any account of the meaning of religious utterances (claims, propositions, assertions) needed to provide an explanation of this phenomenon in the natural history of religion. The speech act theory, particularly as developed by J. L. Austin[2] and John Searle,[3] seemed to us the most promising candidate for this task, especially when we supplemented it with the concept of a conviction.[4]

Now, verificationism seems to have been driven from the philosophical and theological battlefield. Unfortunately, religious pluralism has become an even more serious problem because the resort to violence to "settle" religious disputes has become much more common and more deadly. Nevertheless, I do not propose to return to these issues, at least not directly. Rather, I intend to extend the account of religious convictions in *URC* to some current issues in the philosophy of religion. I believe the concept of a conviction provides a key to understanding these issues and a way of reformulating them in a more fundamental and fruitful way.

I am, perhaps, the only contributor to this collection who has always thought of theology as "without foundation," though, no doubt, not in the same sense of that term as the one in our title. But what sense is that? There are several different ones to be found in the current discussions. Although McClendon and I were not familiar with any (non-pejorative) sense of "without foundations" in 1974, I think I can suggest one which is consistent with our efforts in *URC* and which is to be found in at least some of the current writers.

One way to make religious or theological beliefs acceptable to one who would otherwise not find them so is to exhibit a relationship between those religious or theological claims and some other non-theological and acceptable claims such that from these latter claims it follows that the theological claims are acceptable, and that one who *did* accept the non-theological claims but did *not* accept the theological ones would be, on his or her own terms, inconsistent or irrational or foolish. The classical arguments for the existence of God (especially the Ontological Argument) are attempts to exhibit such a relationship, as are the occasional appeals to "compelling experiences" (Paul on the road to Damascus, Moses and the burning bush, Jacob wrestling with an angel, Pierce observing the heavens). One might say that in relation to these acceptable non-theological truths or these compelling experiences, the theological claims are *necessary* or that those compelling truths and acceptable beliefs are the *foundation* of the theological beliefs. To say that theology is without foundations, then, is to say that there are no non-theological beliefs or experiences that bear that relation to theological belief. If one adds that anti-theological beliefs are a species of theological belief (as we suggested in *URC*), one then can say that there is no body of non-theological principles or experiences which make it irrational to accept theological beliefs or claims. That, at any rate, is a part of the claim of *URC* and, if I have understood them correctly, also the claim of some of the "no foundations" writers now.

Such a view puts these writers (as well as McClendon and me) at odds with the most common way of doing philosophy of religion in the 1950s and 1960s when I was first working in the area. Then, the focus of the discipline was on either trying to establish some foundation for religious belief or to undermine some proposed foundation. (Positivists and their verificationist allies did philosophy of religion only long enough to point out the unverifiable nature of religious propositions.) Since the task was to find non-theological foundations, it was evidently regarded as unnecessary to examine in any detail either the history or the present practice of any actual religious tradition. Rather, religion was treated somewhat Platonically: there was something called religion (whose definition was very hard to come by) and associated with religion were a cluster of ideas: God, attributes of God, worship, religious belief, sin, heaven, hell, immortality, etc. After defining these ideas and providing a basis for their appropriate use, one could, presumably, examine Christianity, Judaism, Islam, Buddhism, Hinduism, etc., to see how they stacked up. A similar story could be told about most of the "Philosophy" of: science, art, politics, language, etc. Happily, I think, such *apriorism* is less and less accepted. But its influence lingers.

In "God and Human Attitudes,"[5] James Rachels tries to show that the anti-theological claim "There is no God" is necessary in the sense just described, i.e., that once one fully understands what is involved in believing there is a God, one can then see that no such belief could be justified. Specifically, Rachels claims, belief that there is a God necessarily involves worship of the being worthy of that designation: once you acknowledge a being as God, it would be inconsistent not to worship that being. And what is worship? To this question Rachels offers a subtle, complex, and lengthy answer which he summarizes in this fashion:

> In short, the worshiper is in this position: He believes that there is a being, God, who is the perfectly good, perfectly powerful, perfectly wise Creator of the Universe; and he views himself as the 'child of God' made for God's purposes and responsible to God for his conduct. And the ritual of worship, which may have any number of ceremonial forms according to the customs of the religious community, has as its point the acceptance of, and commitment to, one's role as God's child, with all that this involves. If this account is accepted . . . worship will be regarded not as an isolated

act taking place on Sunday (or Saturday) morning, with no necessary connection to one's behavior the rest of the week, but as a
ritualistic expression of and commitment to a role which dominates
one's whole way of life.[6]

Is there a being (Being?) worthy of this attitude? Such a being
must, of course, be extraordinary. Rachels again:

> To bear the title, "God" then, a being must have certain qualifica-
> tions. He (sic!) must, for example, be all-powerful and perfectly
> good in addition to being perfectly wise. And in the same vein, to
> apply the title "God" to a being is to recognize him as one to be
> obeyed . . . And to recognize any being as God is to acknowledge
> that he has *unlimited* claim on one's allegiance . . . That God is not
> to be judged, challenged, defied, or disobeyed, is, at bottom, a truth
> of logic; to do any of these things is incompatible with taking him
> as one to be worshipped.[7]

It is this "unlimited claim" that is the basis for Rachels' argument to an atheistic conclusion.

> The role of worshipper takes precedence over every other role
> which the worshipper has . . . But the first commitment of a moral
> agent is to do what in his own heart he thinks is right. Thus, the
> following argument might be constructed:
>   a) If any being is God, he must be a fitting object of worship.
>   b) No being could possibly be a fitting object of worship since
>   worship requires the abandonment of one's role as an autono-
>   mous moral agent.
>   c) Therefore, there cannot be any being who is God.[8]

Note that this argument is independent of any of the characteristics attributed to God and argued for in classical arguments
for the existence of God: omnipotence, benevolence, omniscience,
even "being greater than any other conceivable being." Whatever
the "factual properties" (Rachels' term) of a being are, this argument concludes that that being could not be worthy of worship
(could not be God) because that would imply that we ought to
abandon our role as autonomous moral agents. To make it even
clearer where the main issue lies, consider the following argument:

(a¹) If any being is an autonomous moral agent, she must be able on her own to discover the right thing to do and be moved on her own to do it.

(b¹) No being could possibly have that knowledge and that motivation because of the limits of human knowledge and the imperfections of human desire.

(c¹) Therefore, there cannot be an autonomous moral agent.

The secular moralist will, predictably, reject (b¹), though something very like it is implied in Christian writers from Paul through Augustine, Calvin, further and up to Barth and Brunner. On the other hand, religious moralists (if I may still use the phrase) will reject (b¹) with equal vehemence. I don't mean to conclude (at least, not yet) that we simply pay our money and take our choice. But I do suggest that there is no theologically neutral ground on which to settle the issues and the issues are: What is worship? What is an autonomous agent?

Let us begin with worship. One way to approach the question is to ask what is a "happy" act of worship? "Happy" (and unhappy) are terms used by J. L. Austin to evaluate a speech-act not only in terms of those old philosophical favorites, falsity and inconsistency, but with respect to circumstance, speaker attitude, audience appropriateness and the like. In *URC*, McClendon and I extended these terms to actions generally to indicate a broadening of evaluative categories from right and wrong to the various sorts of virtues and defects which actions might possess. According to Rachels, a happy act of worship is one in which the worshiper gives "a ritualistic expression and commitment to a role which dominates [his or her] whole way of life." Central to that role, as we have seen, is a belief in a worship of a worthy being (God). One unhappy act of worship, then (and one to which Rachels alludes), is the isolated ritualistic performance unconnected to the life of the worshipper, the worship of the "Sunday morning Christian" (and Friday night Jew or Muslim?). On this Rachels is, I think, quite correct. But, within the traditions that Rachels is concerned with (Christianity, Judaism, and Islam), there are other ways that worship can go wrong. One of these ways is for the worshipper to be unaware or careless of what is involved in worshipping. This might happen, of course, if an outsider were to visit a church or synagogue and "go through the motions." But it may also happen if a member of the community blindly commits himself in the absence of recognition of the relation of himself to God.[9] In *URC*, we introduce a slightly technical use of the word "conviction" to characterize the kind of belief that affirming (or denying) the existence of God requires. A conviction, we say there, "is a belief that is persistently held and acquiring or losing which makes one a different person."[10] Thus, the acknowledgement of God (required for a happy act of worship) is not only a matter of knowing (or believing) something about what is out there (e.g., the "factual properties" of God), but also something about oneself. In particular, in the traditions Rachels is concerned with, happy worship requires the conviction that God (i.e., the object of worship) knows one's interest better than oneself, cares about that interest, and is sufficiently powerful to always protect it. To articulate this conviction is to confess, i.e., in its broadest sense, to reveal one's convictions (nice pun there). In short, we might characterize the Christian concept of happy worship as saying "No worship without confession."

It is much more difficult to address the issue of autonomy. As Rachels himself notes, he says little to describe it beyond asserting that it is a necessary characteristic of a genuine moral agent. Another source of difficulty is the absence of a community or tradition, comparable to the Christian or Jewish communities, in which autonomy has a place. Instead, autonomy is a (purely?) theoretical term, contested among Kantians, Platonists, Existentialists, etc. Nevertheless, we can note at least two different strains of thought about it. One strain stresses independence: we are autonomous to the extent that we are free of outside influences. Whether this is a victory to be won (Kant) or a burden to be borne (Sartre) depends on one's theories of the self, action, and responsibility. Another strain emphasizes integrity: we are autonomous to the extent that our actions are a consistent expression of our deepest desires and aspirations. In this sense, one can be autonomous, whether or not one is influenced from outside, so long as he is not frivolous or inconsistent and so long as he honestly and accurately identifies himself with actions.

It is unclear which of these strains Rachels finds essential to moral agency. He begins by saying that, "to be a moral agent is to be an autonomous or self-directed agent—moral precepts are imposed by the agent on himself."[11] And later, " . . . to deliver oneself over to a moral authority for directions about what to do is simply incompatible with being a moral agent. To say, 'I will follow so-and so's directions, no matter what they are and no matter what my conscience would otherwise direct me to do' is to opt out of moral thinking altogether; it is to abandon one's role as a moral agent."[12] But he also writes, "The virtuous man is therefore identified with the man of integrity, i.e., the man who acts according to precepts which he can, on reflection, conscientiously approve in his own heart."[13]

If we apply these criteria for autonomy to the happy (i.e., confessing) worshipper, what do we find? Our worshipper does not, of course, think of herself as imposing moral precepts but as discovering them or having them revealed to her. But on that point, she is (*pace* Rachels) at one with Plato, Aristotle, and most utilitarians. To say that the happy worshipper "follows [God's] directions, no matter what they are and no matter what my own conscience would otherwise direct me to do" is simply to beg this question; for the happy worshiper, in confessing her conviction that God exists is acknowledging (among other things) that God knows better than she what her conscience truly requires so that, in doing what God requires, she is acting "according to precepts which she can, on reflection, conscientiously approve in her own heart." The happy worshipper does not assert what she takes to be God's direction as an excuse or even as defense (oh ye of bad faith); rather she proclaims it as a sound basis for taking responsibility for it. On the whole then, it seems that the happy worshipper has as good a claim to autonomy as one who, say, models himself on the man of practical wisdom.

Finally, let us look at two points about the only example Rachels takes from the traditions with which he is concerned. He contrasts two episodes in the story of Abraham: his willingness to obey the command of God to sacrifice his son, Isaac, and his "negotiations" with God, attempting to save Sodom and Gomorrah. In the first, Rachels claims that Abraham behaves appropriately for a worshipper although outrageously from the moral point of view; in the second Abraham behaves inappropriately for a worshipper although he is on firmer moral ground. The former

41

has driven even some of the devout to question the connection of faith and morality; the second seems to put Abraham in the position of a weak but sensitive moralist bargaining with an outraged, all-powerful and somewhat petulant tyrant.

My first point is simply to note how singular Abraham is even within these traditions. Jewish, Christian, and Muslim traditions contain not only Abraham but Job, not only Jacob but Jonah, both David and Solomon. There is an array of views about how the serious Jew or Christian is to interpret these puzzling and troubling stories.

My second point is really a suggestion. Rachels treats the story of Abraham as though it were the culmination, the paradigm of the tradition. In fact, of course, it is the beginning of the tradition. So far from being an example of an already established and fixed ideal of the relation of worship, it is the beginning of a long and complex struggle (perhaps still unfinished) to define that relation. Thus, whatever one thinks of Abraham (or God!) in these stories, it is a mistake to regard their interaction as the ideal of worship within the tradition in which Abraham is a patriarch. And it is to those traditions that Rachels directs his argument.

My conclusions are of the same irenic sort that McClendon and I reached in *URC*. (Though, I admit, it seems to have produced little peace.) There *may* be some kind of autonomy that is incompatible with worship as it is practiced in Christian and Jewish communities but (a) Rachels does not show that there is, and (b) any such autonomy requires argument as much as the existence of God. No doubt some (Christian or Jewish) worshippers fail to be autonomous in the way we have defined it, but, if so, it is not because they are happy worshippers. Finally, while I do not think there is a being worthy of worship, nothing in Rachels' argument supports me in that claim.

CHAPTER 2

Convictions and Operative Warrant

David B. Burrell, C.S.C.

One of the legacies of Wittgenstein to the study of theology has been a challenge to the enlightenment demand that faith-statements be "justified at the bar of reason." This demand sounded relatively innocuous in the climate out of which it emerged, yet that climate aggressively promoted a vision of human beings to which faith was clearly an addendum. The lean, efficient model would operate by reason alone; extrinsic needs may call for religious faith, but those could never succeed in *justifying* it. By seizing on the fact of convictions as a mediating notion, James McClendon and James M. Smith set out to challenge that hegemony, for it would be difficult to marginalize convictions from the human enterprise. The fruits of their collaborative effort over a period of eight years were published in 1975 as *Understanding Religious Convictions* (University of Notre Dame Press), and the Preface (signed by "McClendon & Smith") sets the tone for this joint effort: "to discuss the discordant elements which divide our own society into fragments and to discover what Wordsworth calls the 'dark inscrutable workmanship' that can make even discordant elements one"(vii).

We are reminded today, of course, of Alasdair MacIntyre's now-famous image of ethical discourse in modernity as splintered into fragments: shards, as it were, of once-sculpted containers of a language fitted to the whole of life. Yet McClendon and Smith do far more than comment on this plight; by their mutual effort (as religious believer and unbeliever together) they hope to model the kind of joint workmanship which can offer avenues for conversation and for constructive collaboration in today's world. It was not then called "post-modern" but their perspectives certainly were. By focusing on convictions and mapping the conditions for their felicitous use, the authors recognize that warrant for statements or confessions is invariably "retrospective" rather than "prospective."[1] That is the key to recognizing theirs to be a "non-foundational" strategy, even though none of these now-modish terms were current then.

They accepted—indeed displayed—the current situation of a plurality of beliefs, and set out with the help of philosophers of language like J. L. Austin and John Searle to discover the conditions required to assess one's expression of one's beliefs. For they understood that expression to be both personal and communal, like any linguistic performance, and were confident that understanding the full context for felicitous expression of one's convictions "is tantamount to their justification"(15). This will need to be unpacked, of course, but part of the strategy of their joint effort is to remind us throughout that it is an effort: expressing one's faith is itself a practice; it can be done well or badly. The mediating notion of *convictions* is chosen to highlight those beliefs (expressly religious or not) which constitute a person, so that altering them changes the sort of person we are or hope to become. (In this sense, they function analogously to Newman's "strongly-held beliefs" presupposed in all that we undertake, as well as to what current "Reformed epistemology" calls "basic beliefs,"[2] though their manner of analysis and attention to linguistic use is closer to Newman and to Wittgenstein than to the Reformed approach.) By insisting not only that convictions are person-constituting beliefs, but also that persons without them would "lack character"(111), and by placing the expression of such beliefs in the communal context which any linguistic expression requires, they also anticipate Alasdair MacIntyre's later analysis of the role of traditions in directing inquiry.[3] Indeed, their fifth chapter is devoted to showing that there is no neutral, tradition-free perspective from which to assess the sets of convictions which direct human communities and persons in their lives. All this already articulated nearly twenty years ago!

Convictions and Truth

By noting how convictions are person-shaping beliefs, they move beyond the pale philosophical skeleton of 'belief' which Wilfrid Cantwell Smith exposes as an obstacle to academic consideration of religious faith, since contemporary parlance treats 'belief' as medievals used 'opinion.'[4] By emphasizing their linguistic expression we are introduced into convictional communities. Yet the contemporary stage is crowded with many of them, so the immediate question posed is: which of them is true? Here again, the mediating notion of *conviction* helps to place the question. Since convictions are person-centered, and others' convictions are not mine to profess, the relevant question is whether *I* can truly profess the faith I do? But does that entail that 'true' must mean 'true for me' or 'true for them'? To some extent, yes (which gives us their avowed "soft perspectivism"): I cannot myself confess what a Muslim can. Yet not totally (hence "soft") since I could one day do so, and I can understand both his or her confessing and (to some extent by analogy) his or her confession, and probably better than one who confesses not at all. Above all, however, what I really want to know is whether I can truly confess what I do believe; anything else is a distraction from that.

It is here that McClendon's theological orientation comes to the fore: he and Smith are concerned with felicitous confession, and not with *truth* overall. Indeed, how could we talk about religious truth overall, without any perspective? They have no advice on that, and wisely so, for attempts to do so reveal how leveling a question it is, leading to attempts to treat religious statements like any other, overlooking the specific dimension of confession. So McClendon and Smith succeed in doing two quite distinct things: (1) reminding philosophers of the peculiar character of faith-statements (using J. L. Austin and John Searle to do so), and (2) reminding theologians that the post-Tridentine polemic between Protestant and Catholic regarding faith as primarily voluntary (trust) or primarily intellectual (assent) was just that—a polemic which the strategic term 'conviction' helps to mediate.

Faith entails beliefs, indeed, but life-shaping ones whose felicitous assertion is always a confession.

A Plethora of Convictions

Their joint effort, then, weds the riches of a baptist tradition of faith-confession to a philosophical treatment which underscores the community of discourse and of practice, thereby further highlighting a feature of Christian life and practice which modern Protestant theology had curiously overlaid with an individualistic bias. The focus on community also incorporates elements of contemporary hermeneutics (Gadamer et al.), emphasizing the operative role of conversation and dialogue. Indeed, the book itself is the result of one, so the progress of the joint argument enacts what it proposes. In that respect, too, McClendon and Smith anticipate a "post-modern" perspective, worked out here (implicitly at least) with respect to unbelief, and, in anticipation, "other-belief." For wondering about one's own religious convictions will spontaneously elicit wonder about those of others, especially when these appear to clash or even cancel each other out. What invariably mediates a head-on clash of belief-perspectives, however, is the reminder that the signs of authenticity of anyone's faith lie in their manner of living it out. George Lindbeck's example of the crusader's cry of faith negating itself in the act of vengeance which it produced is a telling one.[5] Should anyone ask me, a Catholic Christian, whether the Qur'an is the word of God, how could I begin to answer? McClendon and Smith suggest a way of responding: (1) I don't know; God does [Allah 'arafu], and (2) "by their fruits you shall know them." Combining (1) with (2), and given one's experience with Muslims formed by the Qur'an into humble, hospitable servants of God, it would behoove me to treat the Qur'an as though it were; at least, not to deny that it is the word of God.

Note that such an attitude is more akin to Socratic "unknowing" than to "agnosticism" as we know it in modern times.[6] For those who style themselves agnostics today are usually professing not disbelief (more appropriate to atheists) but rather their incapacity to be persuaded by arguments in favor of faith in God, or even more baldly, erstwhile proofs of God's existence. The position of *unknowing* which I have advocated regarding other faiths (or the faith of others) recognizes rather that I am not in a position to make an assessment of the truth of their professions of faith, nor am I able to dismiss them. It is their fruits which are telling. Is this a pragmatic theory of truth? If it had to be so classified, I suppose so. But maybe "theories of truth" are misnomers, since they would have to be self-referential, and to do so, would introduce an unending multiplicity of levels: can the "theory" be employed to assess its own truth? What if the judgment of truth which we exercise were not a theory but a performance? (If so, then people who are constrained to construe it as a theory would call it a "pragmatic theory.") That seems to be the most that someone like Wittgenstein could say. It is also what Bernard Lonergan insists upon in placing *judgment* as a step beyond *insight* as something which we *do*.[7]

It is not easy to summarize in brief compass Bernard Lonergan's treatment of human understanding, but the parallels with McClendon and Smith are striking. While "theories of truth" cannot help, it seems, but treat *true* as a property of statements, and then ask what warrants our predicating 'true' of certain sentences, we have seen where such a strategy invariably leads. Lonergan begins not with propositions but with our shared experiences with understanding, which he identifies as insights: the 'eureka' of Archimedes.[8] It is these which we must then formulate into statements, to incorporate them into the rest of what we can be said to know, as well as test their veracity. The process of testing culminates in an assessment of their worth, a judgment. This process is characterized by a reach for closure, together with an invitation to revision: in wanting to know whether our way of putting it is true, we must seek out potential objections. In that sense, each judgment we make is, ideally, an assertion as well as a plea for correction. Lonergan calls such an activity "virtually unconditioned": while we assert that such is indeed the case (unconditioned), we do so in such a way that subsequent questions will either be deemed irrelevant (because we will be conscious of already having responded to them or recognize them to be off the map), or they will be acknowledged to challenge our assessment. Upon reflection, we can see that our operative convictions are indeed of this sort.

Some such perspective guides McClendon and Smith as well, for it structures the progress of the book. Rather than a theory we have a grammar: a set of rules governing conditions for felicitous assertion. And that strategy returns us to persons confessing in their community of discourse and practice: a rich context for assessment and for mutual correction. This strategy privileges those who live by convictions and are sufficiently aware of them to confess them. But is not such a context the normatively human one, as they themselves suggest? So we can see how this perspective helps to overcome the modern presumption that faith is an "extra" with regard to the normal human condition, to be tolerated to the extent that people need it to find their way, but eminently replaceable by more rational procedures. Yet merely stating it that way rings false in our "postmodern" era. McClendon and Smith have given us the tools for living in our time, in a world where convictions of faith are respected for their inherent worth to persons attempting to live full, human lives. Reason has an eminent role to play, of course, in tracking the conditions for felicitous profession of our convictions. McClendon and Smith gave us a head start on that project nearly twenty years ago, and it is fascinating to review those efforts as we continue to try to find our way in a world whose tolerance of convictions is unevenly matched with strategies for assessing their relative worth.

CHAPTER 3

In Favor of a "Practical Theory of Religion": Montaigne and Pascal

Terrence W. Tilley

Prelude: The Practical Theory of Religion

James Wm. McClendon, Jr., whom we honor in this *Festschrift*, supports what he calls a "practical" theory of religion. He portrays this theory in the following:

> [A] religion is a set of powerful *practices* that embody the life-form-ing convictions of its practitioners. There *is* no 'essence' of religion; religions are neither . . . all more or less true nor . . . all more or less evil. It follows that generalizations about religion are generally mistaken, since religions differ in kind, and only concrete, sympathetic historical and empirical study can tell us about any particular religion. We may call this the *practical theory* of religion . . . in the sense that its concern is the life-shaping (as I will say, the convic-tional) *practices* religions embody. So religions are not to be identi-fied with their abstract teachings, far less with their 'errors.'[1]

In McClendon's usage, "practice" is a technical term, akin to Alasdair MacIntyre's understanding of "practice." McClendon writes:

> [S]ocial practices, like games, strive for some **end** beyond them-selves (health for the practice of medicine, livable space for archi-tecture), require intentional participation on the part of

> **practitioners**, employ determinate **means**, and proceed according
> to **rules**. So a "practice" . . . is a complex series of human actions
> involving definite practitioners who by these means and in accord-
> ance with these rules together seek the understood end.[2]

McClendon differs from MacIntyre in allowing that the *teloi* of
practices are not necessarily internal to those practices and in
claiming that practices, even if one engages in them properly, do
not necessarily require morally good means, develop virtuous
practitioners, or lead to good ends.

In construing religion as a set of practices, McClendon continues to distance himself from the dominant strand in modern
philosophy of religion. This essay first sketches that dominant
strand and its intrinsic defects. Then it returns to the beginning of
the modern era to retrieve another strand which many modern
philosophers have dismissed, misunderstood, or vilified. This
tradition of Montaigne and Pascal is not merely one of conformist
fideism, as it is often portrayed.[3] Rather, I argue that it rightly
construes religions as life-shaping traditions of practices and
rightly sees that when traditions are in conflict the issues which
require solution are not purely noetic, but overarchingly practical.
Third, this essay argues that understanding religion *practically*, as
this alternate tradition does, shows not only where the burning
issues lie in controversies over the 'rationality of religious belief,'
but also the actual force of Pascal's famous "wager argument."
Close attention to this strand shows in the end that 'practical'
philosophies of religion can be constructed which need not and
should not be construed as either 'fideist' or 'irrationalist.'

Religion and Religious Belief in Modern Philosophy

Since the beginning of modernity, philosophers of religion
have focused their attention on religious beliefs abstracted from
religious life. Their debates over "religion" typically have failed
to address the practical issues an embodied person faces, but have
attended almost exclusively to issues of pure rationality suitable
for the academic mind alone. Philosophers have endlessly debated the proofs of the existence of God, the problems of theodicy,
the rationality of holding religious beliefs, and the possibility of
determining whether religious beliefs were meaningful. Most current explorations of the reliability or justifiability of religious

beliefs have continued this tradition. Such abstraction of religious beliefs from religious life has, alas, deformed the philosophers' approach to religion and their attempts to construct a philosophy of religion.

Philosophers of religion are not alone in ignoring the significance of religious life while debating about religious beliefs. William A. Clebsch captured the problem clearly and elegantly when he contrasted conservative apologetics for religious belief in the modern era with the rich religious life of the premodern epochs:

> Religious belief stridently affirming the inerrancy of a miscellaneous assortment of interwoven and overlaid writings was hardly the same as religious life proceeding unself-consciously under the power of certain myths told in those writings. Religious belief denying human cousinhood with simians can hardly be compared with religious life straightforwardly delighting in brotherhood with a god-man. Religious belief trying to hold Christ in the status of a redeemer differed from religious life humbly serving an incarnate and resurrected savior.[4]

Clebsch here reminds us that religious life cannot be reduced to religious beliefs. Arguing over the propositional content of those beliefs cannot stand in for understanding, analyzing, and criticizing religion(s) and religious life. Whether conservative or progressive, most investigations of "reason and religion" have remained mired in abstract debates about "religious beliefs," or intellectual wrangling over the existence of God. They have ignored the far more important question of the reasonableness or wisdom of participation in the richness and complexity of religious life.[5]

Religious epistemology is the center of modern philosophy of religion. Investigations in this area have generally remained bound to the modern focus on religious beliefs as properties or dispositions of individuals without regard to their socially embodied religious life.[6] The individualism and anti-authoritarianism of modernity appear especially in arguments over the 'foundations' of religious belief. If a person's belief is well-founded in the nature of things, based on good evidence or irresistible experience, concluded from a good argument, formed in a reliable belief-forming practice, or developed by the exercise of a properly functioning belief-forming mechanism working in a suitable environment, then that individual or her belief is justified, warranted, proper, etc. If the nature of things does not properly evoke a religious belief, or if the evidence for one's religious 'hypothesis' is inconclusive, or if one's religious experience is unreliable, or if one's argument for the existence of God is not sound or probable, or if one's religious doxastic practice is not reliable or not properly followed, or if one's belief-forming equipment is not performing as designed or is not in the proper environment when one develops a religious belief, then that individual or his belief would not be warranted, justified, proper, etc. The question of an individual's warrant or entitlement to hold specific propositions about religious matters remains the central area of concern in religious epistemology.[7]

Religious epistemologists have tended to accept the modern era's valorization of the individual's quest for cognitive certainty. Yet the modern quest for certainty was not a philosophical Athena sprung full-grown from Descartes' head. Modern philosophy, including philosophy of religion, grew out of a tradition of theology as "scientia," as sure knowledge. From the "golden age" of the thirteenth-century scholastics through Calvin's *Institutes* in the sixteenth century and into the modern period, the theologians' ideal was the formation of a comprehensive *summa* or even system of Christian theological beliefs. But by the end of the sixteenth century, there were many systems in irreconcilable conflict. And by the middle of the early seventeenth century, the tolerance typified by Montaigne and inscribed in the Edict of Nantes (1598) had become untenable. Each of the many other forms of Christian faith became as much a "disconfirming other" for one's own faith as the Jewish tradition had been. Thus, the intellectual elite's "flight from authority" and their quest for certainty which constitutes the Enlightenment project was a flight from *competing* authorities, *conflicting* systems, irreconcilable *scientiae*, and religious institutions *at war* with each other. The prima facie epistemic problem may involve the rationality of individuals' religious beliefs, but in the context of profound social conflict and economic upheaval, the real problems were practical ones.[8]

Modernity in general and modern philosophy of religion in particular have inherited the theologians' approach to solving religious conflict. Theologians were—and mostly are—concerned with showing which are the right (doctrinal) beliefs. Practical questions were erased or shunted to irrelevance. In a similar vein, philosophical rhetoric sometimes has so divided epistemic from "prudential" or "moral" issues that these seemed to have nothing to do with each other.[9] Religious epistemology developed in an arena of debate over whether individuals properly can and do have certainty when they hold religious beliefs. Its practitioners have usually tacitly accepted the basic presumptions of modernity: (1) having abandoned authority, each individual properly quests for her or his own certainty; and (2) religious belief is a "private" affair involving individuals and their beliefs.

The academic study of religion and some recent developments in epistemology have shown that the issues are far more complex than the modern paradigm can accommodate. Even though, in our era, religious affiliation may be, at least politically, a matter of individual choice, it is not clear either that individuals can choose their beliefs freely or that justifying individuals' entitlement to hold specific propositions is necessary or sufficient to show the reasonableness of her religious commitment, practice, and belief. Religious epistemology needs a new practical paradigm. The way forward begins by stepping backward to retrieve the practical insights of the Montaigne-Pascal tradition. We need not reject the gains of modernity (as some postliberal theologians and postmodern philosophers do). We do not need to intensify modern individualism and atomization (as some poststructuralist philosophers and literary theorists do). Rather, we need to recognize both the contributions and the incompleteness of the modern project by incorporating the social, institutional, and practical dimensions of life into its perspective. We need to focus on religious believing as practices of *embodied* persons, not on propositions to be debated by minds engaged in academic exercises. In short, we need to retrieve the *practical* issues of religion without succumbing to an internalist or fideistic position which privatizes religious life and practice.

Understanding the reasonableness of religious belief and practice does not fall in the realm of *scientia* and certainty, but in that of *praxis* and *phronesis*.[10] Religion is not merely a set of beliefs or even a theological or doctrinal system. Religious knowing or believing is not merely accepting doctrines, but living a life shaped by a religious tradition carried by enduring institutions and transmitted through committed communities. Being justified in one's believing is not having warranted basic beliefs, but having the ability to make and to keep a wise commitment to a religious life and to live it fully. The real issue, I will argue below, is to solve the problem of the choice of practices.

Feminist 'epistemologists'[11] point the way in this area for epistemology generally. First, some note that there is a great gulf between academic epistemologies and real issues. "Feminists who expect a theory of knowledge to address people's everyday cognitive experiences and to examine the place of knowledge in people's lives, who expect it to produce analyses and strategies that will contribute to the construction of a world fit for human habitation, can find little enlightenment in mainstream epistemology."[12] Academic epistemologies especially neglect the difficulties that people have in even getting access to positions in which basic information is available. They are blind to, or think irrelevant, class, race, and gender issues. Academic epistemologies ignore the political and social realities which make the very possibility of knowing a practical impossibility for those marginalized in a society and unable to get into position to be able to know.

Being in position to know something is, in general, taken for granted by epistemologists. They simply presume that what I will label "positional defects" are limited to individuals' epistemic 'defects,' disqualifications, or deviations from the "normal case." For instance, a blind person cannot get into a position of "being appeared to now redly" and a deaf person cannot get into a position of "now hearing a high-pitched tone." These are taken to be "equipment defects" which obviously disqualify those with "defective equipment" from being in a position to perceive sights or sounds. Such 'defects' render them irrelevant to academic epistemology. They are simply not subjects in and of that discourse. A person who was neither at the royal banquet last night nor has received any reports of what happened at the banquet is in no position to know how many glasses of red wine the queen drank. This is not an "equipment defect," but an "access problem." Since the person had no access to the relevant information, the question of her knowing or not knowing the proposition about the queen's drinking simply never comes up—it remains "irrelevant to" and out of sight in epistemology. In general, such "positional defects" are (perhaps) benignly, although (all too) blithely, covered by *"ceteris paribus"* or other similar qualifications.

Yet "other things being equal" does not always apply benignly and ought not be invoked blithely. Social and political practices can also give people "positional defects," a factor ignored in academic epistemology. Such marginalized people are also not subjects of and in that discourse. Code persuasively details the problems which women on welfare in Canada (and, analogously, in other nations) have in getting access to services and information as an example of systemic epistemic marginalization. It is not that these women are stupid or lazy or unindustrious, but that the varied demands made on them to acquire and maintain the assistance that they need to provide their families with basic needs makes it impossible also to get in position to acquire the information they need to find a way off the eternal wheel of welfare. When one is required by welfare rules, for instance, to spend the entire day riding buses to follow the regulations for getting to locations where one can obtain needed medical assistance, that same day cannot be used to find a job or child care or to acquire information or education. The fact is that political, social, ethnic, economic, and gender-based patterns, however benignly intended, make it practically impossible for people to get into position to know. Such disqualifications can be malignant in effect. Nor are they the same sort of "positional defects" as noted above. That I could not find out the time of an interview for a job for which I am qualified because I was required by law or regulation to be elsewhere is a "positional defect," but one due not to my own intrinsic epistemic defect or my (uninteresting) lack of information, but to my being systematically forced to an epistemically marginal position. *Ceteris paribus* clauses obscure such practical epistemic problems.

Of course, the epistemologist will claim that such problems are irrelevant to the proper task of epistemology, of finding the conditions under which a person can be said to know. And that may be true. But the fact that it is true *is the very problem*. The problem is that the "proper task" of epistemology is blind to the (contingent, but real and extensive) social factors which empower or disable an embodied, socially located person from getting in position to know. The only subject of the discourse of academic epistemology is the epistemically privileged individual who has no specific social location and no difficulty with access to basic data or information. That such a subject cannot exist outside of the ivory towers of academia means, in practice, academic epistemologists study only very rare cases, not common ones.

Second, in addition to introducing practical "political" elements into epistemology, some feminists advocate the demythologization of the Enlightenment myth that there can be dispassionate investigations, even in science. Alison M. Jaggar has noted that "western epistemology has tended to view emotion with suspicion and even hostility."[13] She goes on to note the consequences of obliterating emotions:

> This derogatory western attitude toward emotion, like the earlier western contempt for sensory observation [now so basic to epistemology], fails to recognize that emotion, like sensory perception, is necessary to human survival. Emotions prompt us to act appropriately, to approach some people and situations and to avoid others, to caress or cuddle, fight or flee. Without emotion, human life would be unthinkable. Moreover, emotions have an intrinsic as well as an instrumental value. Although not all emotions are enjoyable or even justifiable . . . life without any emotion would be life without any meaning.[14]

Jaggar claims that even positivist epistemologies allow a role for emotion in the (intuitive) suggestion of hypotheses for investigation, but rigorously exclude emotion from the processes of justification. However, if (as in the 'naturalized' epistemologies typical of W. V. O. Quine, Alvin Goldman *et al.*) one cannot separate the processes of belief formation from the processes of belief justification, then an epistemology of science itself must incorporate "values and emotions. Moreover, such an incorporation seems a necessary feature of all knowledge and conceptions of knowledge."[15] The consequence is that affect, inclination, intuition, or emotion must be internalized into epistemology, especially into the naturalized epistemologies which focus on cognitional or doxastic practices.

The simple fact is that pure rationalist and empiricist epistemologies have been found wanting both because they fail to explain belief acquisition and because they fail to show the conditions for knowing. The modern separation of "epistemic" from "moral" and "prudential" issues is not merely misguided. Rather it is but a symptom of the philosophical disease of modernity where pure theory is valorized and practical, bodily, emotional issues degraded, where the socially privileged subject is taken as the norm, and where the social locations which shape us all are blithely and not benignly erased. Hence, some contemporary epistemologists have embarked on a practical path which must lead them to consider doxastic practices, the conditions under which they work, and the "noncognitive" ingredients necessary to knowing, including both personal attitudes and social conditions. Religious epistemologists like Alston have begun to make this turn and have started opening this path. Ultimately it leads to a claim that the justification of religious belief is best understood not as demonstrating that an individual is entitled to hold some specific religious proposition, but as showing the wisdom of participating in a religious tradition, and, by implication, the wisdom of accepting the central and distinctive practices and convictions of that tradition. Although the dominant strand in modern philosophy of religion has substituted examining the validity of an isolated, unlocated individual (mentally) holding "religious beliefs" for understanding religion, there is another tradition in modern philosophizing about religion that does not take this path and whose insight can be retrieved as we cut a path into the uncharted terrain of "practical epistemology."

The Legacy of Montaigne and Pascal

Michel de Montaigne, in his "Apology for Raymond Sebond" (1580), wrote that "Christians do themselves harm in trying to support their belief by human reasons, since it is conceived only by faith and by a particular inspiration of divine grace."[16] Montaigne here seems to anticipate the two basic patterns that would come to dominate the modern debates over the justification of religion and religious belief for the next four centuries.

The first pattern can be labeled *externalist*: If reason could provide a solid external foundation or uncover external evidences for religion or show the validity of a revelation, then a reasonable person could and should accept religious beliefs thus externally warranted. Conversely, if rational arguments cannot provide independent or external reasons for accepting religious claims or can show religious beliefs to be irrational, then a reasonable person is not justified in accepting religious beliefs. The dominant tradition in modern philosophy of religion is externalist.

The second pattern can be called *internalist*: Rational arguments cannot be expected to provide an external basis for religion so religious belief properly must rest on faith and grace alone. Whatever "reasonableness" or "evidence" can be found in religion is found within, not before or under, religious commitment.[17]

Montaigne himself has generally been classed with the internalists. He is typically identified as a fideist who is skeptical of reason's power to ascertain religious truth and who advocates conformity to prevailing winds of traditions as the appropriate stance to take in the absence of good external reasons to be religious. He can thus be envisioned as standing near the head of a line which runs through Pascal, Demea (in Hume's *Dialogues Concerning Natural Religion*), and Kierkegaard, and extends to D. Z. Phillips and others in our own time. These 'internalists' do not isolate faith from reason or religion from the rest of the world, as their opponents sometimes claim. Nonetheless, they do find that religious beliefs neither need evidence nor have external rational support. Religion is a matter of grace, faith, committed choice, or expressive reaction to the world. Reasoning and evidence are internal to faith, not its foundations.

The "subject" of Montaigne's essay, the late fifteenth-century author Raymond Sebond, can be seen as an ancestor of the externalists. This dominant modern tradition includes the numerous rational theologians of the seventeenth century, Cleanthes and Philo (in Hume's *Dialogues*), William Paley, and extends, more recently through A. J. Ayer, Bertrand Russell, Father Frederick Copleston, Antony Flew, Hugo Meynell, Richard Swinburne and others. In different ways, such thinkers presume that religious belief needs evidential support or foundational demonstration if a reasonable person is to accept it. They then disagree about whether it has any such support or whether the foundations of theism are sturdy enough to support the religious edifice. To be religious, and more specifically to be Christian, may ultimately be a matter of divine grace; but human reason must at least prepare the way of the Lord.

Yet Montaigne hinted at a possible third approach in an earlier essay: "We should meddle soberly with judging divine ordinances" (1574)—an approach, alas, mostly unexplored in philosophy of religion. In this essay Montaigne recollects dispute over the rationality of believing in divine providence. But here the ground is not the fertile soil where either externalist disputes over whether one should accept God's existence and/or internalist rhetoric about simple acceptance or divine grace or leaps of faith flourish. The context for this essay is not a dispute between belief and unbelief, but a dispute over established patterns of religious practice. The dispute is particular, not general, and practical, not theoretical. Here a rather different pattern and practice of argument emerges.

The argument is about evidence for a belief that God acts in history (an argument which seems externalist), but it presumes the reality of and belief in God (a pattern which makes the argument seem internalist). Montaigne's discussion of "sober meddling" reaches the following judgment about the disputes between contending Protestants and Catholics:

> It is enough for a Christian to believe that all things come from God, to receive them with acknowledgment of his divine and inscrutable wisdom, and therefore to take them in good part, in whatever aspect they may be sent to him. But I think that the practice I see is bad, of trying to strengthen and support our religion by the good fortune and prosperity of our enterprises. Our belief has enough other foundations; it does not need events to authorize it. For when the people are accustomed to these arguments, which are plausible and suited to their taste, there is a danger that when in turn contrary and disadvantageous events come, this will shake their faith. Thus, in the wars we are engaged in for the sake of religion, those [Protestants] who had the advantage in the encounter [i.e., the battle] at La Rochelabeille make much ado about this incident and use their good fortune as sure approbation of their party; but when they come later to excuse their misfortunes at Moncontour and Jarnac as being fatherly scourges and chastisements, unless they have their following completely at their mercy, they make the people sense readily enough that this is getting two grinding fees for one sack, and blowing hot and cold with the same mouth. It would be better to tell them the true foundations of the truth.[18]

The situation Montaigne describes is not one in which believers seek a theoretical foundation or evidence for their faith. Rather, each of two warring groups of believers, Huguenot and Catholic, attempts to develop evidence to show that God is on their side. Each can begin by pointing to a military victory as a sign of divine favor for their cause. Yet when each loses a battle this is not a sign of divine displeasure with their cause or favor for the opponents' cause, but a God-given chastisement of the side the divine providence favors. Montaigne rightly mocks the self-serving dissymmetry of such theological apologies which can construe all events as evidence in support of one's own cause.

It would be easy to construe this account as 'internalist.' Montaigne's skepticism of the Protestants' arguments (and, implicitly of Catholics' analogous arguments) would be another instance of his own skepticism about external support for religion. Like religious externalists' arguments, such evidential claims and counterclaims are inconclusive at best, obscurantist and deceptive at worst.

Yet when one considers the actual dispute Montaigne recollects, it is not typical of the disputes which fire internalists' rhetoric or externalists' theoretical arguments. The issues are not "religion" or "religious belief" in general, or the existence or non-existence of God. Their dispute is over *which* Christian tradition is divinely sanctioned. The context is not an academic philosophical dispute, but a bitter conflict within a family of traditions which share some practices and goals, and a war among the institutions which support them. The audience for the arguments, as Montaigne notes, is not academic skeptics, but already committed believers. Each side tries to find arguments that believers on the other side or wavering believers on their own might find "plausible" supports for allegiance to their own side. The proponents typically appeal to shared beliefs and images, especially biblical ones, which carry substantial rhetorical weight for adherents in both camps. The envisioned audience for such persuasion is not the ignorant masses which elegant rhetoric can easily sway, but people of common sense. Montaigne advises against such "evidential" arguments because the audience might well be able to "see through" the ideological dissymmetry and so find their faith shaken when events conspire to go against their party.

This sort of argument is not usually found in the mainstream of philosophy of religion, but in inter-Christian polemics. This pattern of argument often degenerates into name-calling, proof-texting, and finger-pointing almost before it begins. Sadly lacking here are the issues of rationality, evidence, and argument which light the internalist-externalist fires.

However degenerate the arguments themselves can become, the questions they address are important and practical. Within which form of life ought the hearers live? Which practices ought the audience take up? To which tradition and institution ought they give their allegiance? Internalists' urging them to fideism begs the question when the issue is *which* faith one ought practice. After all, appealing to faith when the dispute is about faiths is like appealing to authority when the dispute is about authorities. The externalists' quest to find evidence is also useless for the 'evidence' is ambiguous at best. Neither approach can help with this practical problem. Their proponents might claim that they were not trying to solve practical problems. And *that is precisely the problem* with their approaches—they are impractical. Their strategies of argument are irrelevant to help resolve the practical disputes.

Moreover, a practical approach doesn't misportray the situation of commitment as internalist or externalist approaches do. The internalists tend to take religious commitment as basic, unarguable, *given*. Like classic Protestant doctrines of predestination and divine grace in which the person has no say over her true status vis-a-vis God, so internalism finds that no ordinary human practices make it possible to give the person a say in *taking* a position or *making* a commitment. But the fact is that people do choose to make commitments in religion as in love; that we can freely choose neither our beliefs nor our lusts does not imply that we do not commit ourselves to chaste marriage or to active religious devotion. Having beliefs or lusts may be necessary, but is not sufficient, for justifying engaging in religious or amatory practices.

The externalists tend to portray the position of the disputants as one like that of 'scientific' neutrality in which neutral investigators seek evidence and in which the convictions the investigators hold are irrelevant. This view is most fully developed by Flew as his methodological presumption of atheism. But that position is simply untenable. The fact is that the investigators are not neutral judges but committed disputants. The issue is not one of simply adding a new belief (belief in God) to our store of already-accepted beliefs, but the question of which central and distinctive convictions we ought hold.[19] Both internalist and externalist accounts misportray the practical-intellectual issues.

But if the usual philosophical approaches are not only wrong in their presumptions about the positions of those practically engaged in argument, but also of little use in practical disputes, is there no practice for resolving overarching and life-determining practical issues except the desultory polemics and the self-serving rhetoric whose posturing is open to Montaigne's withering analysis? Montaigne himself hinted at a different way of disputing such important practical issues. This path avoids not only the antitheses of externalism and internalism, but also the dead end of polemics. In an essay "On the art of discussion"(1588), he offered a practical prescription for a practical disease:

> The most fruitful and natural exercise of our mind, in my opinion, is discussion. I find it sweeter than any other action of our life. . . .
>
> The study of books is a languishing and feeble activity that gives no heat, whereas discussion teaches and exercises us at the same time. If I discuss with a strong mind and a stiff jouster, he presses on my flanks, prods me right and left; his ideas launch mine. Rivalry, glory, competition, push me and lift me above myself. And unison is an altogether boring quality in discussion.
>
> As our mind is strengthened by communication with vigorous and orderly minds, so it is impossible to say how much it loses and degenerates by our continual association and frequentation with mean and sickly minds. There is no contagion that spreads like that one. . . .
>
> I enter into discussion and argument with great freedom and ease, inasmuch as opinion finds in me a bad soil to penetrate and take deep roots in. No propositions astonish me, no belief offends me, whatever contrast it offers with my own. . . .
>
> When someone opposes me, he arouses my attention, not my anger. I go to meet a man who contradicts me, who instructs me. The cause of truth should be common cause for both. . . .[20]

Montaigne points to the delight of the shared practice of mutually seeking for truth in agonistic (not uncommitted, neutral, academic) conversation. This practice requires no external epistemic foundation; convincing people to participate in it, if conviction is necessary, requires practical work and prudential arguments. Modern versions of this practice appear as the "unconstrained communication" postulated by Jürgen Habermas or the "conversation" advocated by Richard Rorty. Beyond the posturing of polemics, such a practice may open up possibilities of reasonable and humane arguing without a false presumption of disputants' uncommitted neutrality. It goes beyond the scope of this essay to show that engaging in such a conversation is an appropriate practice for philosophers of religion (and others) who seek both to understand religious practice and to show that any specific practice is preferable in the situation of diversity in practices and conflict over ultimate beliefs. However, I have elsewhere[21] claimed that the more a religious tradition (and the institutions which carry it and the communities which transmit it) is committed to the pursuit of wisdom, to "the common cause of truth," the wiser it is for people to be committed to such a tradition and the practices which constitute it.

But by most accounts from the mainstream of philosophy of religion, such a view is hardly in the line of Montaigne and Pascal. They are "fideists" who, by definition, are skeptical about rational foundations for faith or even, perhaps, of the reasonableness of "deciding" for faith. They resolve the problem, suggests Penelhum, by recommending conformity to the prevailing tradition as a way of avoiding commitment (Montaigne) or of inducing it (Pascal).[22] Although Pascal's famous Wager is acknowledged to be an argument of sorts, it is often alleged not to be an appeal to reason, but to "prudential self-interest." Although Penelhum calls it "irrefutable" given Pascal's assumptions,[23] we cannot give him those assumptions without making a fideistic choice. Or so philosophers often claim. But, in fact, the Wager is a very subtle, practical argument which points a way to finding a wise commitment. Its force can be seen when one has a practical, rather than an academic and doctrinal, understanding of religion.

The Wager and Religious Practice

The Wager argument is so well known as to need little exposition. First, the Wager is unavoidable: God is or God is not, and your life declares which bet you make. You cannot avoid wagering since you are already *in medias res*. We are all like the stranded mountaineer in James's "The Will to Believe;" we must choose either to follow the path that may be useless or remain where we are. Second, the Wager involves specifiable risks and benefits. If you do believe in God, and if there is no God, you have a finite and temporal loss (perhaps of the 'goods' obtained in 'immoral' practices from which you abstain, although this might be balanced by gaining the goods which religious practices bring, a point Pascal seems not to make). If you don't believe in God, and if there is no God, you gain some finite temporal "goods," which you might have lost had you abstained from practices incompatible with belief. If you do believe in God, and if there is a God, your gain is an "eternity of life and happiness." If you don't believe in God, and if there is a God, you may have a temporal and finite gain, but you miss out on a gain greater than which cannot be conceived. Therefore, since the risks are equal, and the benefits infinitely disproportionate, the wise person will bet on God, for the benefits of that risk infinitely outweigh the benefits of the other risk.

The Wager has recently found some philosophical defenders. Thomas Morris notes that Pascal's is not an "epistemically unconcerned project."[24] The wagerer finds both belief and unbelief relatively on an epistemic par with each other. In this context, most standard objections to the Wager vanish. As Morris put it:

> It is not an assumption of the Wager that God will reward a person for a deliberate, calculated charade of belief undertaken and maintained on the grounds of the grossest self interest. So the famous objection of William James, who was offended by such an assumption, misses the point.[25]

Nor does the Wager require a threat of punishment or promise of reward from God. As Morris notes, the text requires neither. Once one realizes the situation of the wagerer (as the dominant strand in modern philosophy of religion with its academic bias does not), most of the alleged problems with the Wager argument drop out.

The problem that remains, however, is that the epistemically concerned subject who wagers evidently has not two options, but many. This has come to be called the "many Gods" problem: our choices are not between theism and atheism, but between atheism and the many gods proposed by the various religious traditions. Given that there are a large number of possibilities, and given that the Wager is constructed assuming an "either-or" situation, the Wager therefore seems substantially flawed. Penelhum details this well.[26]

However, in one sense, the "many Gods" problem may be rationally solvable by using Anselm's definition of God as "that than which a greater cannot be conceived" as Lycan and Schlesinger point out.[27] The Wager requires not that one choose a god to one's taste, but that the God which one chooses must be the greater than any other, for this God and only this God holds out the possibility of the greatest (infinite) gain. Worship of any other god would be like participating in a practice with finite benefit. Hence, if one has a "choice" among deities, and one cannot worship them all, worshiping that than which a greater cannot be conceived offers one the greatest possible benefit. Devotion to the "other gods" *is* or *entails* disbelief in that than which a greater cannot be conceived. Therefore, the assumption of the Wager is not necessarily a fideistic choice. It can be construed as a forced option: either believe in that than which a greater cannot be conceived or believe in anything else. But only one has the possibility of infinite gain. So the wise person will choose that faith over any other. The problem of "many gods" does not defeat the wager.

But, alas, that may not solve the problem because the problem is a practical one. Many traditions are constituted by radically different practices for worshiping that than which a greater cannot be conceived. Taking the problem of religious diversity as a problem of "many Gods" is the wrong approach because it leaves the real, practical problem intact—*how to* devote oneself to the Infinite. The presumptions of modern philosophy that religious belief is an individual's disposition or property rather than a practice leaves the practical problem of "many gods" finally intact.

However, there is a practical way around this practical problem. One must see clearly the situation in which the Wager comes into play. Two factors relevant to the force of the Wager are rarely considered. Yet these show how the Wager can provide a way for resolving the practical problem, at least for people in specific circumstances.

First, it is important to know the purposes for which Pascal composed the argument and the sort of addressees it was intended to convince. All too often, the Wager argument is taken as a 'neutral' and purely 'philosophical' argument, a rhetorical move in a polite conversation carried on by unconcerned academics in professional journals. If one has such a presumption, as Morris suggests, one cannot understand how the Wager could work as a practical argument. Terence Penelhum provides a description of the addressees in which the *Apology* (of which *Pensées* as we have them are fragments) was to have been issued:

> The *Apology* was [to be] addressed primarily to Pascal's cultivated and freethinking contemporaries, who were assumed to be interested in the dramatic developments in the natural sciences and their implications, to possess some degree of philosophical sophistication and to have been wearied by the bitter religious divisions that had plunged France into civil warfare. Such an audience would have acquired an inclination toward skepticism, and to a self-protective and superficial religious conformity. For such people the writings of Montaigne would have been a major influence, and it is clearly Montaigne from whom Pascal derives his understanding of Skepticism. Pascal is passionately convinced that neither the noble pretensions of rationalist philosophies, be they Stoic or Cartesian, nor the easy-going Conformism of Montaigne can offer man an appropriate antidote to anxiety. And the faith which alone can save them is a passionate surrender of the whole personality. . . . [28]

Pascal's situation is like that described by Montaigne (and, I would add, like that which obtains in the present "secularized" context): religious camps have been at war with each other with dreadful consequences not only for individual believers, but also for both churches and the state. One upshot of this is that the starry skies above no longer show the splendor of God; the book of nature no longer can unambiguously reveal its Author to these jaded unbelievers.

The *purpose* of the argument Pascal makes, and centrally of the Wager, is not to complete an academic quest for truth, but to bring persons to religious faith and practice. The way for them to solve their problem in a situation of uncertainty is not to be found in engaging in more philosophical argument, but in taking up a practice in which they learn *how* to see, *how* to read. Abstracting the argument and its purpose from its specific addressees in their social context, especially if one takes it to be an "academic" argument, may easily distort it and undermine its force.

The second factor is the connection of Pascal's well-known final remedy of "masses and holy water" to the Wager. The remedy may, *in this context*, simply beg the practical question by presuming an answer to what is really at issue. Why *this* practice in *this* religious tradition rather than some other? Huguenots and Catholics have been killing each other, in part to establish whether even an attenuated form of religious tolerance is to be permitted in France or in specific *departments*. Not only are these disputants epistemically committed, they also have political and religious commitments. Doesn't Pascal's remedy beg the practical question in favor of the Catholics?

A close reading of some *Pensées* suggests he might not. In *Pensées*, Pascal's imagined interlocutor *admits the force* of the Wager argument. The interlocutor then continues and Pascal responds:

> " . . . I am forced to wager, and am not free. I am not released, and am so made that I cannot believe. What, then, would you have me do?"
>
> True. But at least learn your inability to believe, since reason brings you to this, and yet you cannot believe. Endeavor then to convince yourself, not by increase of proofs of God, but by the abatement of your passions. You would like to attain faith, and do not know the way; you would like to cure yourself of unbelief and ask the remedy for it. Learn of those who have been bound like you, and who are cured of an ill of which you would be cured. Follow the way by which they began; by acting as if they believed, taking the holy water, having masses said, etc. Even this will naturally make you believe, and deaden your acuteness.—"But this is what I am afraid of."—And why? What have you to lose?

But to show you that this leads you there, it is this which will lessen the passions, which are your stumbling blocks.

The end of this discourse.—Now what harm will befall you in taking this side? You will be faithful, honest, humble, grateful, generous, a sincere friend, truthful. Certainly you will not have those poisonous pleasures, glory and luxury; but will you not have others? I will tell you that you will thereby gain in this life, and that, at each step you take on this road, you will see so great certainty of gain, so much nothingness in what you risk, that you will at last recognize that you have wagered for something certain and infinite, for which you have given nothing.

"Ah! This discourse transports me, charms me," etc.

If this discourse pleases you and seems impressive, know that it is made by a man who has knelt, both before and after it, in prayer to that Being, infinite and without parts, before whom he lays all he has, for you also to lay before Him all you have for your own good and for His glory, that so strength may be given to lowliness.[29]

This specific section is exceedingly rich and needs to be unpacked.

(1) Pascal has a psychological diagnosis of the interlocutor's unbelief: his passion is getting in the way of his reason. Having accepted the cogency of the Wager argument, how can the interlocutor *not* believe? The problem cannot be intellectual; thus, it must be passional. The interlocutor's "acuteness" is not intellectual, but passional, scruple.

(2) Pascal has a therapy for the interlocutor. Pascal is certainly not presuming that our beliefs are fully within our control. His therapy is indirect; it does not *directly* give the interlocutor a belief or require an act of will to believe. Pascal is prescribing a specific set of *practices* which, properly and dutifully undertaken, will likely bring about belief. Presumably, the interlocutor's practices have led her not to be religious; through her vicious practices she has acquired a taste for poisonous pleasures. Her practices and her practically-shaped character obstruct her intellect and get in the way of her accepting religion. If she will give up the practices of seeking glory and wealth and take up religious practices of seeking God, she can become a person who can develop a taste for those satisfactions religious practices bring, especially a taste for communion with God. And in engaging in practical religion, she will naturally develop beliefs about God and God's worshipfulness. The Wager argument, to which the interlocutor has 'notion-

ally' assented will come to elicit her 'real' assent (to use John Henry Newman's terms) and become authentic faith not because more arguments are piled up, but because she has become, through engaging in religious practices, a rather different person, one who can be awestruck by *les espaces infinis* and see through the book of nature to the Mind which wrote it. She will become a person of faith whom God graces, not a devotee of poisonous pleasures.

(3) So, although the "presenting complaint" of the heartsick interlocutor is intellectual, his real problem is a hidden disease of the passions. Pascal prescribes a set of practices which will not merely bring about external conformity (as James thought) or contrived faith, but reshape the interlocutor's desires so that the religious life he comes to lead and the rewards it promises become desirable to him. His character will acquire the shape that will make an infinite gain be no mere external compensation for conformity, but an appropriate 'internal' satisfaction growing out of and properly crowning a life of truly religious practice.

(4) Finally, the Wager Argument is not a monologic demonstration, but an implicit dialogue. Engaging in the Wager is not here portrayed as an isolated individual privately betting his life. Rather, the Wager is a shared practice, a conversational remedy in which more than one voice is needed.

However, even granted these points, given the conflicted context, Pascal's therapeutic answer at this point in *Pensées* does indeed seem to beg the practical question badly. But part of the social context and thus the conditions in which religious indifference, conformity, and skepticism is a 'live option' is the multiplicity of competing traditions and practices. Pascal here simply seems to *presume* that the Catholic practices will properly bring the interlocutor to be the sort of person who can accept the Wager argument in a real, not notional, way. In a situation in which practitioners vilify each others' paths, no practices may seem attractive. Why prefer to take up this practice or set of practices rather than another? Pascal seems to ignore this question here.

However, in *Pensées*, two further themes suggest hints toward a resolution of this practical problem. First, Pascal spends considerable space to argue that *"the true Jews and the true Christians have but the same religion."*[30] Although Judaism *seemed* to consist in external practices, true Jews practiced the same religion as the true Christians: "the love of God."[31] Pascal works hard to distinguish the carnal from the spiritual and discussing the figures and types which are found in the "Old Testament." The upshot of these meditations is that Pascal suggests that true religion is not found as much in the institution, community, or tradition to which one is attached, as in the *way* religion is practiced and the sort of God to which the practice is devoted. Combining these points with the noetic solution to the "many gods" problem we can say that good religious practices may be found in more than one religion if the intentional object of those practices is that than which a greater cannot be conceived.[32]

Second, Pascal does give some (rather weak and, by present standards, uninformed) arguments against Islam and the religions of China. But the point of these is to argue that there are some religions which are inferior to Judaism and Christianity:

> I see then a crowd of religions in many parts of the world and in all times; but their morality cannot please me, nor could their proofs convince me. Thus I should equally have rejected the religion of Mahomet and of China, of ancient Romans and of the Egyptians, for the sole reason, that none having more marks of truth than another, nor anything which should necessarily persuade me, reason cannot incline to one rather than the other.[33]

In Jamesian terms, these are not "live options" for Pascal. They do not even qualify to enter the race, much less to have a chance to be the subject of a wager.

This is the shape, then, of a practical religious epistemology, exemplified by Pascal. The situation is this: true heathenism (religious indifference, moral laxity, love of the carnal) and true religion (as evinced in authentic practice of the love of that than which a greater cannot be conceived in Judaism and Christianity) are live options on a relative epistemic par for engaged epistemic subjects. Pascal, like us, is not an epistemically unconcerned subject. His intellect is no religious *tabula rasa*. He is a situated subject who has reduced the live religious options to two—finite and infinite, worldly and 'spiritual' devotion. The question is which path to take. And that *is* the situation in which the Wager is valid, the assumptions on which the Wager is triumphant. If that is the reader's situation, then she should properly find the argument sound! She should be led by rational and practical argument in a committed and human conversation finally to take up whatever practices she actually can from among those which do constitute devotion to or worship of that than which a greater cannot be conceived. There are other people in other situations with different diseases who need different therapies and undertake different practices. But that need not concern her, for she is not embodied "there," but where she is. Nor is she alone, for others share her situation. Together they can explore the significance of their live options.

Here then is a practical resolution of the real problem of religious diversity. It is not "simple conformity," but an acknowledgement that the problem is a situated one. The embodied persons struggling with practical issues acknowledge the authoritative patterns of practices which make some appeal for their commitment. That the disembodied academic mind can toy with other patterns is fine, but irrelevant. The real problem is one of commitment and the Wager is the wager of life. While the academic mind may investigate unappealing practices and construct theoretical arguments, the person in which that mind is embodied makes her Wager, not as much by her isolated investigations, as by her pattern of commitments to practices. In short, Pascal's Wager argument suggests that there is a way to construe the tradition of Montaigne and Pascal, not as "internalist" and "fideist," but as practical. They show how to engage in the practice of engaged conversation about wise religious practice in a conflicted situation in order to come to a practical resolution of such real religious problems.

Postlude: Toward a Practical Religious Epistemology

A viable alternative to the fading modern, individualistic, academic, externalist practice of religious epistemology is not to make a fideistic choice or leap of faith. Rather, the alternative is to engage in practical religious 'epistemology,' the shared practice of seeking the wisdom of a religious commitment, to abandon the academic practice of unengaged jousting in mainstream philosophy of religion, and to enter into one of the shared religious practices of a committed seeking of the Truth valorized by Pascal in the wake of Montaigne.

This sort of practical tradition points the way beyond internalism and externalism in philosophy of religion. We need to find or create practices in which we can dispute reasonably, creatively, proddingly, joustingly, engagedly, and agonistically about practical religious wisdom. The burning religious question is a practical question. It is an 'ethical' one in the broad sense. The issues addressed in exploring the ethic of 'belief' are practical ones: *Since practices shape us as persons, into which practices shall we place or continue to place our bodies, our minds, our selves? A practical religious epistemology is the discipline to which we submit to answer that question.*

The disciplinary practice begins with unconstrained conversation. To use McClendon's definition of a practice, the *end* of this practice is religious wisdom. Its *practitioners* begin wherever they are. We differ from the points at which we start and the paths which we walk. Other people will begin in other places. Within the practice, different people may find wildly different paths to be live options. Perhaps some will find themselves with more than two live options. But why expect otherwise? The real world is messy. What practitioners have in common is that they enter the conversation not as disinterested academics, but as engaged believers, perhaps even engaged nihilist, atheist, agnostic, or 'heathen' believers. Those who do not seek wisdom need not join the conversation. But who are they? Only those who refuse to think about their lives and commitments, who prefer the unexamined life. But perhaps they can be brought to the initial step of the Wager as a *means* of initiating folk into the practice.

Once they are brought to recognize that they do Wager, then our work uses various *means* governed by practical *rules* to narrow our choices to the most plausible ones. But this is not merely a noetic matter, but a contextual one of taste, attraction, and affect, a matter for shared exploration. As Jaggar wrote, "Emotions prompt us to act appropriately, to approach some people and situations and to avoid others, to caress or cuddle, fight or flee. Without emotion, human life would be unthinkable."[34] The *end* is to embody the best available practices in our lives, practices affectively attractive and intellectually satisfying. I claim, although I cannot argue this point here, that any tradition which fails to empower and seek to draw in those who were not (yet) in position to participate in the practice of seeking Truth should be avoided. The traditions which empower people to do and to seek truth would be constituted, in part, by an authentic "peaceableness." As Code finds academic epistemology woefully inadequate because of its failure to include social and political aspects, so I would further claim that a religious tradition which did not include practices designed to overcome the marginalization and dislocation of those without privileged position would not be authentically "peaceable" and thus could not be a candidate for that best practice.

Perhaps one person will have to consider the "proofs" and "moral demands" of Tibetan Buddhism and Shi'ite Islam, and another those of Methodist Christianity and heathenism. And each may come to different choices. But it is possible that the practices we properly undertake in varied religious traditions are analogous enough so that we can come in different ways to different forms of eternal happiness and joy, even if not to the same belief.

The extension of the Wager argument considered here suggests that the wise person will choose to be part of a tradition which has the central and distinctive practice of the love of or devotion to that than which a greater cannot be conceived. Such devotion will be tradition-specific and particular, but have a universalizing goal and intent. In practice, the traditions will have different conceptions of the Greatest as well, but may carry analogous practices. And by engaging in practical conversation, members of such traditions can even come to practical agreement or mutual enlightenment—to which the happy chance which inscribed Buddha in the Catholic martyrology, the influence of that story on Tolstoy,[35] the well-known influences of Tolstoy on Gandhi and of Gandhi on M. L. King, Jr., witnesses. Others may engage in practical attempts to live and think in two traditions as exemplified, for instance, in the work of Raimundo Pannikar. In the messy world of particular commitments, perhaps more cannot be sought, certainly not in theory.

The practical approach of seeking the wisdom of religious commitment is one in which proper beliefs are not the external foundations of practices nor merely the practice-relative beliefs generated by a conformist fideism. Proper beliefs arise out of the practices of the love of that than which a greater cannot be conceived. If this is correct, then the problems of religious epistemology generated by religious diversity cannot be resolved by externalist arguments undertaken by uncommitted academic philosophers of religion, but practically dissolved by Montaignian conversation and resolved by Pascalian wagering, that is making a commitment to the practice of unlimited truthfulness and peaceableness as practical constituents of the religious devotion to that than which a greater cannot be conceived, insofar as this practice can be incarnated in religious institutions, traditions, and communities which support such Truthful religious practices.

THEOLOGY WITHOUT
FOUNDATIONS

CHAPTER 4

Walk and Word: The Alternatives to Methodologism

John H.Yoder

The academic discussion of moral reasoning—like the academic discussion of almost anything else—tends to be dominated by a search for first principles.[1] Once that pattern of work has been established, it being agreed that somehow "before" or "beneath" the debate of which one is aware there is another, then a metadebate opens up, contrasting with one another the various participants' proposals as to *which* first principles are most fundamental.[2]

As If One Could Go Back to Start from "Scratch"

Epictetus is usually credited[3] with the statement that "philosophy" has to do with three questions:

- That we ought not to lie;
- Why we ought not to lie;
- Why that (i.e. the answer to the first "why?") counts as a demonstration[4]

It is from the proliferation of alternative answers to the third question that the several "first principles" debates about moral discourse have arisen. What I propose here is that we would have something to learn from a fuller description of the relationship between the third level and the other two, looking not first at logic but at the real experience of valuing communities.

Epictetus would not have minded admitting that each of his three simple questions breaks down into a network of subquestions without which it cannot be discussed. Just for starters, the following further elements belong in the picture:

1. We ought not to lie
    1.1 What is a lie?
        1.1.1. Why is that the right definition of a lie?
            1.1.1.1. If the reason that this definition of a lie should be accepted is the authority of an interpreter of community tradition (e.g."My mother told me"), why does she have that authority? Does every interpreter of every tradition have the same authority?
            1.1.1.2. Can a human lawgiver redefine, "correct" the tradition?
            1.1.1.3. What other definitions does that one overlap or collide with?
            1.1.1.4. How do you know the difference between a good and a bad definition of a lie? This is like Epictetus' question 3 but it already arises within a smaller area here under question 1.
        1.1.2. Is everything a lie that looks like one?
            1.1.2.1. Is silence sometimes a lie?
            1.1.2.2. Is lying in ambush a lie? (relevant for just war ethics)
            1.1.2.3. Is saying nothing when someone assumes I should speak the same as a lie?
                1.1.2.3.1. If so, whose "assuming I should speak" is authoritative?

2. Why we ought not to lie
    2.1. If the reason given is that someone objects, what is their standing?
        2.1.1. Does the person whom my lie victimizes have special standing? (relevant for victimless sins)
        2.1.2. Does "my mother told me," i.e. the voice of tradition (1.1.1.1 above) prove something?
        2.1.3. Does a human legislator's decree make a lie wrong?

2.1.3.1. If so, who has the right to legislate?

2.2. If the reason given is an appeal to some other value which lying militates against, how are conflicting values to be weighed against one another?

3. Why is the answer given to all of the above a demonstration? Obviously we would have to spread out this question as well into even more subquestions.[5]

This exercise of ramification, breaking each question down into subquestions, will never reach a plateau. Further complexity will always keep showing up. Each question breaks down into several more.

But before the outline began, there had to be things going on which Epictetus took for granted without naming them. There had to be a human social fabric, in which people's relationships were mediated by communication, through various kinds of signals but most evidently in words. There had to be in that social fabric experiences in which the difference between reliable and unreliable communication became evident. There had to be experiences in which specific actions of communication were the objects of blame if they were lies or of praise if they were true.

Attempting to itemize all the possible subquestions which could be found within Epictetus' outline would expand our agenda to infinity. For now, projecting that scenario hypothetically just this much suffices already for our purposes to illustrate how limited is its utility. Instead of taking that path, which some call "foundationalist,"[6] I propose to begin again with what might be called a phenomenology of the moral life. That term is avowedly ambiguous—as is every claim to do "phenomenology"—in that it suggests the reliability or commonality of appearances as I see them, as if my proposing "simply to describe" were a recourse to "objectivity" and thus not subject to anyone's second guessing.

Nevertheless this kind of description is less subject to *a priori* bias than one which claims through some prior definitional ("foundational," methodological, "meta-ethical") move to have avoided the pitfall of particular identity, or to have sheltered itself against the challenges of the relativists.

So I begin by stepping "back behind" Epictetus' outline. There is, as a matter of empirically undeniable fact, a human social fabric characterized by communication. Much communication is non-verbal but for our purposes we can take the verbal as representative. For the society to be viable, most of this communication has to be "true" most of the time; i.e. it has to provide a reliable basis for structuring our common life, counting on each other and not being routinely disappointed. Sometimes some communication is false and no one discerns that fact or suffers from it.[7] Sometimes it is false, and someone suffers from that fact, and blames the teller of the non-truth. As a society develops, the ways of saying "do not lie" become solidified as tradition. The society develops some equivalent of the definition of a lie (1.1 above; probably concretized as sinning against some simple notion of "correspondence" between words and reality), and perhaps modes of disciplining offenders.

All of this is all going strong long before anyone gets around to Epictetus' third question. The fabric exists, and functions more or less well, before anyone asks for an accounting about why it works. The "accounting" that we can do is therefore not "validation" but *a posteriori* elucidation.

Let us keep "my mother told me" as our cipher for the most fundamental level of moral learning, whereby the young human mind/psyche normally appropriates, from an authority which is both overwhelming and benevolent, the simplest sense of "the way things are." In such a micro social setting, moral culture can be taken as univocal. Epictetus' third question "why is that a demonstration?" does not arise.[8] The question "why should I obey?" (Epictetus 2) does arise, and the answer varies from simple motivations of reward for the child, or "because I told you," to more complex or "mature" notions of "honor" or "duty" or making mommy happy or concern for harm to self or others.[9]

The third question does arise when with more than one generation in dialogue, or with more than one culture interfacing, differences demand adjudication and the concurrent appeals to self-evidence and to authority cannot convince. Now Epictetus' third question cannot be avoided. Now the meta-ethical spectrum does spread out, and we can discuss the relative adequacy of ends, means, contract, virtue, story, and/or whatever else as modes of elucidation or even of validation. All of the standard agenda of the textbooks in moral method can be located somewhere in the thicket of ramifications from Epictetus' three basics. But that is not where it started.

That third story is the level on which the bulk of the discipline of academic moral philosophy goes on.[10] Most authors may be read as responding to the question (implicitly or explicitly) why one kind of moral language is better than another. I do not wish to deny the utility of those arguments; I do doubt their absolute necessity, or their priority, or their decisiveness, and in some cases their possibility. There is no reason to be sure that it is better *generally* to use one of those modes (or to use only one) than another. There is nothing necessarily wrong with real life, in which all five of the above (ends, means, contract, virtue, story), along with some other weaker ones, like habit, intuition, inspiration, "mother," and "just because", are mixed together helter-skelter, with no need for one of them always to have priority.

In particular conflict settings, the clash among competing modes of validation is adjudicated by the power of a legislator or a confessor. In settings of intellectual controversy, it can become very useful to sort out the several strands, discussing whether (as Kant argued) there is a clear notion of ultimate obligation utterly independent of considerations of motivation or consequences, or whether (as some contemporary Roman Catholic moral theologians argue) the hard decisions for which the "double effect" rules used to be applied can now be boiled down to "proportionate reasoning" which measures goods and evils by a single (though complex) yardstick.

In most more complex cases, however, the modes interlock. It is possible e.g. to argue on Kantian grounds that in certain settings it is right to maximize benefits; or to argue on pragmatic grounds that a culture or a church reasoning in a Kantian mode is most likely to be socially "together" and therefore effective.

I thus gladly grant the usefulness of these debates in particular settings. Each of them would fit somewhere within the shrubbery created by ramifying Epictetus' three questions. I grant the usefulness of reviewing past personalities and positions as part of the formation of the morally committed person's grasp of issues and pitfalls. All that I need to deny is that any overwhelming reason exists for having to choose only one idiom or for always ranking the several available kinds of resources in the same order.

81

No one can work empathetically within the Hebraic heritage without respect for "divine command" as a master metaphor; yet that does not exclude a morality founded upon "the nature of things" or on "discipleship". No one can work empathetically within the Hebraic heritage without respect for the style of Wisdom, which accumulates aphorisms side by side with no concern for whether they all reason in the same way. No one can have been formed in our culture and discuss moral issues without considering costs and benefits. That does not make any of those modes more foundational than any other.

The life of the community is prior to all possible methodological distillations.[11] The role of the distillation process, which lifts up this or that dimension for this or that purpose internal to the community's identity, cannot be to short-circuit the appeal to all of the community's resources.

Instead of standing in judgment upon the ordinary people who use now the language of virtue, now that of command, now that of ends to press their praise and blame on one another, it is rather the methodologists who ought to bear the burden of proof. When and why does it contribute to the community's fidelity that one should have to decide that virtue language is always better than command language? When and why need we decide between the prophetically revealed will of God and our own conception of human flourishing? Why does it help to put the difference between "nature" and "supernature" or between the moral and the "non-moral" at the foundation of a discussion?

I do not mean this question to be merely rhetorical. I believe that it can be answered; that there would be several good answers, depending on the setting.[12] For some purposes the critical impact of the Kierkegaardian critique may be helpful;[13] for others not. For some purposes Aquinas's claim to contain everything under one tent in the name of Aristotle may be appropriate;[14] for others it is both silly and presumptuous. What we can fruitfully debate is the relative strengths and weaknesses of the contribution of each mode to the mix, and what the real values are which are involved when people think (mistakenly) that they can advocate just one of them against the others.

The Message Is the Medium

If then different meta-questions have priority in different settings, how are we to know which one is fitting when? One set of answers to that question will properly be procedural. The community of moral discourse counts upon several functions, fittingly discharged by different members, of whom the apostolic testimony says that they are severally divinely authorized and empowered.[15] There should be open conversation in which each person can take the floor.[16] The fact that the heritage of normative *halakah* has been relativized for Pauline Christians by recognizing that it is not the basis for "salvation" does not put an end to moral obligation, but only reformulates it.[17] Spirit utterance is to be expected, but it is also to be questioned; ". . . test the spirits to see whether they are of God."[18]

Let these simple apostolic aphorisms stand as specimen ciphers for the mutual interpenetration of medium and message. The divine command to walk in the communion of the Spirit is not in another compartment separate from procedural guidelines about how that communion works as an epistemology. Pluralism as to epistemological method is not a counsel of despair but part of the Good News.[19] Ultimate validation is a matter not of a reasoning process which one could by dint of more doubt or finer hair-splitting push down one story closer to bedrock, but of the concrete social genuineness of the community's reasoning together in the Spirit.

Does It Make a Difference?

It would be self-refuting if I were to seek to exposit an understanding of the shape of moral discourse without reference to particular specimens. Other approaches may not need to show the same respect for concreteness. Jensen and Toulmin surveyed the history of casuistry to make some points about the limits of rules, but did not demonstrate the pertinence of their analysis by arguing a single currently contested case.[20] Jeffrey Stout can write a book on *Ethics After Babel* without considering it important to show that his (admittedly partial) resolution of the problem of relativism can transculturally validate concrete moral choices.[21] The same is even true for the majestic corpus of historical review provided by Alasdair MacIntyre.[22] The immediate impact which the methodological depth awarenesses of these giants of our time will have on deciding when one should tell the truth, or shed blood, give to the poor, insult someone, or have sex, is not apparent.

James Gustafson's *Ethics in a Theocentric Perspective* does deal at some depth with four problems of application,[23] but not in such a way as to have provoked much critical comment, nor in such a way as to have demonstrated that the particular choices he favors are dictated by his work's major agenda. The major agenda of the first part of the study was the way Gustafson had redefined what he calls the "theocentric" context of ethics. That is not drawn upon in any decisive way in the concrete cases.

I submit that a methodological debate which makes a difference for concrete choices would be more illuminating than one whose argument can be carried out without reference to cases. This contradicts directly the assumption which often dictates the flight to the level of methodology, namely the "liberal" notion that if questions of method or procedure could be discussed first, in a more abstract or "purer" or less conflictual form, then differences about concrete behavior would thereby already be partly resolved.

It should thus not be surprising that when in other works I have debated the moral issue of war, criticism often used me as representing a debatable method option,[24] even when it was not my intention to be proposing a specific mode of reasoning. It has been used by others[25] as a specimen from which to reach "back" to fruitful discussions of method issues. I do not grant that mine is a single-issue stance; its application to truth-telling or promise-keeping or economic sharing would cover an analogous range of debatable choices. On the level of argumentative method, the case for promise-breaking or for lying or for polygamy or for letting-die can be quite parallel to the case for war, even though the scale is quite different.[26] On the other hand, there is no obligation to reason in the same way on all subjects. Augustine was deontological about lying and teleological about killing.[27] Today's Roman Catholic bishops give the faithful binding concrete guidance about fetal life but they leave judgment about killing in war to the individual.

Apostolic Suspicion

The great advocates of hermeneutic suspicion in our age are supposed to be Darwin, who taught us to doubt "creation", Marx, who taught us to mistrust the owner, and Freud, who taught us to mistrust our self-awareness. They mightily updated the fundamental questioning stance for which we blame Descartes. Yet more fundamental is the much earlier apostolic warning about the wiles of language itself which we find in the later New Testament writings.[28] If the word-spinners are left to themselves, i.e. if the process of redefining terms and drawing deductions from those definitions goes on without "ordinary language" testing, then the world they make can become self-sufficient, a law unto itself. They proceed *as if* a form of words could be found that would truly describe everything and would cohere in itself; and *as if* the kind of coherence thus constructed would then itself constitute a kind of certainty needing no validation by anyone "out there" having to recognize that "that is what we mean by right and wrong."

James and the author of *II Timothy* are right; language as an autonomous power is not to be trusted. Language is never self-contained unless it be, like algebra, the product of a mind abstracting from moral community. No term is self-defining, no absolute is without footnotes and collisions, no maxim is bedrock, nobody's mother told him the whole truth. If you think you have mastered a language, it has mastered you. Ontological "realism," making the claim that to every noun there corresponds an idea in the mind of God, trying thereby to extend the linguistic self understanding of the monocultural village into metaphysics, is one of the nobler forms of this mistake, but there are plenty of others.

Yet once we have learned how the word-spinners mislead us, we must also recognize that their skills are the only ones we have with which to defend ourselves against their temptations.

A recent specimen of the danger of a new language game's spinning off into autonomy was the "situation ethics" flurry of the 1960's. Its advocates did not claim to prescribe radically different behaviors, but rather to offer a better way to reason morally. Yet there was no careful definition of how moral reasoning should succeed, once its "situation" was defined. How long or broad or deep a "situation" is was left undefined. Should evaluation in the situation proceed by intuition? By applying either learned or innate criteria to make utility judgments? Subjective good intentions ("love is the only imperative") give little guidance.

An older specimen of the same problem was scholastic protestant orthodoxy. University theologians went off on their own in the seventeenth century, to synthesize some biblical language with their greco-roman learning, and expected the resulting mix to stand still.

Whether the argument claiming to take over the field be an old one or new, to suspect the adequacy of the game is a liberating ministry. In that ministry of suspicion we may be helped more by the disciplines which interpret social process and communication than by reviewing classical debates; yet the latter exercise can help too, when its purpose is not to demonstrate that after all one of the old schools was the right one.

This generally critical perspective, downgrading the appetite for intellectual thoroughness in favor of the wholeness of community culture, does not belong peculiarly in the realm of ethics; yet ethics puts it most evidently to the test, since it is the field where wrong thinking most immediately may lead to hurting someone. Similarly the themes of social ethics are the most appropriate test areas, since it is there that the insufficiency of language-centered arguments is more easily observed, there that the presumptions on the side of custom and consensus are most evidently strong.

Each in Its Place

Instead of making the case for the priority of one style, what I have argued is thus that all of them are needed, precisely because none of them may be dominant. Deontological rigor à la Kant is necessary, in the defense of the claims of the absent (God, the neighbor, especially the enemy), but it is wrongly used if it is taken to follow therefrom that in every setting there is only one imperative with no collisions.

Consequential rigor in the style of the utilitarians is a necessary acknowledgement of our responsibility for the length-dimensions of our actions. We are responsible to name and to measure what is at stake; it is our duty to understand and respect considerations of causal connectedness. It is wrong, however, if it be thought that the costs and benefits, as well as the causal connections which enable calculating them, can be transparently known.[29] It is also wrong if it assumes that "I", i.e. the moral agent, am the king, able and bound to impose the best cost/benefit tradeoff as I see it on every conflict within my reach. It is wrong in its failure to recognize that every (pretendedly "pragmatic") way to weigh costs and benefits is subject to a prior set of ("deontological") value judgments.

The language of virtue is fine to acknowledge the depth dimensions of personality and culture, defending those dimensions against "punctualism";[30] it is wrong when it suggests that the virtuous person can operate without the resources of the other orders, as if there were a sort of built-in moral compass, unfallen or easily repaired despite the Fall. It is also wrong in that if taken thoroughly it would disqualify as subhuman the large number of persons whose life experience never formed in them the qualities which the doctrine affirms.[31]

Instead of seeking to settle on the one right idiom, the greater value will inhere in the skills of mixing and matching according to the shape of a particular debate.[32] The exercise of that skill, within the complementarity of the various components of adequate moral discourse, might be called a virtue; but it will also be a duty, and it will also be useful.

Form Follows Function

The invitation to which the preparation of this essay initially responded[33] suggested that I should advocate "biblicism" as an alternative to other standard philosophical views about metaphysics, epistemology, or norms. Precisely because of my commitment to a community which in turn is committed to canonical accountability, I saw no way to squeeze such accountability into such a strait jacket. There is no such thing as "biblicism." It is none of the above and not an alternative to any of the above. Is canonical accountability a distinctive way of being? Of knowing? Of norming? Why need it be any of the above? Why not all of them, and more?

I have thus attempted to deviate from the grid of the traditional approach to these issues in order to demonstrate why the grid seems to me to be philosophically misleading. Having sought to do that, I should now return to ask whether my low view of the utility of standard disjunctive approaches in methodology is cor-related with my using the Bible in ethics as I do.[34]

Certainly the two dimensions of my stance are mutually com-patible and reciprocally supportive. Skepticism about methodo-logical reductionism and respect for the "thick" reading of any real history, in which the Bible belongs, go naturally hand in hand. The Bible is itself, in its role as common memory of the God movement, full of a multiplicity of styles of praising and blaming. It is the prototypical narrative—although since then we have had nearly two millennia more of the same—of how a value-bound community exercises all kinds of moral discourse, mixing and matching its modes rather than being concerned to please the philosopher for whom one idiom must be shown to be more acceptable than another.

Dramatically since the fifteenth century, as had been the case less deeply before that, the Bible has functioned not merely as our deposit of moral memories but also as critical fulcrum for "renais-sance" and "reformation." By common consent, something had gone wrong with the Christian movement. The different diagno-ses and the different prescriptions for healing had in common the notion that the origins of the Christian movement, to which the Bible testified, possessed a permanent pertinence as testimony to what the movement had initially been sent by God to do,[35] and should be restored to doing.

Unfortunately, before long the notion of employing a critical fulcrum within history to correct the course of an historical move-ment was hijacked by a particular scholastic style, and the Bible was transformed by Protestant scholasticism into a collection of inerrant propositions freed from the conditions of human fini-tude. Those infallible propositions, it was assumed, could then be—had to be—carried into the theological subdiscipline of ethics as a compendium of undiscussible divine commands. That pre-emption of the Bible by scholasticism[36] transformed a living nar-rative into a collection of timeless norms and made it difficult even to this day for a non-Fundamentalist use of the Bible to be listened to. It opened the door for a new set of foundational methodology debates about how to prove that the kind of God who on other grounds could be proven to "exist" would have chosen to "reveal" through these texts.

A more pointed variant of the "reforming" role is the "prophetic." Sometimes it is not enough to correct a loss of vision or vigor; sometimes the need is to denounce idolatry or inhumanity, or to offer a hope reaching beyond present possibilities. The worst form of idolatry is not carving an image; it is the presumption that one has—or that a society has, or a culture has—the right to set the terms under which God can be recognized.

The oddity of the stance of those for whom my reading the Bible as ethical resource is noteworthy is that they sense no need to validate with the same rigor the *other* resources (i.e. their own views on "nature" or "reason") to which they and others appeal instead. Yet those other authorities are no less idiosyncratic, and they usually represent a younger and a smaller community.

To the "reforming" role has been added in our age an "ecumenical" one. The discrepancy between theological affirmations, which all "confessions" make, to the effect that the faith community is one, and the empirical dividedness of churches has provoked in our time renewed commitment to dialog about differences. Ethics is included in this dialogue, although only very marginally.[37] In such conversation no community can impose its separate past path on the others. Roman Catholics cannot ask Protestants to share the decisions of Trent. Lutherans cannot expect the "anabaptists," whom their *Confessio Augustana* condemns five times, to share that text as an identity marker. The canonical Scriptures are, at least on pragmatic grounds, the primary court of appeal.

Neither the reforming use of the canon nor its ecumenical use is dependent on the theories about the special revelatory status of the texts in which the Protestant scholastics invested, theories to which today's liberals are still reacting.

My challenge to methodological disjunctions would make sense quite independently of this background in the fruitfulness of canonical accountability. An intelligently humane atheist could make the same point as I do about the way moral thought works. Nonetheless I have more reason than the atheist to press the argument. It is I who had my canon kidnapped by the methodologists three centuries ago. It is my faith which claims to be good news for those whom the way it was interpreted in the recent past has kept from hearing it.

Form must follow function in the sense that *if* the function in question is the continuing accountable common life of a people, whose members call one another to renewed faithfulness to the call of the God who has entered human affairs to save, *then* the forms of that community's discourse must be no narrower than the story itself. The normal way to sustain the identity of the community, so that the appropriate praising and blaming procedures—which might be called "pastoral care" if very concrete, and "Christian ethics" if more general—can be accountable, must then be to remember together the common heritage. Not all of the heritage is biblical; there are also the saints of the centuries since then; they were committed to the same fidelity. Not all of the concepts need to be biblical; good news can be translated. All that is needed is the confessed readiness to be part of the edifice of which the canon represents the ground floor.

CHAPTER 5

"I Will Ask *You* a Question": Interrogatory Theology

Ched Myers

The primary theological task of an indigenous theology in North America is to provide a frame of reference for the prolonged and intense experience of negation. We have concentrated on being an answering theology, and this is our undoing in an age when answers can have only a hollow ring. Now we must concentrate on providing a place to which to refer the questions.

—Douglas John Hall[1]

At a crucial juncture in his mission, Mark's Jesus was confronted by members of the ruling Jerusalem establishment, who demanded that he present his political credentials:

By what authority are you doing these things; and who gave you this authority? (Mark 11:28)

"These things" refer to the dramatic challenges Jesus had just made to the scribal status quo: his theatrical, militant march into the capital city followed by his public disruption of commerce in the Temple (11:1–25). As far as the guardians of civic order were concerned, things had gone far enough. It was one thing for this Nazarene to have made a name for himself playing the prophet in distant provinces, quite another to have created a protest spectacle in the city of David—especially during the feast days, that tension-ridden season in the nation's life when old symbols of liberation, uneasily latent, always threatened to erupt again. It was time to force this country preacher to divulge just what he was up to.[2]

By what authority, and who gave it to you? In all times and places, this is the central challenge put by governments to dissidents. Those in power recognize no authority they have not defined, brokered, or mediated. Conversely, any who would contest the dominant arrangements must justify themselves. It is the circular genius of State logic: There can be no protest except by permission. How will Jesus counter? He pauses, eyeing his antagonists, understanding that to defend his practice is a losing proposition as long as *they* are framing the issue. Measuring his words carefully, he goes on the offensive:

> I will ask *you* one question; answer me, and I will tell you by what authority I do these things. (11:29)

Here is Jesus' most powerful weapon, with which he lays siege to the citadel of self-referential authority: questions that drive a sharp wedge into the cracks of the social order in order to pry open its internal contradictions.

Where do you think John's authority came from? Jesus' opponents stiffen and gulp hard, huddling. The case of the recently martyred rebel prophet John is a delicate political matter indeed. They can hardly delegitimize the work of so popular a national hero; yet if they eulogize John, their own duplicity—as the administration that consented to his execution—will be unmasked (11:30–32). Jesus has, in effect, thrown the challenge back in their face: *Tell me whose side **you** are on, and we'll talk.* The breeze shifts, and an awkward silence settles heavily over the scene. Finally, like all official spokespeople under pressure, they issue no comment, refusing either to confirm or deny.

> We do not know. (11:33)

So Jesus shrugs, and walks. The moral of the story: If we want to know what Jesus stands *for* in the conflict-ridden world, we had better be prepared to be questioned *by* him about our own alignments.

Should Theology Rationalize
or Problematize Social Reality?

In the Markan vignette, Jesus is challenged by the political authorities to justify his direct attack on their institutions of law and order. But instead of rationalizing his position, Jesus problematizes *theirs*. This ought to disturb North American Christians. In the U.S. today, State officials have no reason to question by what authority we act, because our actions do not question their authority. Our churches, both liberal and conservative, exhibit a peculiar constellation of dread and reverence toward public authority. We are thus like Mark's scribes—essentially noncommittal about our political alignments in the historical moment. Indeed, we tend to view religious movements that *do* challenge the State—whether Christians for Socialism in Chile or Islamic "fundamentalists" in Algeria—with utmost wariness.

There are many reasons why we U.S. Christians have sought refuge in political ambivalence. We experience enough material comfort and privilege, and are sufficiently insulated from those for whom "the system" does not work, to be relatively content with the social order and comparatively untroubled by its contradictions. We assume that our socio-political structures are, if flawed, nevertheless the lesser of evils—at least we cannot think of a better alternative. Sometimes we figure that contemporary political issues are just too complicated for the church to deal with. But what I wish to address here is the way in which our political ambivalence is rooted in an ideological bargain we have struck with modernity. The bargain is this: Christians have conceded to the State authority over the public sphere in hopes of retaining a modicum of authority over the private sphere. This is why our theology has tended to rationalize rather than problematize social reality.

Many complex historical forces have created and sustained this bargain. McClendon and Murphy[3] show how the philosophical forces of the Enlightenment moved theological concern away from traditional problems of collective character ("What is expected of us?") to modern problems of personal existence ("Who am I?") and epistemological doubt ("How can I know?"). Meanwhile, the socio-economic and technological forces of capitalism were facilitating the steady privatization of consciousness and the disintegration of community ("I am what I produce/consume"[4]). The bargain in the U.S. was reified politically by the Deist architects of our oligarchic republic in the Constitutional "separation of church and State." In the eighteenth century this was understandably attractive to minority Christian traditions fleeing the oppressive neo-Constantinian arrangements of Old Europe. But though intended to protect church and State from each other, this social contract has functioned over time to marginalize the former and exalt the latter. By the end of the nineteenth century the forces of the secular, monist faith of Progress and the national ideology of Manifest Destiny had thoroughly displaced older Puritan or Baptist visions of how to build a moral and plural society.[5] Twentieth century forces of bureaucratic centralization have rendered religion almost irrelevant, while steadily sacralizing the State. This was clearly evident in socialist countries, but is no less the case with U.S. democratic centralism.[6]

However gradual and complex the evolution of this public-private trade-off has been in modernity, it is every bit as Faustian a bargain for the church as was the ancient deal it cut with Constantine. It is a deal with the devil *not* because the political power of the institutional churches has been broken, or because postmodernity has brought theological pluralism. Those are *promising* features of our historical situation from the perspective of non-Constantinian theology. No, it is Faustian because it has led the church into idolatry. As Thierry Verhelst put it,

> Western modernity is in pursuit of a "false infinite," that is to say a quantitative in-finite according to which one constantly produces, consumes and "progresses" more and more. Today, the consequences of this Faustian undertaking are devastating. As Raimundo Pannikkar has said, Western modernity produces a substitute for transcendence.[7]

Moreover, by conceding that faith is essentially a private matter discontinuous with public life Christian theology has forfeited its critical vocation at a time when technocratic totalitarianism is rapidly dehumanizing every aspect of life, public *and* private. We need look no further than Desert Storm or the 1992 Los Angeles uprising to see that churches in the U.S. continue to be preoccupied with personal morality or self-realization while equivocating on politically contested issues such as militarism or racism.

Conservative theologians need not question the social order because Jesus is "the answer" to all personal dilemmas. Their Jesus shrugs at public crimes while obsessing about sexual behavior. In reaction, political theologies too often simply reverse the equation, emphasizing social struggle and dismissing individual piety as irrelevant. In between, liberal theologians forever find it easier to question the existence of God than the authority of the State. And neo-liberals today carry on the "Christian realist" tradition of rationalizing U.S. power and privilege in the New World Order.

This is perhaps why Critical Theorist Walter Benjamin wrote earlier in this century that theology has become like a troll; though wise, it is "small and ugly, not risking itself to be seen in public."[8] Indeed, the days are long past when theology was royalty in the court of critical disciplines. This is a good thing insofar as it relieves theological discourse of the untenable burden of trying *always* to speak universally and comprehensively. Yet many contemporary theologians—unsure of their role in postmodernity—are clearer about what theology can no longer claim to do than about what its task might legitimately be. Fortunately there are theologians such as Jim McClendon who *do* understand both the legitimacy and importance of the task. He has offered excellent guidelines for those of us who would do theology from the more modest but more authentic perspective of a determinate convictional community.[9] His "three-stranded" *Ethics* and trinitarian *Doctrine* suggest ways in which we can begin to undo the Faustian bargain.

I am one who wishes to follow McClendon in reconstructing a "baptist" theological discourse that is non-Constantinian, postmodern, and above all, biblical. But given our historical context, in which an omnivorous State simply ignores internecine theological debates, this old/new discipleship tradition needs even greater encouragement to follow Jesus in problematizing social reality. There is, after all, a certain baptist reluctance when it comes to politics.

Freedom, understood by traditional Baptists as the State's non-interference in the affairs of the church, is usually given priority over the demands of justice, which may require the church's interference in the oppressive affairs of the State. Anabaptist communities, meanwhile, have tended to withdraw from what Cornel West calls the "public conversation." But sectarian theology merely accommodates the Faustian bargain in a different way, which is why in the U.S. baptist churches are as politically domesticated as mainline ones.

Christians need not feel responsible *for* the State, but we must be able-to-respond *to* it. We are instructed by the example of Jesus—and, for that matter, by the militant Baptist tradition of Martin Luther King, Jr.—to engage the Powers wherever and whenever *anyone* in the body politic is marginalized or oppressed. And this requires a problematizing theology.

From Confession to Quandary: Jesus as Interlocutor of Church and World

I recently read the 1992 "Birmingham Confession" issued by the Cooperative Baptist Fellowship, being distributed by the Baptist Peace Fellowship for wider endorsement. The statement apologizes for the Southern Baptist Convention's failure, three decades earlier, to reach out to the Sixteenth Street Baptist Church in Birmingham, Alabama after it was fire bombed in September, 1963, killing four young African American girls. While this document is still overly vague in its understanding of the demands of repentance and reconciliation, it nevertheless suggests a model for Christian acknowledgment of both historical and continuing complicity in the sin of racism. I cite it here because it reflects a growing concern among baptist-type Christians to develop a theological discourse that maintains a political edge and speaks with an eye toward the public conversation.[10]

This same spirit is reflected in three recent Third World *kairos* documents, in which Christians facing oppression in such places as South Africa and Central America seek to name both the sins and the signs of hope in their historical context.[11] These documents have in turn stimulated renewed interest in "confessional" theology in the U.S. Bill Wylie Kellermann describes this tradition:

> In church history, especially Protestant tradition, it is recognized that there are extraordinary times when the church's very identity is imperiled. If its confession is not made unequivocally clear, nothing less than the meaning of the gospel with the church and before the world is at risk. This special time, a *status confessionis*, is brought on by a historical crisis within the church or without. It is

incumbent on the community of faith to discern and name the crisis and to distinguish, as clearly as it possibly can, between truth and error, even between life and death.[12]

He points to two such efforts (relatively unsuccessful) in the twentieth century: the Barmen Declaration in Germany under Hitler, and subsequent attempts in the U.S. and Europe to make opposition to nuclear weaponry *status confessionis*.[13] Following his mentor, the late William Stringfellow, Kellerman has argued that the North American church needs a confessional theology today, accompanied by a practice of public witness. Recently a number of ecumenical peace and justice groups have taken up this challenge, promoting a call to a *kairos* process in the U.S.[14]

There is much to commend confessional theology to the church's quest to rediscover its vocation of problematizing the Faustian bargain made by capitalist religion. Public confession engages us both politically and personally, and clearly certain historical moments demand it. The 1992 Los Angeles uprising, for example, was in my opinion one such moment.[15] Yet that is precisely the problem for the North American church: We live in the shadow of a long legacy of scribe-like equivocation that has refused to make collective declarations of allegiance in specific situations. Issues such as slavery, war, and the equality of women have in the past and continue today to split our churches. Even if we today *could* achieve unity—declaring "Here we stand" concerning, say, homelessness or genetic engineering—do the Powers even take into account what the churches say any more?

There are other problems as well. Do not theological declarations run the risk of being tainted with triumphalism when uttered from the context of imperial culture? Are categorical pronouncements even helpful, given the terrible ambiguities confronting our society today? Above all, there is the matter of whether confession can be translated into concrete action—what Yoder calls "making the tradition credible."[16] The case of the 1983 U.S. Catholic Bishops Peace Pastoral would indicate that local congregations are ill-prepared to adjudicate the practical imperatives arising from a "confessional" position. In light of these ambiguities, I wonder whether confessional assertions represent the *most* appropriate theological discourse for the North American church. Canadian theologian Douglass John Hall shares my doubts. For two decades he has been contending that a truly contextual theology for North America must adopt a discourse of negation rather than affirmation. In a 1976 essay he wrote:

> Our culture is sick, and because it is also very powerful, its sickness infects the whole world. On the brink of overt nihilism in our public life, and neurotically clinging to the positive in our private existences, we fear an open confrontation with the contradiction between our optimistic expectations and our increasingly depressing experiences. The repression of this contradiction is costly in life and truth. Its repression at home inevitably means that it breaks out in strange places with names which quickly become household words: Vietnam, Bangladesh, Chile. . . . There can therefore be no more responsible theology than one which tries to provide a climate in which men and women in this society may feel able to expose themselves to that contradictory state.[17]

In his recent *Thinking the Faith* Hall continues to argue that "there is no greater public task for theology in North America today than to help to provide a people indoctrinated in the modern mythology of light with a frame of reference for the honest exploration of its actual darkness."[18] I agree with him. But what kind of theological discourse can best promote such exploration?

In good baptist style we turn to the Bible for help; I believe that Mark's gospel offers us clues for constructing such a discourse. More than three-quarters of the pericopes in Mark are composed around questions to, by or about Jesus—from his inaugural challenge to scribal authority (1:24) to the story's closing quandary (16:3). Jesus is presented not as a sage who explains life's mysteries, but as the great interlocutor of reality. His queries lay bare the "inner conflicts" of disciples and opponents alike (Gk. *dialogizesthai*; 2:8; 8:16f; 9:33f; 11:31). Sometimes they are sharply rhetorical: "Can Satan exorcise Satan?" (3:23); "What will the owner of the vineyard do?" (12:9). Other times they are wrapped in metaphor or parable: "Is a lamp brought indoors to be put under a basket?" (4:21); "Should wedding guests fast while the bridegroom is with them?" (2:19). But always they challenge both the ideology of the dominant culture ("How can the scribes say . . . ?" 12:35) and the theology of disciples ("Do you not yet understand?" 8:21). Above all—and baptists should appreciate this—they call into question our biblical literacy: "Have you never read . . . ?" (2:25; 12:10); "Is it not written . . . ?" (9:12; 11:17).

But Jesus the Interlocutor is neither a Grand Inquisitor nor a Devil's Advocate. He is rather the great pedagogue of what Paulo Friere calls "conscientization." Friere's work in promoting literacy among the poor showed him that the empowering teacher provides the right question, not the right answer: "The educator's role is to propose problems about the codified existential situation in order to help the learners arrive at a more and more critical view of their reality."[19] Mark's Jesus is indeed such an educator, problematizing the world view of his followers and his opponents because it is problematic from the vantage point of the Kingdom.

Jesus questions the world.

In the tradition of the Hebrew prophets Jesus is a relentless interrogator of those in power. With deadly rhetorical aim he exposes the duplicity behind official piety: e.g. theological legitimations of elite social power that appeal to heaven (8:12), or to intellectual traditions (10:3), or to Temple State nationalism (12:35). When challenged by the authorities, Jesus turns the tables with brilliantly crafted counter-questions that unmask their ideological agenda, such as their attempts to control the economy of redemption (2:9) or their subservience to Roman interests (12:16). Even when in legal jeopardy and cornered in a public showdown, Jesus acts as prosecutor, not defendant: "Is it lawful to do good or to do harm on the Sabbath, to save life or to kill?" (3:4). So skillful is he at severing the identification of State authority with the sovereignty of God that in the end, Mark tells us, Jesus' opponents stopped debating with him:

> When Jesus saw that the scribe had answered wisely, he said to him, "You are not far from the kingdom of God." After that no one dared anymore to press questions to him (12:34).

Jesus' actions, too, challenge the structures of authority. His practice of exorcism seeks to name the very demons of empire trying to name and control him (5:7–9). It challenges a "House divided" (3:23) and symbolically enacts the denouement of an ancient prophetic plot:

> The Lord whom you seek will suddenly come to his temple . . . But who can stand when he appears? . . . Then I will draw near to you for judgment, to bear witness against sorcerers and adulterers, against those who swear falsely and who oppress hired workers in their wages, against those who thrust aside the alien, the widow and orphan. . . . (Mal. 3:1ff)

In his direct action in the Temple[20] Jesus assumes the role of a divine litigator indicting public crimes:

> Is it not written, "My house shall be called a house of prayer for all the peoples?" But you have made it a "den of thieves" (Mark 11:17).

Jesus cross-examines Israel's most inured institution before the bar of Yahwist justice and finds it wanting: "Do you see these great buildings? There will not be one stone left upon another . . ." (13:2). Mark's Jesus is thus portrayed not as the *answer* to our private questions but as the *question* to our public answers.

Jesus questions the church.

Jesus' also directs his queries toward his own disciples.

Who is my mother and my brother? (3:33)
What is the kingdom of God like? (4:30)
Why are you afraid? (4:40)
Why are you both arguing with the scribes? (9:33)
Can you be baptized with my baptism? (10:38)
Why do you bother this woman's good deed? (14:6)
Could you not keep watch with me? (14:37)

Jesus' questions open up painful and awkward uncertainties for disciples: "Do you have eyes, and fail to see? Do you have ears, and fail to hear? And do you not remember?" (8:18). Moreover, his teaching and practice provoke our incredulity (10:24,32). But this is precisely his pedagogical strategy—to break the spell of credulity the dominant order casts over its subjects, to force a crisis of faith. Incredulity can be subversive, for doubt about the world is a "necessary condition" to joining the struggle to transform it.

At the structural center of Mark's story is Jesus' famous double question to his disciples, upon which all Christian theology turns:

"Who do the people say that I am? . . .
Who do *you* say I am?" (8:27,29a)

Here Mark boldly transforms the foundational declaration of Hebrew faith—"God said to Moses, 'I am who I am!'" (Exod. 3:14)—into a query. Significantly, Peter sees in this remarkable solicitation a happy occasion for confessional orthodoxy: "You are the Christ!" (8:29b). Yet Jesus responds to Peter as if he were merely another demon attempting to "name" him—he *silences* him (8:30; cf. 1:25; 3:12; 9:25).

This precipitates what I have called the "confessional crisis" in Mark (8:31–33).[21] Jesus repudiates Messianic triumphalism by invoking the political vocation of the Human One; Peter attempts in turn to repudiate such a "negating" theology. Jesus then utterly problematizes the matter by aligning the Petrine confession (which was, let us not forget, the creed of the churches to which Mark wrote, and which still read him today) with *Satan!* The struggle concludes with Jesus' invitation to his disciples to a practice of the cross (8:34ff). Mark thus displaces Peter's confession with Jesus' quandary about losing life in order to save it. The later trial narrative reiterates this theological displacement. Jesus is "not ashamed" of the Human One before the Powers—and loses his life (14:62ff); at the very same moment Peter is "ashamed" of Jesus while trying to save his own hide (14:66ff). The courage and commitment to the public order lay at the heart of Jesus' courtroom "confession"; conversely, the dread of and reverence for authority lay at the root of Peter's courtyard quandary—and ours today.

Finally, in Mark the interlocuted also become interlocutors. The disciples do not say much in Markan theatre. Their few lines function to reveal the shadowy hues of their humanity—duplicity (10:39), equivocation (14:19), or plain foolishness (9:5). Their incredulity does however cause them to ask questions of their own, even if they are leery (5:31), leading (10:35), or pleading (4:38) ones. Their quandaries resound perhaps most sharply in the hollows of our readerly stomachs, for in them our own deepest anxieties about discipleship are laid bare. Who of us has not wondered why Jesus seems absent in the midst of storms that threaten to sink us (4:41)? Have we not many times puzzled resentfully over how to respond to the overwhelming needs of the poor, given our meager resources (6:37; 8:4)? Awed by the legitimacy of the rich and powerful, do we not constantly check our bearings according to their maps (9:11), unable to imagine a history freed from their control (10:26)? Do we not rage against our impotence (9:29) and doubt in our innermost selves whether the world can really ever be changed (13:4)? Battered by disappointment and failure, do we not agonize over our own betrayal (14:19) and too often despair that we have come to the end of the line (16:3)? Mark's Jesus, then, offers believers not certitude but queries that force us to encounter our individual and corporate darkness.

Jesus has been variously named by the church—Christ, Sophia, Suffering Servant, Good Shepherd, Word of God. Whatever else he may be, however, he is Lord only insofar as he is Interlocutor of church and world. Mark's gospel, the prototype of Christian narrative theology, suggests that the church's own theological discourse should also be *interrogatory*. Unfortunately, when the early church struck its deal with Constantine, it moved decisively away from questioning reality and began its long theological orbit around the propositional discourse of dogma, institutionalized in the great declarative confessions.[22] As long as the church understood Christ to be mysteriously present among the poor, and itself inhabited the margins, no ruler's authority was beyond question, no social system beyond critical scrutiny. But once Christ was located on a heavenly throne and Christians were advisors in earthly courts, the grounds on which theology could (or dared) challenge the authority of emperor, pope, or king narrowed considerably. The mountain of ecclesial doctrine thus long ago buried the voice of Jesus the Interlocutor in our churches.

Like Peter in the palace courtyard (Mark 14:54), we North American Christians today warm ourselves by the fire of imperial certainties even as we are chilled to the bone by the protracted historical quandaries swirling around us. Our domesticated theologies have exchanged the messianic commission to question public authority for the empire's sanction to peddle private religious answers. We, too, make our confession too soon and realize our denial too late. But the subversive genius of Mark can help the church again learn how to engage itself and the world with problematizing quandaries that animate rather than with rationalizing answers that pacify. Recovering the disturbing and disrupting character of interrogatory theology could not be more important. We live in a socio-political universe of high mystification that can only be "de-coded" (as Friere would say) through relentless inter-rogation. The convolutions and duplicities of our public dis-courses—whether commercial ("Chevy is the heartbeat of America") or political ("It's morning in America")—are designed to preclude critical apprehension and mire us in a culture of consuming credulity and political passivity.

Theology must learn again to ask questions. Below I suggest two discursive traditions that I believe can help us. One is a philosophical and prophetic tradition that spared no question of the world. The other is an ecclesial and pastoral tradition that models how the church can persistently question itself.

Prophetic Negation: Critical Theory

"A refusal to cut off further relevant questions even when they lead us into the darkness of negativity"—this was the central thrust of the mid-twentieth century intellectual tradition known as Critical Theory, according to its foremost North American theological interpreter Matthew Lamb.[23] Critical Theory was founded by the "Frankfurt School" of philosophy: Max Horkhe-imer, Theodor Adorno, Walter Benjamin, and best-known in the U.S., Herbert Marcuse. It "emerged from a distinct crisis in Euro-pean bourgeois culture" in the aftermath of World War I, writes Paul Mendes-Flohr, that deepened through the experience of the Third Reich and the Cold War: "The modern world had indeed witnessed the creation of a splendid, majestic edifice, but it was held to be a Trojan horse hiding within insidious forces bent on humanity's spiritual and psychic emasculation."[24]

Adherents of Critical Theory articulated a profound disillu-sionment with the optimistic creeds of modernism—Enlighten-ment rationalism, technocracy, and above all, history-as-Progress. They were among the first to understand that these positivistic myths could be countered neither by pessimism nor skepticism, but only by a thoroughgoing discourse of negation. Through its so-called "negative dialectics," Critical Theory challenged the most basic assumptions of modernity:

In their *Dialectic of Enlightenment*, Adorno and Horkheimer develop the antithetical or "inverse" insights into how scientific reason is mythic, how enlightened liberal morality is barbaric, how technological progress is retrogression. Benjamin caught this inverse insight imaginally: "Marx says, revolutions are the locomotives of world history. But perhaps . . . revolutions are the grasp by the human race travelling in this train for the emergency brake."[25]

"If the twentieth century vaunts an ideology of life, liberty, and the pursuit of happiness," continues Lamb, "then critical theory poses the uncomfortable question of why no other century has witnessed such massive destruction of human life by human beings." If the Frankfurt School set its face against modernity, it was nevertheless squarely within the Enlightenment tradition of rational criticism—in much the same way that Anabaptists were within the spirit of the Reformation. In both cases, these radical minorities refused to suspend their criticism once the reformist movements that spawned them began to compromise with systems of domination.

The modern era began when the "Age of Reason" overthrew the sacred totalism of the "Age of Faith" through scientific inquiry into how the physical universe was ordered, breaking the grip of the old cosmologies. At the same time, nascent industrial capitalism sought to transform traditional economic culture while the emerging bourgeoisie questioned the divine right of kings and launched new republican experiments in democracy. But once the old feudal order was shattered, liberal thought became increasingly unable or unwilling to turn criticism back upon its own constructs. "The old order of sacral hierarchy gave way to a new order of secular bureaucracy in which the myth of identity between reason and reality would be legitimated by an empirical science increasingly constituted by 'value-free' observation and quantification as the only valid form of rationality."[26] New totalist and instrumentalist theories of the universe, society, and the human being were now legitimating colonial projects, advancing military technologies, and undergirding industrial profiteering.

Marx launched a second phase of criticism by challenging the absolute claims of liberal capitalism. He formulated his theory of human alienation by studying how an uncontrolled economy controlled all social relations, "practising a new form of dialectical analysis which exposed the basic economic contradiction inherent in capitalist relations of production" and introducing the notion of class struggle.[27] Marx thus inspired a new round of struggle for freedom and justice throughout the industrializing world, though his theory of revolution ironically found its most dramatic expression in semi-feudal Russia. Again, however, once Marxist criticism was reified and canonized in state socialism, its revolutionary power atrophied, as Leninism yielded to Stalinism. Hegemonic Marxism, like liberalism before it, became a legitimating ideology for bureaucratic totalism. By the mid-twentieth century, then, European civilization seemed to offer only "the cynical choice between monopoly-controlled states or state-controlled monopolies."[28]

The Frankfurt School thus launched a third tradition of criticism, arguing that the mass cultures of western and eastern blocks were more alike than different. The "conveyors of packaged images and symbols"—whether Soviet propagandists or Madison Avenue hucksters—were strangling political imagination.[29] Marcuse understood clearly the monistic character of technocracy:

As a technological universe, advanced industrial society is a *political* universe, the latest stage in the realization of a specific historical *project*—namely, the experience, transformation, and organization of nature as the mere stuff of domination. As the project unfolds, it shapes the entire universe of discourse and action, intellectual and material culture. In the medium of technology, culture, politics, and the economy merge into an omnipresent system which swallows up or repulses all alternatives. The productivity and growth potential of this system stabilizes the society and contains technical progress within the framework of domination.[30]

Negative dialectics attempted to resist this totalism by deconstructing its foundational myths and interrogating its social and intellectual conventions in order to free political imagination again and re-animate the struggle for human liberation.

Critical Theory was, predictably, berated from the political Right for its "sour grapes" about modern society. But there were objections from the Left as well, the most telling complaint being that its thoroughgoing negativity undermined efforts to construct concrete social alternatives. Indeed, many Critical Theorists were leery of political activism, with the notable exception of Marcuse. Yet during the 1960s Critical Theory was rehabilitated as part of the intellectual underpinning of the New Left, student anti-war protests and the counter culture. But as these movements began to unravel in the 1970s, doubts were again raised about the politics of negation. A notable chapter in this debate was the often-heated dialogue between North Atlantic political theologians inspired by Critical Theory and Latin American liberation theologians influenced by Marxism-Leninism.[31] Political theology, disillusioned by the atrophy of human rights in Eastern Europe, rejected socialist positivism and "every identification of utopian thinking with Christian eschatology."[32] Writing from the perspective of insurgent Latin America, Juan Luis Segundo countered that this seemed "much more akin to the Cartesian theoretical revolution based on methodic doubt than to real practical revolution."[33]

An analogous debate rages in current cultural theory, which is awash in Deconstructionism. "It is remarkable how parallel deconstructionism is," notes Marxist Terry Eagleton in his study of Benjamin, "to the later Frankfurt school [in its] rage against positivity, the suspicion of determinate meaning *as such*, the fear that to propose is to be complicit."[34] Deconstructionists rightly insist that the mystifying discourses of capitalist culture must be dismantled.[35] But the exclusive focus on discourse leads Raymond Williams to call them merely "textual revolutionaries" who posit "the universality of alienation, the position of a closely associated bourgeois idealist formation."[36] Eagleton contends that this tendency can be traced to the failure of radical student politics in Europe in the late 1960s: "Unable to break the structures of state power, post-structuralism found it possible instead to subvert the structures of language."[37]

A theology of discipleship must indeed be leery of theoretics that give primacy to discourse-critique over practice and that are thus reluctant to make political choices and forge constructive social programs. At the same time, the political developments of the last decade suggest that neither our practice nor our criticism has been nearly critical *enough*. On one hand the failure of many Third World revolutionary movements has chastened theologies of liberation. On the other hand, North American political theologians have had to come to terms with the fact that the only option facing those freed from authoritarian socialism is peonage to the most totalitarian system of all. This is what Marcuse called "society without opposition"—the iron rule of mercenary capital and its ideology of global open markets and open shop. The New World Order is rapidly destroying what remains of the integrity of both labor and the environment, while the triumphant military machine of the West now proceeds unobstructed in its "low-intensity" wars on the poor, from Panama to Somalia.[38] If indeed we are seeing the steady ascendancy of what Bertram Gross calls capitalist technocracy's "friendly fascism," Critical Theory and its legacy offers encouragement to our quest for interrogatory theology in at least three respects.

First, Critical Theory's uncompromising emphasis on philosophical "non-identity" with totalist ideologies echoes the First Testament's prohibition of images and the Exodus God's refusal to be named (Exod. 3:13ff). This caused some to refer to the Frankfurt School as "theological Marxism." The great "refusal" (Marcuse) to close ranks with modernity also encouraged both political theologians (e.g. Moltmann) and liberation theologians (e.g. Sobrino) to rediscover the "negativity of the Cross." Jesus' cross, argues Sobrino, "calls into question all knowledge of God based on natural theology":

> God on the cross explains nothing (but) criticizes every proffered explanation. The cross is not a response; it is a new form of questioning. . . . It is not so much people asking questions about God; rather it is primarily people being called into question concerning themselves and their self-interest in trying to hold and defend a specific form of the deity.[39]

This represents a major step in moving theology from a rationalizing to a problematizing discourse.

Second, Critical Theory's critique of history-as-Progress inspired a whole generation of philosophers (e.g. Bloch) and theologians (e.g. Metz) to challenge the sacred assumptions of social Darwinism, from Adam Smith's "invisible hand" to Marx's "historical necessity," and to sever hope from optimism:

> Against the conservative hope in restoring some semblance of balancing contradictions after the fashion of the eighteenth century's *ancien regime*, critical theory hopefully despairs. Against the liberal hope of engineering contradictions after the fashion of nineteenth-century industrialization and urbanization, critical theory hopefully despairs. Against the radical hope of exploiting

107

contradictions for the sake of revolutionary resolutions after the fashion of twentieth-century state socialisms, critical theory hopefully despairs.[40]

Many in the Frankfurt School were deeply attracted to Judeo-Christian eschatology because "its teaching of a radical disjunction between history and redemption serves to illuminate the 'metahistorical' ground of human existence and destiny."

On a deeper level, Critical Theory was a quest for transcendence that was conceived not in metaphysical but in metachronic terms. Truth . . . is not in heaven but in the future. This conception of the truth endowed the Frankfurt School, according to Horkheimer, with "the hope that the earthly horror does not possess the last word." This hope, in turn, permits one to utter a confident "No" to the existent order. Or, as Adorno asserted in terms self-consciously theological, "the only philosophy which can be responsibly practiced in the face of despair is the attempt to regard all things as the way they would present themselves from the standpoint of redemption."[41]

During the 1960s theologians were also re-reading Critical Theory, and some broke from the liberal consensus to reconsider the tradition of biblical apocalyptic as a discourse of radical transformation. Carl Braaten, for example, contrasted the "evolutionary monism" of modern development theory with Jesus' "revolutionary dualism . . . contradicting all history which wishes to build the future out of its present."[42] Apocalyptic hope can give baptist theology today the vision to see beyond the failures of both orthodox Marxism and laissez-fair capitalism, and to grasp the opportunity of this historical moment to promote desperately needed political imagination and social innovation.[43]

Third, Critical Theory has helped re-establish the ground for conversionist theology by asserting the universality of historical guilt. In the well-known dictum of Walter Benjamin, "There is no record of civilization that is not also a record of barbarism."[44] Some, such as Marcuse, called in their own way for repentance, arguing that people can "find their way from false to true consciousness only if they live in need of changing their way of life."[45] In fact, the following passage from Marcuse's *Essay on Liberation* is not unlike Jesus' call to radical discipleship:

"Voluntary" servitude (voluntary inasmuch as it is introjected into the individuals), which justifies the benevolent masters, can be broken only through a political practice which reaches the roots of containment and contentment. . . . Such a practice involves a break with the familiar, the routine ways of seeing, hearing, feeling, understanding things so that the organism may become receptive to the potential forms of a nonaggressive, nonexploitive world.[46]

In its rejection of modernity's pretensions to innocence and its exhortation to resistance, Critical Theory moves from the detachment of denunciation to the engagement of alternative practices.

In sum, Critical Theory's insistence on toppling the idols of modernity, its non-progressive historical hopes, and its conversionist orientation each can encourage North American baptist theology to recover an interrogatory discourse, and with it the prophetic vocation of the church. We live in a time, asserted Edward Abbey in his "Writer's Credo," when it is

not merely heretical but treasonous to question our own government's policies, to doubt the glory of planetary capitalism, to object to the religion of endless economic growth, or to wonder about the ultimate purpose, value, and consequences of our techno-military-industrial empire. Those who persist in raising doubt and question are attacked by defenders of order as the "adversary culture." Very well: let us be adversaries.[47]

Jesus the Interlocutor was such an adversary, and faced its consequences. Can the church do differently?

It takes courage to follow Jesus in questioning the public order. It takes just as much courage, however, to turn our criticism of the world back upon ourselves. There is no room for self-righteousness, for Jesus is also the questioner of the church. Where can we find resources for an interrogatory theology that insists with equal vigor upon the discipline of self-examination?

Pastoral Inquiry: Quaker "Queries"

As an historical generalization it is fair to say that the more social status and privilege the church has assumed in a given social order, the more its theological discourse has taken on a defensive, apologetic and abstract character. Conversely, when the church has had less status, or was willing to risk losing it, its theology has tended to be more offensive, critical, and practical.

We see this, for example, during the Reformation. Luther and Zwingli began as "protest" theologians, first questioning and then breaking with the Roman church. Once they decided to forge political alliances with governments, however, the tone of their discourse quickly became apologetic concerning matters of civil order, as evidenced by Luther's decision to side with the princes during the Peasant uprisings, and even more so by second-generation magisterial Calvinism.[48] Catholic theology, meanwhile, awakened from its complacency by the Protestant threat, recovered an *offensive* zeal in the Jesuit Counter-Reformation.

The most *consistently* evangelical, prophetic, and eschatological theological discourse of the period however belonged to the various movements of the Radical Reformation. Anabaptists were persecuted by Catholic and Protestant magistrates alike for their practical and theological challenges to prevailing religious, economic, and political orthodoxies. Walter Klaassen has rightly characterized Anabaptism as the most concerted attack on the Constantinian arrangement in the history of the church.[49] As McClendon has pointed out, the descendants of the Radical Reformation have continued to give priority to discipleship over dogma.[50] It is not surprising therefore that in *this* family tree we find a branch that came closest to adopting an explicitly interrogative theological discourse. I am referring to the discourse of "Testimonies, Advices, and Queries" that takes the place of theological doctrine among the Religious Society of Friends, or Quakers.[51]

Testimonies, Advices and Queries represent a "cluster of practices intended to encourage Friends, individually and as groups, to hold up their lives to the Light."[52] This discourse, according to Quaker historian T. Canby Jones, first appeared in 1682 in the form of three questions posed by London Yearly Meeting to determine the "state of the Meeting":

> What friends in the Ministry, in their respective countries, departed life since last Yearly Meeting? What friends imprisoned for their Testimony have died in prison since last Yearly Meeting? How has the Truth prospered among friends since the last Yearly Meeting and how do they fare in relation to peace and unity?[53]

Meant to inspire reflection on costly discipleship, these *Queries* were institutionalized in 1723, and others added over time. A century later, London Yearly Meeting developed *Advices*, "short counsels and positive suggestions for the improvement of the life, conduct and witness of Friends . . . conceived of as supplementary and subsidiary to the Queries."[54] *Testimonies* were in turn developed to articulate "corporate convictions, concerns which we are committed to put into action as a community of faith."[55]

Jones defines the three elements of this discursive tradition as follows:

> A Testimony is a standard of faith, ethical behavior or Gospel Order which a group of people covenants together to observe. . . .
> A Query is a sharply focused question designed to challenge persons or a group to live up to a corporately adopted standard of faith and behavior. . . .
> An Advice is friendly counsel from the group on what it means to live by a commonly accepted testimony.[56]

Friends look to *Queries* to help clarify the meaning and requirements of the various Testimonies. "Meetings were asked to read out the Queries and have their members examine their consciences in regard to such questions as the taking of oaths . . . the witness against paying tithes . . . the keeping of slaves . . . the penal system . . . (and) whether they held their lives free enough from the excessive cumber of acquisitive vocations."[57]

But Queries are not "loaded" questions; their purpose is to facilitate an examination of the community's conscience.

> Suited to the searching mood of Friends at their best, they are broad, open-ended questions to promote self-examination under the leadership of the Spirit. They are non-dogmatic, non-hortatory . . . not intended to discourage but to encourage.[58]

Unfortunately, this desire not to condemn has often diffused efforts by Quaker meetings to take a firm position. Herb Lape points out that John Woolman's long campaign to get Friends to reject slavery "would not have gotten very far if the framework for . . . deliberations had been 'love and tolerance' rather than discerning the 'will of God'."[59] Indeed it was Woolman's opponents who appealed to meeting unity in their arguments not to exclude slave owners.[60]

As the vehicle for community self-assessment, then, Queries try to preserve a delicate balance. They are questions to our life, not accusations, yet they are *hard* questions, not merely rhetorical ones.[61] Advices grow from the community's experiences of fidelity (and infidelity) to its testimonies. They are eminently practical encouragements, not legalisms. Pacific Yearly Meeting's current *Faith and Practice* does not require silence during meeting for worship, for example, but rather urges Friends "to give adequate time to study, meditation, prayer, and other ways of preparing for worship, and to arrive at meeting with an open and expectant spirit."

To see the contrast between this interrogatory, practice-centered approach to theology and traditional dogmatic discourse, let us look briefly at a concrete social issue. Because Christian pacifism has been a keen interest of McClendon's, let us take the example of the most well-known, and probably first, Quaker Testimony. The Peace Testimony was articulated by George Fox in his Declaration of 1660: "We do utterly deny all outward wars and fighting, whether for the kingdoms of this world or for the kingdom of Christ, and this is our testimony to the whole world." This practice is understood by Friends to express their conviction that "there is that of God in every person."[62] This radically egalitarian notion was applied by early Friends to small matters as well as large, including both dress and address (Plain Dress and Plain Speech). It represented a direct threat to established seventeenth-century conventions of social hierarchy as well as political conformity, and for this Friends were fiercely persecuted.

In today's democratic cultures, the notion of the divine in each individual has, as an abstract theological proposition, become palatable; indeed it would be affirmed by most Christian traditions. These other churches would not, however, predicate the idea on an ethical practice—so resistance to militarism does not necessarily follow. Thus, outside of the opinions of professional ethicists or the dictums of pastoral letters, mainstream Catholic and Protestant churches offer few vehicles for community self-examination on weighty matters such as war.[63] In contrast, the Peace Testimony has anchored a long Quaker tradition of active nonviolence and noncooperation with authority.[64] Indeed, mainstream church acceptance today of the individual right of conscientious objection is attributable largely to Mennonite and Quaker advocacy.

Pacific Yearly Meeting *Faith and Practice* includes the following Query concerning the Peace Testimony:

> Do we live in the virtue of that life and power which takes away the occasion of all war? Do we refrain from taking part in war as inconsistent with the spirit of Christ? What are we doing to remove the causes of war and to bring about the conditions and instruments of peace?[65]

To be sure, one could argue that this traditional language is too vague. Given our present context of technological militarism and the brutality of economic oppression, we might sharpen this Query for example as follows:

> How are we complicit in structural violence without ever taking an aggressive personal action? How can we politically resist institutions of domination while still "seeing that of God" in those who control them? What does it mean to be in solidarity with victims of violence despite the fact that they may seek just redress through violent methods?

Advices concerning the complex and difficult matter of fidelity to the Peace Witness have not always been clear and courageous. Yet historically Friends have formulated some quite specific Advices, with Woolman again a good example. On the eve of the French and Indian wars in 1755, he and 21 others issued an epistle noting that paying tax monies for military purposes was "inconsistent with our peacable testimony."[66] War tax resistance has been an arena of struggle for many Friends ever since.[67] We need not idealize the discursive practices of Testimonies, Queries and Advices. Friends, like every other community of faith, have compromised the best of their own tradition. There are two notable problems. One is the fact that this tradition, like any other, can and has degenerated into a formalized discourse that inspires the memorialization of discipleship rather than the reproduction of it. Jones points out that by the third generation of the Quaker movement, after the Toleration Act of 1689 halted official persecution, Advices and Queries began to function more to encourage sectarian conformity than practical formation, and that in the nineteenth century, under the influence of evangelical pietism, they became increasingly devotional.[68] Today much of the discourse one hears in meeting strikes me as vague and overly solicitous. For example

113

London Yearly Meeting's 1964 Advices on peace sound more like sanctimonious exhortation than practical counsel:

> Seek, through his power and grace, to overcome in your own hearts the emotions which lie at the root of conflict. In industrial strife, racial enmity and international tension, stand firmly by Christian principles, seeking to foster understanding between individuals, groups and nations.[69]

North American Quakers know well how the sharp edge of community self-examination has been dulled by prosperity and comfort.

A second problem is the tendency of contemporary liberal Quakers to disconnect their discursive tradition from its biblical moorings. Unprogrammed Friends have too often ignored Rufus Jones' warning that the authority of the Inner Light should not replace "the slow verification of truth by historical process; nor is it a substitute for Scripture."[70] The result over time has been theological ambivalence, followed by confusion of identity, followed by ethical drift. When our queries arise only from within ourselves there is a danger they will be confined by our own fearful horizons, cut off from the unboundaried questions of Jesus the Interlocutor and the radical biblical vision of the kingdom of God.

Still, imagine how different our churches would be if as part of our regular worship we reflected on queries concerning war, peace, and Christian witness—rather than, say, reciting ancient theological creeds! We non-Quaker Christians would do well to consider the historically attested tradition of Testimonies, Queries and Advices as a model for interrogatory theology. It has three characteristics that reflect the concerns of postmodern theology. First, it puts the concrete before the theoretical; like theologies of liberation, it seeks unity in orthopraxy rather than orthodoxy. Second, it puts the communal before the private, and depends on the vitality of corporate discernment; this is why Friends have developed a patient (if painfully slow) process of coming to "unity."[71] While the attendant questions of community formation, discipline, and decision making are beyond my scope here, they are the *right* questions from a baptist perspective.[72] Third, this discourse relies by design on the reflective rather than the declarative, and is thus open to constant rearticulation; in the words of

Philadelphia Yearly Meeting's *Faith and Practice*, Testimonies, Queries and Advices represent "landmarks, not campsites."[73] Testimonies endure, but should be reinterpreted into new contexts. Queries stand ever in need of honing so they do not become rote or irrelevant. Advices, by definition, must be revised as the times change so they will be practical, not rhetorical.

A discourse of queries offers a pastoral corrective to the prophetic negations of Critical Theory by turning Jesus' questions back upon ourselves. This insistence on self-examination prevents us from imagining we can somehow stand apart from the ambiguities of the world, smugly reproaching the compromises of practical politics, and reminds us how compromised we ourselves are. Sadly, hyper-critical attitudes are widespread among radical Christians today—and represent the biggest reason why the baptist movement is so fragmented. It is a great irony that alternative communities who are deeply critical of the "great" orthodoxies of the established church so often end up constructing "little" orthodoxies to replace them. We then relentlessly apply litmus tests to each other, and end up succumbing to the grand sectarian legacy of the North American Left—defining ourselves according to our differences with those closest to us.

It is a good thing for baptist communities to talk about their work and witness—this is the stuff of *testimonies*—as long as one's own practices are not held up as the *only* legitimate expression of discipleship. We need to offer each other practical suggestions about how to live more simply, or nonviolently, or justly—this is the stuff of *advices*—as long as this does not deteriorate into a new kind of "purity code." The *query* that ought to circulate among us is not "Who is the most faithful?", but rather "How can we all deepen our journey of discipleship—wherever we are starting from?" In the biblical narrative, radical judgment is accompanied by radical grace; this dialectic should also characterize baptist theology.

Conclusion

I have contended that Mark's Jesus invites the church to rediscover the authority of questions in order to recover our vocation to question public authorities who rationalize idolatry, injustice and violence. I have further suggested that we can find support

115

for constructing an interrogatory theological discourse in the older ecclesial tradition of Quaker Queries and the newer philosophical tradition of Critical Theory.

In our culture of credulity, apathy, and presumed innocence, our task will not be easy, as Cornel West has pointed out:

> Criticism is about discomfort—it's unsettling, it's about being transgressive in the sense of calling what one has assumed into question. America does not take well to that. Socrates said that the unexamined life is not worth living. But we could say the examined life is painful.[74]

McClendon himself makes the same point when he opens his *Ethics* by acknowledging that "theology means struggle":

> The struggle begins with the humble fact that the church is not the world. This means that Christians face an interior struggle, inasmuch as the line between church and world passes right through each Christian heart. It nevertheless means that the standpoint, basic point of view, the theology of the church is not the standpoint, basic point of view, theology of the world.[75]

McClendon understands, in other words, that the vocation of theology is at once prophetic and pastoral.

As a teacher of such theology, Jim McClendon has never spared his students hard questions and never settled for easy answers. Most importantly, he has stipulated that the scholarly study of Christian theology entails "enlistment as students of this strange and demanding master," Jesus. The Christ who is our Interlocutor stands before history, problematizing the church and the world from the vantage point of the kingdom of God, and inviting his disciples to do the same.

CHAPTER 6

Ethnography-As-Theology: Inscribing the African American Sacred Story

Theophus Smith

The theologian, like the ethnographer . . .

George Lindbeck[1]

The combined term, "ethnography-as-theology," may appear to violate the boundaries of both disciplines until a prototype is invoked: James Wm. McClendon's *Biography as Theology*. Like that predecessor project, the present essay seeks to illuminate the exemplary character of its subjects as displayed in their *lived* theology. I too investigate my subjects' religious convictions by attending to their ethics of character, and to the story-shaped images that frame those convictions and that character. In this successor project, however, the subjects are not individual lives but ethnic and religious communities. Specifically, I treat black North American communities beginning in slave religion and extending to recent developments in black religious experience.

Moreover, ethnography-as-theology explores the role of the theologian as a kind of ethnographer (Lindbeck, Schreiter), and draws the implications of that role for the ongoing evolution of black theology as a still developing discipline. The subtitle, "Inscribing the African American Sacred Story," signifies the convergence of the two roles as a combined literary performance. Here the ethnographer's performance of describing and "inscribing" culture (Geertz), or "writing culture" (Clifford),[2] cooperates with the narrative theologian's distinctive craft: to inscribe the sacred story that grounds and shapes a community's convictional character, moral practices, and social-religious constructions. However, I will also be attentive to the way in which the descriptive and inscriptive tasks of the theologian exceed those of the ethnographer. Here ethnography-as-theology means ethnography as a correlative discipline in the task of charting the religious depth and dimensions of a people's storied universe.

Autobiography-as-Theology

The Scripture stories . . . seek to subject us, and if we refuse to be subjected we are rebels . . . we are to fit our own life into its world, *feel ourselves to be elements in its structure* of universal history.

[The Bible] is tyrannical . . . it excludes all other claims. . . . All other scenes, issues, and ordinances have no right to appear independently of it, and it is promised that all of them, the history of all mankind, will be given their due place within its frame.

Erich Auerbach[3]

The initial influence on my own efforts to inscribe black America's sacred story was Paul Tillich's project of "theology of culture." I first encountered that project as a seminarian in the mid-1970s. Tillich presented theology of culture as a newly developing contemporary source of systematic theology. He sought a method for treating cultural and historical materials as theological sources for systematic construction, analogous to the treatment of biblical materials as sources by the biblical theologian. Tillich described this method in aesthetic and hermeneutic (interpretive) terms as a matter of 'reading styles' at the level of a culture's "ultimate concern." With similar intent the present study reads black America's representations of ultimacy and transcendence in terms of its ethnological styles and performances, its ecstatic worship, its magical healing traditions, and its emancipatory and transformative practices.

118

The key to the theological understanding of a cultural creation is
its style . . . It is an art as much as a science to 'read styles,' and it
requires religious intuition, on the basis of an ultimate concern, to
look into the depth of a style, to penetrate to the level where an
ultimate concern exercises its driving power.[4]

In recalling this programmatic formulation I acknowledge the
Tillichian sources of my scholarship; that is, my initial construal
of black theology as a theology of culture.

That pursuit was intercepted in the late 1970s, however, by my
discovery of black theology as a liberation theology. In this regard
Robert Schreiter has usefully distinguished liberation approaches
in his study, *Constructing Local Theologies*. Schreiter observes that
liberation theology seems to work "best when acute social transformation is needed. It has been less successful as a means for
sustaining identity. It still exhibits difficulty in dealing with the
complexities of popular religion." He then proceeds to present
alternative theological approaches that are more conducive to a
people's spirituality, designating them variously as "ethnographic approaches," "theology as variations on a sacred text," "theology as praxis," and "theology as wisdom."[5] Ethnographic
approaches focus on cultural and religious identity, as conveyed
by indigenous forms of oral as well as literary discourse, by ritual
practices and social organization. Liberation approaches on the
other hand, like theologies of praxis, seek social transformation.
The most dynamic movements and informed analyses, as Schreiter himself acknowledges, encompass both approaches—as I endeavor to do below.

An existential turn 'from system to story'[6] was the next decisive element in my own approach to black theological construction. Here the autobiographical background to my scholarship
became foreground. As a graduate student in the early 1980s I had
immersed myself not only in liberation theory but also in an
emancipatory practice. This was a practice that bridged psychotherapy and social activism, and to which I began to look increasingly for spiritual sustenance and vocational formation. As not
uncommonly occurs in graduate school, the stresses of study,
economic hardship, and interpersonal developments resulted in
the dissolution of my ten year-old marriage and small family.
Divorce was a major shock for me. It eviscerated my ego, my

self-possession, and devastated my spiritual-intellectual foundations. Precisely to the degree that my marriage had served as a capstone of my Christian identity and religious world-view, to that degree I felt myself adrift in the universe, abandoned by God and by love. I entered (not for the first time, but never so totally before) the profoundly alienated condition known in Christian mysticism as "the dark night of the soul."

In this lamentable state I was able to find no resources for psychosocial relief or spiritual consolation in the liberation theories and practices that had framed my former pursuits. Those pursuits, empty husks now, mocked my desperate and futile efforts to find resources for the present or hope for the future. I turned then to the fragmented remains of my Bible-based Christian convictions. Within that still sounding universe I finally heard benediction (blessing) in the form of judgment: this shattering of my world was blessed judgment on my former, misguided efforts to ground my life on the inadequate foundation of emancipatory axioms, principles, and imperatives. Admittedly, the ensuing 'shaking of the foundations' was compounded by the rigors of dissolution and divorce, but those foundations had failed the test of tribulation anyway. In any case I was compelled to reexamine my allegiance to liberationism as framework for my life and vocation. Painfully and so slowly, I found the reconstruction of my life and faith within a familiar biblical narrative framework: that of the wandering believer whose loving God calls me back from every idolatry that counterfeits my true identity, my spiritual-human authenticity, and my ultimate allegiance. It remained to follow-through this 'rescue' by biblical narrative within the compass of my intellectual endeavors.

Ethnography and Biblical Narrative

The model of post-modern ethnography is not the newspaper but that original ethnography—the Bible.

Stephen A. Tyler[7]

My most elaborate effort thus far to articulate this narrative turn is the book-length study, *Conjuring Culture: Biblical Formations of Black America* (Oxford, 1994). I begin that book like Lindbeck's theologian who employs the ethnographer's method of "thick description" (Geertz). In particular, I detail the spirituality of black North Americans as an ecstatic and conjurational spirituality that employs biblical narrative in order to inscribe black experience in sacred figures. By ecstatic spirituality I refer to spirit possession and its centrality in numerous Afro-Atlantic worship experiences. Conjurational spirituality, on the other hand, derives from an African American tradition of folk magic and healing called conjure, hoodoo, or rootwork. Conjure practitioners or "doctors" transform reality by means of spells or incantations uttered with or without the use of efficacious materials (herbs, powders, fluids, for example) or spiritually charged substances. The intention to transform, or the 'will-to-transformation,' is the central feature of conjuring as a mode of spirituality. By tracing that intention throughout its socio-cultural and theological-political manifestations, the book brings to view more extensive phenomena of "conjuring culture." These are transformations in the social-historical reality of black North Americans through the narrative appropriation and ritual reenactment of biblical symbols and figures.

McClendon pointed my way to such an approach by his biographical treatment of Martin Luther King, Jr. as a socio-political performer of strategically selected biblical stories and images. Speaking of the dominant images in King's life as "the key" to his biography, McClendon illustrated how "the convergence of such images in a particular person helps to form his characteristic vision or outlook."

> King understands his work under the image of the Exodus; he is leading his people on a new crossing of the Red Sea; he is a Moses who goes to the mountaintop, but who is not privileged to enter with his people into the promised land. These are major images, and . . . there are others as well.[8]

This figural portrait of King is an illuminating moment of "biography as theology," McClendon's program for understanding individual lives and their characteristic vision as informed by religious images. In the remainder of this section I too display some major biblical images or figures. But by contrast, as promised, I attend to collective rather than individual instances in black North American religious formation.

Most useful for this purpose are the figural or typological codes that predominate in Afro- and Euro-American biblical hermeneutics. In this regard Northrop Frye has observed seven major codes or "phases" deriving from the Bible and comprising a typological system as in the following schema: "Old Testament"—(1) genesis (creation), (2) exodus ("revolution"), (3) law, (4) wisdom, (5) prophecy; "New Testament"—(6) gospel, (7) apocalypse. In this schema each phase or figure is a "type" of the one following it and an "antitype" of the one preceding it. The type-antitype relationship between these codes is evident when one considers, for example, Genesis as a (proto)type of Exodus, and Exodus as a (second) type which recapitulates or fulfills Genesis. The most elegant statement of this relationship is the one formulated by Erich Auerbach: the first type signifies the second, while the second comprehends or fulfills the first.[9] I now proceed to illustrate that typological relationship in terms of some of the major biblical types that configure black religious experience.

Genesis and Exodus

A recent expression of the typological relationship between Genesis and Exodus has been provided by literary historian Werner Sollors: "typological ethnogenesis."[10] The term designates the formation (genesis) of peoplehood through the hermeneutic of biblical typology. With this term Sollors refers to the premier interpretive tradition that has shaped the self-understanding of both African and European Americans. Each people or *ethnos* has envisioned and reinvented its existence in terms of characters and events found, most notably, in the Exodus story. By means of figural participation in that narrative each has engendered and later regenerated its corporate identity as an antitype of ancient Israel. Such identity formation in North America has focused repeatedly and intensively on the Exodus themes of liberation and promised land in biblical narrative. Accordingly, both black and white Americans identify their New World existence with ancient Israel's transfer from the experience of bondage and oppression on the one hand, to new freedom and a promised destiny on the other.

Exodus and Law

Just as the Exodus modality in black American experience also constitutes a type of Genesis experience—the beginning of a new citizenry and peoplehood in North America—so the figural experience of Law serves as a form of Exodus recapitulation. Typically, black Americans have employed legal processes and strategies as instruments for achieving manumission or emancipation and, subsequently, civil rights. To employ the term introduced earlier, law was *transformed* from its original role in the Americas as an instrument for legitimating and enforcing African American bondage, to a countercultural instrument or an 'exodus' device for setting captives free. In this regard the justice intentionality and emancipatory potential of law has been partially realized or fulfilled as an Exodus modality in black experience. That is, law has served to secure access to a "promised land" of freedom and full citizenship.

Wisdom and Prophecy

Similar resonances operate between the figural modes of Wisdom and Prophecy, Prophecy and Gospel and, finally, Gospel and Apocalypse. In African American experience the Wisdom figure emerges in the form of folk wisdom or "mother wit" (Dundes).[11] Under this figure are included the bicultural proficiencies, survival strategies, and trickster skills of black Americans as displayed in their ongoing efforts to outwit oppression and deprivation. Black religious prophetism has achieved a measure of fulfillment of these skills. As prophets of social change, African American leaders have been required to become proficient in "transcendence as well as wit over force" (Badejo). Like the premier folk hero and trickster figure, High John the Conquerer, the black social prophet "knows the society in which he operates. He is a student of its strengths and weaknesses and his actions manipulate them."[12]

Here we should compare the public persona of Martin Luther King, Jr. with other heroic and prophetic figures in black history who have likewise displayed trickster characteristics, such as Harriet Tubman, Sojourner Truth, David Walker, Nat Turner, Henry McNeal Turner, Marcus Garvey, Booker T. Washington, Adam Clayton Powell, Jr., Malcolm X, and Eldridge Cleaver. Such leaders have functioned as agents of social-political transformation by means of skillful manipulation of the strengths and weaknesses of the society around them. Their wit and trickster acumen, however, consisted not simply in their own employment of guile or deception but rather in confronting and outwitting their society's use of force and deception. Consider here one of the meanings of 'conjure tricks,' where a practitioner is skillful in countering and reversing the spells of an opponent (as in the folk proverb, "using the slavemaster's tools to dismantle the slavemaster's house"). The slaves' "symbolic reversal" (Outlaw) of the Exodus story offers a clear instance of using the Bible, often employed to sanction slavery, as an instrument of liberation instead. In their Exodus figuration, "as Vincent Harding has observed, the imagery was reversed: the Middle Passage has brought his people to Egypt land, where they suffered bondage under Pharaoh. White Christians saw themselves as a new Israel; slaves identified themselves as the old."[13]

Prophecy and Gospel

Now let us observe in black social prophetism a fulfillment of the narrative trajectory and intentions of the Christian gospels. Such fulfillment is ready to view in the Afro-Christian project to find a nonviolent 'cure' for racism and racist violence. That project climaxed with the King movement in the 1960s. However innovative he was, King also inherited his people's centuries-long, transgenerational experimentation with pharmacopeic (healing) and conjurational (magical-transformative) proficiencies at the level of socio-political realities. In Martin Luther King, Jr., the Afro-American prophet as trickster found vocational fulfillment as a nonviolent practitioner who (homeopathically) used a disease to cure a disease; that is, used victimization to cure victimization.

The movement contrived civil rights marches and demonstrations as social rituals that enabled victims to be transformed from mere sufferers (from their *status quo*) into activist heroes. Thereby it countered their internalized self-disesteem and, at the same time, induced observers and erstwhile protagonists to become converts and allies rather than persecutors. The freedom movement contrived such demonstrations in the form of agonized (compare the Greek, *agon*) festivals, during which masses of participants and, vicariously, an observant nation were initiated into an 'ecstatics' of repentance, self-sacrifice, and reconciliation. Television viewing of police brutality against participants 'awoke the conscience of a nation' (King), leading to federal legislation and a new public ethos that has irrevocably transformed the previously normative, *de jure* victimization of black Americans.

The conjurational and pharmacopeic nature of black social prophetism can be appreciated, again, with reference to the employment of images or figures. Thus, James M. Glass has correlated prophetic and political vision in his formulation of the political leader as a "shaman" who successfully employs socially transformative "signs." Political vision is shamanic when it employs incantatory signs in the therapeutic effort to address a "diseased situation."

> What the shaman does, how he enters into a diseased situation, depends on his capacity to construct 'signs,' to devise an incantation that will reach the unconscious . . . [an ability] as critical to the political vision.[14]

Socio-pharmacopeic projects remain a feature in the ongoing struggle of black Americans: the struggle to countermand the most toxic forces impacting our communities, both internally and externally. Those (external) forces include the entire range of dominating, scapegoating, and victimizing processes at work in history and society. Unfortunately but inevitably, those same processes are also internalized and compounded within black America itself. So toxic are these doubled effects that communities require practices and discourses that deliver them from the toxicity of their own traditions, institutions, and practices. A stereoscopic view allows us to see a convergence here between the curative, healing interests of black culture and its negative, counter-conjurational tasks. The use of an opponent's conjure trick to outwit or frustrate that opponent's purpose, or the use of a toxin to cure its own poisonous effects, suggests the kind of negation that is called for and that is distinctive in the ethnography of black folk traditions. I return to this issue of internal negation in the concluding paragraphs below.

Gospel and Apocalypse

> The Biblical image which has been at the heart of the black [American's] faith in the eventual appropriation of the American myth must be replaced . . . a possible new image is that of an African Diaspora based on the Biblical story of the Babylonian Exile and the final Jewish Diaspora. It is to the end of the Biblical history of Israel that black America must look rather than to the beginning.[15]

I turn finally to the terminal figure of the Apocalypse. Here it is opportune to note that the sequence of biblical figures need not correspond to black social history in a linear, chronological manner. Rather, biblical configurations of experience can be partially, proleptically, or retrogressively occurring at any period in social or (for that matter, personal) history. Black slaves sang spirituals that strongly displayed Exodus figuration, for example. On the other hand, more literate freepersons (so-called Ethiopianists) were writing at the same time with prophetic expectation of a messianic deliverer from their "Babylonian captivity." (While Exodus is early in biblical Israel's chronological history, the Babylonian exile and other experiences of diaspora are late occurrences). Remarkably, the Babylon figure reemerged in the 1960s prophetic criticism of Elijah Muhammad (Nation of Islam) and in the revolutionary rhetoric of Eldridge Cleaver (Black Panther Party). Similarly, two widely separated historical epochs—the 1860s emancipation of the slaves and the 1960s civil rights movement—have been represented by the same biblical figure: Exodus. In this regard we must bear in mind the configural feature that theologian Harold Dean Trulear calls the "flexibility in the Black story." As Trulear insists, "conceptualizing the Black story . . . does not mean that it is plagued by the linear rigidity and teleology of western philosophy of history."[16] Nonetheless it is necessary to address the eschatological trajectory of all the preceding figures toward their narrative consummation in the closing text of the Christian scriptures: the Book of the Apocalypse.

The figure of the Apocalypse is conventionally appropriated as if identical with the Greek figure of Nemesis (from *nemo*, to give what is due), the goddess of retribution. A Christian displacement of that convention operates in biblical narrative, however. This much overlooked displacement allows the Apocalypse to be read typologically as a fulfillment of the Gospel narratives. Here I press into service René Girard's "nonsacrificial" reading of gospel texts, in which the revelation of a nonviolent God corrects conventional readings that identify Christianity with the violent sacred.[17] That (mis)identification certainly operates in black religious experience, as this slave peroration evinces:

> Thar's a day a-comin'! Thar's a day a-comin'. . . . I hear de rumblin' ob de chariots! I see de flashin' ob de guns! White folks blood is a-runnin' on de ground like a riber, an' de dead's heaped up dat high! . . . Oh, Lor'! hasten de day when de blows, an' de bruises, an' de aches, an' de pains, shall come to de white folks, an' de buzzards shall eat 'em as dey's dead in de streets. Oh, Lor'! roll on de chariots, an' gib de black people rest an' peace. Oh, Lor'! gib me pleasure ob livin' till dat day, when I shall see white folks shot down like de wolves when dey come hongry out o' de woods![18]

One can certainly empathize with the impulses that drive such victims to seek resolution of the violence inflicted on them by their tormentors. However, the Apocalypse as read through the lens of the gospels can be seen as providing a radically different resolution. This is the therapeutic, or rather pharmacopeic, (or again, homeopathic), resolution of using a toxin as its own antidote. Thus Adela Yarbro Collins argues that the Book of the Apocalypse is best decoded via an Aristotelian schema of catharsis. Hence she entitles her study, *Crisis and Catharsis: The Power of the Apocalypse.*

> There is a certain analogy between Aristotle's explanation of the function of Greek tragedy and the function of Revelation. In each case certain emotions are aroused and then a catharsis of those emotions is achieved. Tragedy manipulates the emotions of fear and pity; Revelation, primarily fear and resentment. Aristotle's term "catharsis" is a medical metaphor. In its medical sense it refers to the removal from the body of alien matter that is painful and the restoration of the system to its normal state.[19]

The pharmacopeic expurgation of fear, powerlessness, and resentment is the prescriptive intent or "medical" function of the Book of the Apocalypse, according to Collins. In its *sitz im leben* (situation in life), she argues, the book performed a cathartic function for Christian communities who were currently undergoing the brutalities of Roman persecution.[20]

We do not require the corroboration of historical-critical scholarship in order to appreciate the trajectory of Collins's hypothesis. Her interpretation offers the welcome opportunity to 'save the appearances' of the Apocalypse as a text coterminous with the nonviolent import of the Christian gospels. In this connection a nonviolent reading of the gospels calls us to complete such a trajectory over against conventional interpretations of Apocalypse. We proceed by attending to the revelatory intention of the gospels as the canonic norm of the Christian Scriptures. If we invoke Luther's hermeneutic formula, 'scripture interprets scripture,' then we are summoned to a hermeneutic appropriation that fulfills Collins's hypothesis by fulfilling the Gospel trajectory of Apocalypse.[21]

To discern such an appropriation in the context of black religious figuralism brings us to the figure at the end of the Book of the Apocalypse: the figure of Diaspora or 'dispersion.' In Revelation 21 and 22, New Jerusalem appears as that end-time city in which a remnant has finally been freed from entanglement in worldly systems of injustice and oppression; they have been liberated from the world's "principalities and powers" (Eph. 6:12). That liberation is apocalyptically prefigured where, as history ends with the death knell of Babylon the oppressive city, the remaining people of God are summoned out of their long exile; out of their last captivity: "Come out of her, my people," the heavenly voice rings out, "lest you take part in her sins, lest you share in her plagues" (Revelation 18.4).

Here I argue that black Christian and other nonviolent communities are rightly represented as co-participants in a global configuration of all Abrahamic communities currently experiencing Diaspora.[22] In their diverse configurations these communities, 'Abrahamic' (that is, Jewish, Christian, Islamic) and others, provide both traditional and innovative strategies for fulfilling the Bible's prophetic vision of social justice, universal security, and enduring peace. (Consider here King's triad of anti-racism, anti-poverty, and anti-war ideals, elaborated as the most radical challenges facing the global community today.)[23] Whether regarded as rooted in or rather captive to their host cultures, diasporan communities are undergoing the challenge of myriad forms of social transformation and human solidarity. We should especially note the operation in such communities of various expressions of activism in society, solidarity with victims, and resistance against all forms of prejudice and oppression. Most promising, however, is the prophetic awareness of being summoned or called by the possibilities of post-national transcendence. Diverse peoples of faith are called to "come out" from excessive allegiance to various forms of nationalism, and to "come out" from the oppressive conditioning of their host cultures, in order to acknowledge, support and advance the trans-national humanity of peoples everywhere.

Ethnography as (Systematic) Theology

At the root of a theological position there is an imaginative act in which a theologian tries to catch up in a single metaphorical judgment the full complexity of God's presence in, through, and over-against the activities comprising the church's common life. . . .

David Kelsey[24]

In this concluding section I return to the ecstatic, conjurational and pharmacopeic elements in black religious experience, as the distinguishing ethnographic features of its sacred story. We have seen how that story comprises the incantatory and conjurational appropriation of biblical figures and narratives (from Genesis to Apocalypse). Moreover, such figures have been appropriated for emancipatory and pharmacopeic projects and purposes, as manifested in ecstatic performances and ritual reenactments. At this stage I contemplate in a proleptic way the possibility of systematic theological construction on the basis of this ethnographic, figural, and narrative perspective. What would such a constructive theology look like? What would it require in terms of method, sources, and organization? What style(s) of discourse would be most appropriate for its subject matter, community of origin, and audience? What must it achieve to be authentic to its ethnic, religious, and broader literary communities and, concomitantly, what must it be certain not to do?

It is impractical to answer most of these questions before the fact. As a thought-experiment (Kierkegaard), therefore, I essay in accord with Kelsey's formulation "to catch up in a single metaphorical judgment the full complexity of God's presence in, through, and over-against the activities comprising the church's common life" (Kelsey). In my judgment, the most felicitous and inclusive metaphor for such a demanding purpose is a metaphor that denotes transformative cure, healing or wholeness. The term "pharmacopeia" appeals to me for that reason. Below I show how it takes into account some of the stylistic and ethnographic imperatives of African American cultures, demonstrate its usefulness for black theological construction.

Pharmacopeia: An African American Ecstatic Theology

What if theological doctrines too can be rendered efficacious for healing and transforming souls, life situations, even entire cultures? Surely that question arises (if only tacitly) for a people whose spirituality makes prominent the use of medicinal and curative practices. The traditional cultures of West Africa fostered such peoples before many of them were transferred to the Americas by the Atlantic slave trade. Here I note in passing only two such cultures whose traditions and practices are significantly present on both sides of the Afro-Atlantic world. I refer to the Yoruba people of Nigeria, whose *orishas* (spiritual personalities) each possess their own leaves or herbs for healing, sustenance and preservation, and who are still venerated today in African-derived religions in Cuba, Haiti, the Caribbean, and Brazil. I also refer to the Kongo peoples of the Congo-Angola region, whose sacred medicines or *minkisi* provided the material-spiritual prototypes for black North American conjure paraphernalia and rootwork.[25] After considered reflection upon the remarkable acculturation and transformative practices of those peoples and their descendants in the Americas, I hazard the following informed hypothesis. Have biblical texts and theological beliefs served as surrogate materials or adaptive elements for more extensive curative projects? Can texts and doctrines be rendered useful as *materia medica* and *materia sacra*, and bear a similar transformative intent as other, more traditional pharmacopeia?

Consider, as a readily available example, the use of the Christian doctrine of forgiveness. Historian Timothy Smith's research has led him to argue that forgiveness and reconciliation toward enemies were the central doctrines of slave theology. The basics of that theology, Smith claims, were "first, forgiveness, awe, and ecstasy . . . the experience of forgiveness and the doctrine of reconciliation were primary."[26] He then proceeds to observe how theological doctrine converged with the psychological and existential needs of the slaves. On this view, their theology of forgiveness addressed the existential agony of impotence and the outrage that they experienced in the face of severe oppression. In particular slave converts to Christianity acknowledged their need to be 'saved' from an internal cauldron of violent impulses. "Black converts knew they had a lot to forgive. A long stream of testimony and reminiscence records their outrage at the injustice and hypocrisy of Christians who held them in bondage." Thus in the following testimonies we find instances of an extraordinary disposition of forgiveness directed toward white Americans.

> A fugitive preacher witnessed open discrimination against Black people at successive church services conducted by Baptists, Presbyterians and Methodists in the little town of Coxsackie, New York. He declared he had suffered more in spirit that day than at any time since ridding himself of slavery's chains. Nevertheless, "in pity and tears of sorrow," he wrote, "I commend them to the blood in which they must be cleansed if they ever reign in glory, and like Jesus I say from my soul, 'Father forgive them for they know not what they do'."

In acceding to the doctrine of reconciliation with enemies, black believers endured internal struggles in order to practice forgiveness toward their white oppressors. And in addition, wherever they discovered the efficacy of such forgiveness they reflected upon, celebrated, and proclaimed it to others:

> Sometime after 1812 the members of the African Baptist Church in Savannah, Georgia, recorded on the tombstone of their first pastor, Andrew Bryan, that when at the outset of his ministry thirty years before he had been "imprisoned for the gospel without any ceremony and . . . severely whipped," Bryan told his [white] tormentors that "he rejoiced not only to be whipped, but . . . was willing to suffer death for the cause of Christ."

131

Smith argues that such forgiveness became central in the practice and theology of early black Christians, not because of abstract idealism or sheer religious zeal. Rather, such doctrinal formation was commended to them by "the psychic necessity of finding means to resist inwardly injustices they could neither condone nor for the moment curb." Therefore, he quotes one representative speaker in conclusion, to the effect that they found that it was "'a great mercy to have all anger and bitterness' removed from their minds."[27]

This historian's correlation of theological doctrine with existential situation and religious psychotherapy is plausible and convincing, but offers a partial account. By way of extension, consider that what is also operating here is a correlation of doctrine with ritual and incantatory (or conjurational) practices, and with pharmacopeic or healing strategies. Observe in this regard some of the expressions of Christian conviction that Smith quotes and highlights, and which evidently evoke the Christian scriptures: "willing to suffer death for the cause of Christ"; "Father forgive them for they know not what they do"; "a great mercy to [remove] all anger and bitterness." Is it doubtful that such phrases, ritually intoned and repeated in hymns, sermons, and prayers, function in ritual contexts as incantations? When internalized by the victimized believer who is struggling to achieve an interior disposition of forgiveness toward enemies, their effects cannot be distinguished from the efficacy of spells and trances. The point here is not to reduce these invocations to magical phenomena, but rather to observe correlations between them and the pharmacopeic intention that operates in such phenomena.

The African American correlation of folk magic and folk pharmacy appears prominently in the traditional designation of an expert practitioner as a "conjure doctor." Such designations sharply differentiate black American from popular use of the term, "conjure," to mean only imagination on the one hand or only sorcery, witchcraft, or occultism on the other. But the folk synthesis between magic and healing evident in the notion of a conjure doctor suggests a comparable synthesis between religion and healing, manifested for example in the black preacher as a community therapist (Smith).[28] If we consider that such a second-order synthesis with religion might include in its purview social-historical 'cures' or transformations (activism as therapeutic, as an extension of folk cures and healing practices), then the following theological opportunity arises. It becomes possible to formulate in theological terms a rule-governed 'grammar' by which projects of social-historical transformation are distinguishable and comprehensible as Christian pharmacopeic projects.

The category, 'theological pharmacopeia,' emerges here in the pursuit of what George Lindbeck calls a postliberal theology based on cultural-linguistic approaches. Accordingly I am not concerned to create, in Lindbeck's terms, yet another category in the "cognitivist" or "experiential-expressivist" approaches to theology. That is, I do not intend (in cognitivist mode) that we propose doctrinal belief as psychosocial therapy on the basis of adherence to propositions of faith: belief in the Trinity, for example, as a transcendental referent for the beatific reordering of group relationships. Nor am I attempting (in experiential-expressivist mode) to propound curative or pharmacopeic experiences, or the religious expression thereof, as the essential feature in theological formation or reflection. Rather I am proposing (in cultural-linguistic mode) that we investigate 'theological pharmacopeia' as a category for explaining the distinctive manner in which African Americans appropriate biblical texts and religious doctrines.

> The task of descriptive (dogmatic or systematic) theology is to give a normative explication of the meaning a religion has for its adherents. . . . Meaning is constituted by the uses of a specific language rather than being distinguishable from it. Thus the proper way to determine what "God" signifies, for example, is by examining how the word operates within a religion and thereby shapes reality and experience rather than by first establishing its propositional or experiential meaning and reinterpreting or reformulating its uses accordingly. It is in this sense that theological description in the cultural-linguistic mode is intrasemiotic or intratextual.[29]

Thus the preceding section described, in accord with Lindbeck's emphasis on intrasemiotics or intratextuality, the biblical signs (Greek: *semeía*) or figures that provide the (textual) codes or grammar of black religious discourse and practices. But here I would qualify Lindbeck's formulation of the "descriptive" theological task as culminating in the "explication" of such meanings.

I suspect that normative *explication* of religious meaning, as an analytic or hermeneutic task, is still conditioned by cognitivist or experiential-expressive interests in *explaining* religion. Rather, I juxtapose to this postliberal approach the kerygmatic insistence of Karl Barth on church dogmatics as *presentation* more than explanation. In Barth's terms the theologian's craft consists in the presentation of the 'event' which is the community itself; the community as an instantiation of the lived reality of its founding truth (here I retrieve Barth's theological interest in the narrative presentation of the community's convictions, as intersecting Lindbeck's cultural-linguistic trajectory). The theological task (balancing Lindbeck with Barth) then becomes the normative presentation of its lived reality as displayed by a community's cultural forms and linguistic practices.[30] More concisely stated, description and explication must be rendered in the service of religious presentation. Ethnographic (or in other projects, phenomenological) description then serves theological 'profession', in both senses of that word: to espouse a cause, and to practice a discipline. Here, the discipline is theology understood as a community's articulated self-disclosure of its apprehension of (and its apprehension by) ultimacy, or the transcendent, or the extraordinarily powerful.

In the preceding section on ethnography we have seen that the cultural forms and linguistic practices that characterize black Christian communities in North America are governed by a pharmacopeic intention. To repeat, that intention consists in the will-to-transformation as manifest in a intergenerational quest for psychosocial and sociopolitical cures—curing slavery, curing racism, curing violence. The curative intention has governed black religionists' characteristic uses of biblical narrative and, by hypothesis, their uses of Christian doctrine. In concluding this section I try to substantiate that hypothesis, in the form of a normative presentation of a Christology based on this theological-pharmacopeic approach.

A distinguishing feature of black America's Christological discourse and practices is their curative focus on the imitation of Christ. In the *imitatio Christi*, Jesus as "Suffering Servant" (Isaiah 53) provides an exemplary model for the nonviolent transformation of victimization. On the basis of that model African American communities have devised 'homeopathic' strategies in order to 'cure' violence in the form of racism at the level of social change. For black religionists, finding such a cure has presented an ongoing problem of praxis and survival, not theology alone. It is the problem of curing racist Christianity as a deformed cult; that is, healing Christianity itself of its deformation as a religion of sacralized violence that is contrary to its own founding truth in the gospel revelation of God in Jesus Christ.

A crucial aspect of that black Christian heritage has been its mimetic or imitative features—its derivation from a long tradition of Christians practicing the *imitatio Christi*. A pharmacopeic problem has plagued that practice however. How do conventional victims imitate Christ without exacerbating or augmenting the scapegoating excesses of their dominant culture, a culture (in this case) which chronically misconstrues Christianity precisely as a sacrificial cult or a scapegoating religion? On the one hand black Christian activists have faced the difficult problem: How do I overturn my victimization without creating a new class of victims (that is, how to resist nonviolently)? But they have addressed as well an equally agonizing problem in black religious history: How do I transform victimizers without inviting and incurring the internalized effects of abuse? The solution that emerged from their practice was a (conjure) prescription that consisted of the embodied person as a tonic/toxic *pharmakon*. The cure prescribed was homeopathic on the basis of a nonviolent model, in which the victim's own body and person serves as *materia medica*—toxic to the victimizer if violation ensues, but tonic if victims are saved. To that end the 1960s freedom movement crafted public displays of victimization in which any violation of the victims' bodies would clearly reveal their scapegoat status. In such displays precisely what was toxic for victimizers if abuse occurred—that is, public recognition of their identity as persecutors and scapegoaters—became tonic if scapegoating was terminated and prospective victims were spared, rescued, or 'saved.'

Embedded in this schema of Christological transformation are three pharmacopeic modalities: *pharmakon*, *pharmakos*, and *pharmakeus*. Our English cognate forms like pharmacy, pharmaceutic, pharmacology, and pharmacopeia, all derive from the Greek

135

word, *pharmakon*. Recently the double-valenced use of this word, to mean either medicine or poison or both at once, has been brilliantly expounded by Jacques Derrida in his essay "Plato's Pharmacy."[31] Derrida's essay skillfully elaborates the three variant meanings of the Greek form: not only *pharmakon* (medicine/poison), but also *pharmakos* (victim or scapegoat), and *pharmakeus*, a sorcerer or magician. In this section we see how all three variants are significant for understanding African American religious formation. We have already observed the applicability of the *pharmakon*, or the medicine/poison variant. Now it is illuminating to recall the second meaning, *pharmakos* or victim/scapegoat, and also to develop a third variant, *pharmakeus* or sorcerer/magician.

In the folk culture of black North Americans the figure of the *pharmakeus* is most evident in the indigenous forms of the "conjuror," "conjure doctor" or "hoodoo doctor." On this view, Martin Luther King, Jr., for example, was not only a *pharmakos* (victim) but also a *pharmakeus* (practitioner). By the term *pharmakeus* I refer to his shamanistic ability to achieve the nonviolent amelioration of conflicted situations for his client communities, specifically black communities undergoing legalized discrimination and civil rights violations. The two features of shamanism most prominent in King's vocation are (1) the shaman's self-cure as a condition *sine qua non* of curative ability in relation to clients, and (2) the shaman's use of his or her own body as a site of "symbol production" in the curative process.[32] The former feature designates King's internal overcoming of feelings of self-doubt and fear as a victim himself of race hatred; the latter refers to his self-representation as a 'Moses' figure and, by extension, a messianic deliverer.

As a practitioner of nonviolent religion in the Afro-American tradition, King reenacted the gospel story in a salvific rather than a sacrificial mode. More precisely: the movement induced participants and observers alike to perform their own imitation of a nonviolent model who saves rather than sanctions new victims. The movement achieved this distinction by crafting, on the streets and before the public media of the nation, ritualized reenactments of the gospel story in which a victim secures salvation for co-victims and victimizers alike, without thereby requiring or initiating the creation of new victims. Indeed, civil rights history attests that such performances were catalytic and widely transformative for current and future communities of victims and victimizers.

However, the pharmacopeic efficacy of the *imitatio Christi* is not limited to the external projects of such communities. The model or figure of Christ also serves as an exemplary *pharmakon/pharmakeus* with respect to the interior dimensions of black American experience. In concluding this Christological sketch, I focus only on the most challenging problems in the internal constitution of black religious communities. One chronic problem, highlighted earlier in the section on prophecy and gospel, consists of the toxic forms of internalized self-hatred, intragroup mistrust, and the dysfunctional behaviors that any group experiences as a result of prolonged domination by another group. Alongside those internalized disorders is another complex that calls for pharmacopeic treatment: the endemic tendency of every community and tradition to reify its own constitution; to establish rigid behaviors and practices based on the exclusion and marginalization of perceived 'others'; and to construct hegemonic structures deriving from such forms of self-absolutization. A crucial requirement in treating these matters is a praxis that anticipates them, and thus intrinsically incorporates forms of self-negation.

That is to say, a praxis is needed that inhibits a community from sedimentation into its own forms of ideological rigidity. Such a praxis would be conducive to a permanent 'diaspora' in which one is always undergoing dispersion from monocultural structures to more inclusive formations. Thereby it would effectively subvert and retard sedimentation—whether sedimentation of thought or of social structure. As in Dr. Martin Luther King's metaphor of the "world house" in *Where Do We Go From Here?* such a praxis would serve to disperse communities continually beyond themselves to engage, for example, "black and white, Easterner and Westerner, Gentile and Jew, Catholic and Protestant, Moslem and Hindu."[33] In our contemporary context we would add persons and groups who are conventionally excluded or marginalized on the basis of gender identity, class background, sexual orientation, physical challenges, age, addiction, and other categories. A broad programmatic intention, then, to negate the endemic tendency to self-absolutization, is the pharmaconic praxis envisioned here.

That intention has been lucidly elaborated by Marxist feminist scholar Erica Sherover-Marcuse, as a principal feature in "a practice of subjectivity" that seeks to mitigate dogmatic and ideological formations even in a community's emancipatory projects:

> The emancipatory *intent* of a subjective practice cannot guarantee that its own activity in the service of liberation will be free from domination. . . . An emancipatory subjective practice would thus have to struggle continuously against its own reification, against the incremental sedimentation of liberatory processes into fossilized procedures, against the distortions of domination which ingress into all attempts at liberation. It could only do so if its own praxis nourished and encouraged in individuals a critical intelligence and a sense of self-worth *in the context of a developing solidarity.* . . . Therefore an emancipatory practice of subjectivity must posit as its goal not the immediate realization of 'the (given) self,' but the *emergence* of a 'self-in-solidarity.'[34]

Such a formulation, the *self-in-solidarity*, is convergent with Dietrich Bonhoeffer's Christological formula of Christ as "the man for others." Indeed, these are both ecstatic formulas espousing the wholeness and interconnectedness of humanity and the passionate desirability of manifesting our connectedness. However, what is salvific (Latin: *salvus*, to make safe, healthy) in such a Christology is not sheer belief in such formulas as Christological dogma (as mere cognitive assent to a proposition of faith). Nor does its pharmacopeic efficacy require a foundational experience or authentication based on expressions of conversion or sanctification. Rather, what 'saves souls' is a lived instantiation of such a model or exemplar in the practices of individuals and their communities of reference. This perspective yields a performative Christology, therefore, in which belief in doctrine and experiential-expressive contents are (not negated but) elements in, or inducements to, exemplary practices.

Here we should recall in conclusion that such practices, and their corresponding discourse, do not inhere in those communities in some abstracted, metaphysical way, but rather in narrative modes of lived experience. It is through the stories that a people tells itself, and tells about itself, that its practices become internalized, definitive and formative for their character. In this regard the sacred story of black Americans is the story of a pharmacopeic people whose enslaved ancestors received the divine gift of a prescriptive repertory or formulary, the Bible. With this formulary we have been empowered to prescribe for ourselves, and for other communities, healing models and processes for treating our own afflictions, and those of our nation and the world. The signal figure in that formulary is the Christ figure: a model for curing oppression and violence that enables us to embrace (to save) our enemies rather than destroy them. God grant that our theologies too may assist in rendering us even more proficient in ecstatic realizations of that model.

Non-Foundational Theology and Narrative

The Church's One Foundation is Jesus Christ Her Lord; Or, In a World Without Foundations: All We Have is the Church

Stanley Hauerwas

Practicing Theology in a World Without Foundations

James McClendon has been teaching us how to do theology in a world without foundations before anyone knew what anti-foundationalism was. That he has done so is due partly to his philosophical astuteness as developed in his and James Smith's book *Understanding Religious Convictions*.[1] I suspect, however, that his "anti-foundationalism" owes more to his determined stance to do theology in the baptist tradition.[2] The baptist tradition never sought a "worldly" foundation since it knew there is no foundation other than Jesus Christ.

To do theology with no other foundation than Jesus Christ strikes many as dangerous if not irresponsible. Such a theology, it is claimed, surely must be relativistic and fideistic since it lacks any "rational" basis. Moreover it has no means to speak to the wider world, thus robbing Christians of any way to serve their non-Christian neighbor. Even worse, such a theology invites a triumphalistic attitude incompatible with Christian humility.[3]

I have no intention to try to answer such criticisms on McClendon's behalf. He has already dealt with them time and time again. Instead I am going to offer three exhibits—three sermons—of what Christian practice might look like in a world without foundations. I take such a strategy to be commensurate with what McClendon has taught us, for in a world without foundations all we have is the church. That such is the case is no deficiency since that is all we have ever had or could ever want.

The Church, moreover, but names those practices through which the world is known and given a history.[4] Thus McClendon begins his "systematic theology" not, as recent theology, with doctrine but with ethics. But the ethics he develops is not that of a "theory," since ethics for him is constituted by those practices that make the church the church.[5] Therefore my use of sermons is an attempt to use a practice central to the church's life in which form and matter are one.

The three sermons I put on display are also meant to exhibit McClendon's account of the strands—the bodily, the social, and the anastatic—that shape his *Ethics*. The first sermon is meant to display the bodily, the second the social, and the third the anastatic. Yet as McClendon emphasizes, the strands cannot stand alone but constitute the rope of Christian existence.[6] Accordingly each of the sermons also have elements of the other two strands.

Though I think each sermon can stand on its own, I will begin each by setting its context and conclude each, not with an explanation, but with further reflection on why and how I think it exemplifies how we can and should go on in a world without foundations.

Body Stories

The following sermon was delivered at Aldersgate United Methodist Church in Chapel Hill, North Carolina, July 18, 1993. I followed the lectionary reading appointed for the day. Since I am a member of Aldersgate, I used the occasion to challenge the gnosticism so endemic to American Protestantism as well as direct attention to the importance of the eucharist.[7]

Jews and the Eucharist

Genesis 28: 10–22
Romans 8: 12–25
Matthew 13: 24–30, 36–43

We are not a church that often celebrates the eucharist. I regret that and would like us to move toward celebrating every Sunday. There are many reasons Protestant churches do not regularly celebrate Eucharist, but I think the main reason is most of us no longer believe our salvation comes through the Jews. I realize this claim will strike many as fantastic but by the time I finish I hope it will at least make sense—as well as create in us a hunger to feast with our God.

The text we heard from *Romans* is, of course, part of the problem. The text itself is not the problem, but how we hear it. We are told not to live according to the flesh, "for if you live according to the flesh, you will die; but if by the Spirit you put to death the deeds of the body, you will live." Our problem is that such a text reinforces our presumption that Christianity is about the "spiritual" and on the whole we like it like that. By spiritual we usually mean it is about stuff too deep to understand, but nonetheless important.

We also think the spiritual is the contrast with all the things that make life good. To be spiritual is to be anti-body, anti-sex, anti-pleasure. So to be spiritual means to be good, but dull. This really does not sound like terribly good news, but then if Christianity is really about the spiritual then we are pretty much left alone to do what we want with the stuff that really matters—that is the body, sex, and money.

That we associate Christianity with this sense of the spiritual is not surprising given the world in which we live. If we did not put God in something like the "spiritual realm," we would not know where else God might be. We know that no matter how much our belief in God might matter to us—and I know that it matters a great deal to most of you—most of us live our lives as practical atheists. We think we need God to give "meaning" to our lives, but if in fact it turns out that God just is not God, most of us would not have to change how we live. We could go on doing pretty much what we are doing.

145

For example Paul tells us "the creation waits with eager long-ing for the revealing of the children of God . . . We know that the whole creation has been groaning in labor pains until now; and not only the creation, but we ourselves, who have the first fruits of the Spirit, groan inwardly while we wait for adoption, the redemption of our bodies." Think about how that set of claims would play in any public school in America. All creation—rocks, plains, mountains, trees, cats, dogs, moles, weeds, and even us—is longing, Paul says, for the revealing of the children of God.

We may think this a colorful way to see the world, but we do not have the slightest idea what difference such a view might make for the way we conduct our science or our everyday life. We need our nature dead, subject to the laws of cause and effect, so we can subject it to our purposes—purposes that are, of course, meant to serve human well being. We do not believe that what we call nature is best understood as creation. In this sense, the crea-tionists are right to suggest that the way children are taught to view "nature" in the public schools makes irrelevant any claim that we and the world are God's good creation. I know we would like to believe that we and the universe exist as gift, as God's good creation, but it is hard to know what creation means once we have learned to view the world "scientifically."

So Christianity becomes that name for a set of beliefs we cannot "prove;" that is why we call it "faith." Faith is a kind of "knowledge," but it is personal. It means a lot to me, but I cannot presume anyone else ought to share it. Most that come to church probably believe some of the same stuff, but I cannot say that anyone who does not believe it is any the worse for it.

The story of Jacob's dream stands in stark contrast with this understanding of "faith." One of the worst sermons I ever heard was on this passage. The preacher tried to make Jacob meet our understanding of Christianity as spiritual, as a meaningful expe-rience. He noted that Jacob was on the whole a pretty unsavory character—a kid spoiled by his mother, a thief who steals his brother's birthright, a schemer who deserves to have Laban as a father-in-law—but this preacher said Jacob had this wonderful dream that changed his life. Such dreams, he assured us, were the way ancient people described important religious experiences.

The way we know Jacob had been changed by this wonderful experience was that the first thing he did on awaking was to pray.

The only problem with this way of viewing this story is it fails to attend to the content of the prayer. Jacob is not in the least changed by his dream. All the dream taught him was that God is present in this place in a peculiar manner, but he is not a bit intimidated by that knowledge. He is the same old Jacob, so he sets out to strike a bargain with God: "If you will give me what I want, take care of my food and clothing, then you will be my God and I will even erect a house for you and give a tenth of what you give me." This is a man who knows how to strike a deal.

As moderns we try to naturalize such passages by giving them a spiritual meaning. By doing so, however, we miss that Jacob, unsavory though he is, recognizes that God is here at Bethel in a way that God is not everywhere. This place is different because this God is not some generalized spirit we need to give meaning to our lives. No, this is the God of Abraham and Isaac. This is the God of this land, the land of Palestine, which is given to Jacob who is going to need it because he is going to have many descendants.

Moreover the people of this land, Jacob's descendants, are God's people in a way no others are God's people. All the families of the earth will be blessed through these people, but they are different from such families. For God says though you, that is the Jews, will spread abroad, you will not escape me. I am going to bring you back to this land because I keep my promises. You may learn to like Babylonia, Spain, or America but as a people you belong in Palestine. Given all they have gone through since the time of Jacob, understandably the Jews sometimes think: "Is this a promise we want?"

Let us confess that the Jacob story bothers us. Is not God everywhere? Yes, but however God is present everywhere does not mean that God is not present in Palestine in a way that is different.

But surely it is an arrogant and elitist claim to suggest that God is peculiarly the God of the Jews (or in a way different from being a God for everyone). It may sound arrogant to those of us who like to think God is the great democratic politician running the bureaucracies fairly. But I tell you this, if God is not the God of the Jews then our faith is in vain. Put as starkly as I can put it: if

Christian envy of the Jews ever leads to the destruction of the last Jew from the face of the earth then God will destroy the earth. Our God is not some generalized spirit, but a fleshly God whose body is the Jews.

That God, the God of the Jews, is the God we Christians believe has come in Jesus of Nazareth. We should not be surprised that the God of Abraham, Isaac, and Jacob would so come since God has no fear of the material—after all it is God's own creation waiting in eager longing. God came in this man, Jesus, to engraft us Gentiles into the promise to Israel. God is present in Jesus in a way God is present nowhere else. Through that presence we have been made part of Israel's blessing so that we too might be a blessing to the nations. God does not save us—Jew, Christian, and everyone else—by giving us a better set of philosophical ideas about how to live; God saves us through setting up this rock in Palestine called Jesus. Through Jesus' life, death, and resurrection, we have been made part of God's life with the Jews. All creation rejoices in our creation as God's people for we are what God has always desired as the end of creation.

That God's salvation is so fleshly, so material, is why we are here to worship God in one another's presence. We know we cannot hear the word as isolated spirits, but rather we hear God's word as God's body. Through the hearing of the word God creates a unity unknown anywhere else. Of course that is why nothing could be more scandalous than for Christians to kill one another. When we do so it is not just like committing murder, it is suicide.

That unity God creates by making us the body of Christ is most vividly present in Eucharist. Through that bread and wine, which is the body and blood of Christ, we become God's body. Such presence is made known because our savior is no dead hero, but the resurrected Lord. Resurrection does not mean Jesus, after laying a few insights and ideals on us, took a flier, leaving us alone to deal with this mess. Resurrection means that when the words are said—this is my body, this is my blood, pour out your Holy Spirit on these gifts—there is nothing we can do to prevent God from being present.

It is frightening is it not? As Jacob says, "Surely the Lord is in the place—and I did not know it." And then we are told: "And he was afraid." I do not blame him in the slightest. God is frightening.

Indeed I sometimes think the reason that Protestants, and in particular Methodists, are more likely to believe in the "real absence" rather than the "real presence" is that God just scares the hell out of us—and for good reason if God just is this God of Abraham, Isaac, Jacob, and Jesus.

Yet God's unrelenting refusal to be "spiritualized" is particularly threatening in the light of our Gospel for this morning. The parable of the wheat and the tares has been used particularly in recent times to challenge Christian presumption that we are better than other people or know something others do not. We are, thus, told that in this time between the times we really do not know who has been good and who has been bad until next Christmas. We are comforted by the suggestion that "until the end of the age" we really cannot tell who are the children of the kingdom and who are the children of the evil one. So who are we to judge—particularly ourselves. We are all equally sinners—which is good news because I am freed from thinking that how I live matters to God.

But once this parable is read eucharistically we see it is no accident that the kingdom of heaven is like a good field of wheat. Wheat becomes bread and bread becomes, through the Spirit, the body and blood of Christ. God is present here in this meal in a way God is present nowhere else. We are that wheat, we are that bread that the families of the world need if they are to know God. We are the people on which the peace of God depends. We are God's eucharist, we are those children for which creation had been longing. In the celebration of this meal God lifts us up, as he lifted Christ on the cross, so that the world might see the beauty of God's creation made real in a people at peace with their world. How can we not hunger to share this meal and share it often? May God continue to make us hungry for it. Amen and Amen!

It is my hope that this sermon displays how the Church is storied by God and accordingly stories the world. This, moreover, is a bodily matter that requires Christians to acknowledge that our existence only makes sense as we recognize God's presence in the people of Israel, that is, the Jews. Just to the extent Christians are tempted to tell our story separate from the story of Israel we become something less than God's body. Thus McClendon not only rightly reminds us of the significance of the body in his *Ethics*, but also makes the continued existence of the Jews a central issue for his Christology in his *Doctrine*.[8]

A Community's Stories

This sermon was preached on August 8, 1993 at Broadway United Methodist Church in South Bend, Indiana. Adam, my son, and I belonged to Broadway our last years in South Bend.[9] This year Broadway was celebrating its centennial and the congregation asked some of us back to preach. I again followed the lectionary for the day.

Our Many Stories and the Unity We Seek

Genesis 37: 1-4, 12–28
Romans 10: 5-15
Matthew 14: 22–33

It is wonderful to be back. It has been almost ten years since Adam and I were sent out from this place. I use the strange locution "sent out" to remind you that you prayed with us to discern whether we should go. I still remember David saying to me: "I think it all right for you to go if you will put before the seminarians you train what we have taught you here."[10] I have tried to do that, but I cannot tell you that the word I have spread about Broadway has been well received. I know you think I idealize Broadway, and I am sure my memory is selective, but the story of Broadway, even with the most unflattering subplots revealed, remains a challenge for most mainline Protestant denominations.

I do not mean to pour cold water on the celebration of our 100 years, but I would not be faithful to you if I did not speak the truth. The plain truth is that Broadway survives as part of a larger church that is dying. Mainstream Protestantism in America is dying. Actually I prefer to put the matter in more positive terms: God is killing Protestantism and perhaps Christianity in America and we deserve it. By "dying" I do not mean that the institution will not continue to exist. But it is not clear what relation the institution that survives will have to the great tradition we call Catholic Christianity. Paul Ramsey was fond of quoting the Methodist Bishop who, during an intense debate at conference, rose to the defense of the church with the claim: "Long after Christianity is dead and gone Methodism will be alive and well." I suspect the Bishop was unfortunately right if for no other reason than that the ministerial retirement fund will continue to pay dividends whether God exists or not.

In fact I think this is the reason that the story of Broadway is such a challenge to mainstream Methodism. For if the God we worship does not exist then this church makes no sense.[11] As David once put it when asked what is the most important thing we do as a church: "Why we come here every Sunday and celebrate the Eucharist." What could be more important than making God present here on Broadway Avenue in this neighborhood at this rather modest church Sunday after Sunday?

I have to tell you, however, that your answer to that question— "that nothing could be more important than the celebration of God's presence in Eucharist"—is not the answer most Methodists give. Most Methodists think it more important that their churches be friendly than that they manifest the unity that comes only through Eucharist. What matters to us Methodists is that we are an inclusive church: we do not want to believe anything or engage in any practices that might offend and thus exclude anyone.

We think that our practice of being inclusive is underwritten by texts like we heard in Romans—"there is no distinction between Jew or Greek; the same Lord is Lord of all and is generous to all who call on him." We think Paul is telling us we should not discriminate on the basis of race, religion, or sex. We read Paul's proclamation of the creation of a new people made possible by Jesus' death and resurrection as the equivalent of democratic egalitarianism.

If you are unsure that Jesus is the second person of the Trinity you can be a Methodist. If you think that God is just as likely to be absent as present in the Eucharist you can be a Methodist. If you think that Christian participation in war raises no moral questions you can be a Methodist. If you see no connection between God's presence in the Eucharist and war you can be a Methodist. But you cannot be a Methodist if you think it proper to exclude anyone else on any of the above grounds.

Such an inclusive church would seem to be one well fitted for success. Yet it is dying. I suspect it is so because people fail to see why they should belong to a church built on being inclusive since any volunteer service agency will do just as well. Moreover such agencies are usually better run.

I do not mean for my remarks to sound harsh. In the absence of practices such as the Eucharist that provide compelling examples of unity, it is easy to see how inclusivity could be confused with unity. The unity of which Paul speaks, that between Jews and Greeks, is made possible through the common confession that Jesus is Lord who has saved us by being raised from the dead. That unity is not based on the acceptance of everyone as they are because we want to be inclusive, but rather comes from the fire of Christ's cross through which we are transformed by being given distinctive service in God's kingdom.

I remember how John[12] created a hunger in us for this communion by reminding us in sermon after sermon that through word and sacrament God was making us a new people. Then, of course, we would not have the Eucharist but we knew we had missed something we needed. He reminded us that in this feast of the new age we became part of God's life and thus of one another's lives—we became united.

Yet what does that mean? What does it mean for us to be united in Christ. We can say, "The claim of Christian unity is a mystery" by which we mean it is hard to explain. But, of course, that means it is not a mystery since true mysteries are not explanations but realities that can be known only through proclamation—Jesus Christ is Lord.

I think the unity made present in the confession that Jesus is Lord is quite simple, but no less mysterious. It means I will never be able to tell the story of God's formation of my life without the story of Broadway United Methodist Church. This is where Adam was confirmed. This is where John made me go through a year of training before I could join the church since, as he put it, "Your history does not give me much confidence you understand what it means to be a member of the church." This is where I wandered back into Protestantism, which I am sure made it possible for me to even think about teaching seminarians at Duke, and which resulted in my being married to Paula, a Methodist minister.

Of course I did not come to Broadway as a cipher. I came bringing other stories that in one way or another had claimed me. Certainly the story of being a theologian was important, but that was just a peg on which to hang much more significant engagements. Adam and I, after all, came to Broadway from worshiping God at Sacred Heart. We came, that is, about half-Catholic. Moreover I had been touched by the witness of nonviolence of the Mennonites through John Howard Yoder. In your willingness to include us as part of your stories those other stories also became part of what it meant to be Broadway. Of course, those stories, Catholic and Mennonite, simply cannot be avoided if you live close to Goshen and a university called Notre Dame.

That Adam and I are no longer here does not mean that our story does not matter. Sarah was quite clear that she did not regard my unwillingness to join a church in Durham as good for my relation with Broadway.[13] So now Aldersgate United Methodist Church in Chapel Hill, North Carolina is part of your story. You want to know who Paula is and what Adam is doing, whom he is marrying, not simply because you are curious, though certainly that, but because you know your lives are united with ours. And you know that what God does with our lives makes a difference in how you tell your stories and how we together tell the ongoing story of Broadway.

Our unity is constituted by our inability to tell our stories without one another's stories. It takes time to do that. Indeed such unity is the way God's patience creates time by providing us the space to have our stories conformed to the story of Christ. Such a conformation does not obliterate our story, but rather it shapes how the story is told so that it may contribute to the upbuilding of Christ's body—so that finally our stories will be joined in one mighty prayer.

That our unity is so constituted is a great mystery, but here is even a greater mystery: what it means for our lives to confess that Jesus is Lord is that we, finally, are not the best teller of the story of our lives. When we confess that Jesus is our Lord our lives are no longer our own, our possession. We are now constituted by a history that we do not create, but the story of our lives comes through others. This means that those with whom we confess and commune may well know us better than we know ourselves.

That, of course, is why we are such an evangelistic group: we want our lives expanded through telling others of the stories that constitute our lives. Paul makes clear that no one can believe who has not heard; no one can hear unless someone proclaims, and proclamation cannot occur unless someone is sent. So we send one another away from Broadway that those who we do not as yet know become part of the unity of God's peace.

But what does this have to do with celebrating our one hundredth anniversary in the context of a denomination that is dying? I think something like this: the church lives on memory. In celebrating our anniversary we remember all those who have constituted this congregation. We believe they are celebrating with us today.

I think particularly of Gary.[14] When Gary was ill and unable to be with us I often felt a kind of dis-ease about whether we should celebrate the Eucharist, unsure if we were whole. I particularly missed him because it meant I was left alone to sing off key. Of course we no longer need to worry about Gary being present as we know Gary is in that communion of saints and no illness will ever again prevent his being with us. Our celebration, our continued survival, is a memorial to Gary and all the others who have made us possible by God's grace. We fear the dying of our church because we want the Gary's remembered.

It is, therefore, a good thing we have been here a hundred years to be a place of memory. A hundred years is a long time in places like Texas. This church, moreover, has been through some tough times but it has survived. Current theology is enamored of the image of liberation, but I confess in the world in which we live survival seems to me to be the greater good. Of course we do not survive just to survive, but so we might be God's speech for those who have not believed.

Yet I am not confident that we will be here in a hundred years. By "we" I do not mean just this particular church, but what we now call "Protestantism" and, perhaps, Christianity. That we Methodist-Protestants were called into existence and survived I am confident was God's doing. But I am not sure how God will have our story told for the upbuilding of the Kingdom. Perhaps God sold us into Egypt that we could prepare the way for the survival of a church that will still have to face, no doubt, a quite different but no less significant Exodus.

Or it may be that we are like Jesus' disciples whom Jesus "made" get into the boat while Jesus went up on the mountain to pray. The disciples found themselves battered by waves and wind, but then saw Jesus, who seems to have just been out for a stroll, walking, like the Spirit at Creation, on the sea. That he walks so prevents them from "seeing" him because they have not fathomed that this is the one who alone has the right to command the sea and the stars.

Peter, ever one to test things, says, "Lord, if it is you, command me to come to you on the water." In response to Jesus' command, Peter walks on the water until he notices the wind, becomes frightened, and begins to sink.

I suspect our situation as Protestants is not unlike that of Peter. We were, perhaps, rightly commanded to step out of the ark of Peter to walk on water. We did all right while we were not that far from the boat, could continue to presume its existence, and we remained focused on the one who had commanded us to leave. But then we noticed the wind. Put quite simply, when we became fearful about our survival, we sank.

For notice when Jesus and Peter rejoined the others in the boat the wind ceased, and they worshiped Jesus, saying, "Truly you are the Son of God." That, of course, is the heart of the matter: we are not here to call attention to ourselves, to insure our own survival, but quite simply to worship Jesus. Only such a one is capable of constituting us into a unity, of making us a new people, so that the world might know the God who rules the sun and the stars is the one found in Jesus Christ. If we try to base our unity on anything other than this one, we will by necessity become fearful and sink. Once Protestantism becomes an end in itself, presumptively believing we can tell our story without the story of our sisters and brothers in the past and present called Catholic and once we no longer long for the unity only God can give, God will kill us.

But the good news is this: that here in this place we have been made God's own. In a hundred years this building may well not exist, Broadway United Methodist Church may not exist, Methodism may not exist, Protestantism may not exist, but we will be remembered through the unity God has created here through word and sacrament. For never forget that God makes us God's own through faithful worship; and our story together cannot, therefore, be lost. So let us rush to this table, to climb back into this boat, so that we can once again worship our God.

McClendon has reminded us of the importance of the narrative character of Christian convictions. "Jews and the Eucharist" was the attempt to display the cosmic story Christians tell and to celebrate God's creation. In this sermon I have tried to remind us how our "smaller" stories are part of the story of God's creation that longs for the unity of God's kingdom. Just as I tried to suggest in "Jews and the Eucharist" that Christians cannot tell our story without the Jews, in this sermon I wanted to remind Protestants that we cannot tell our story without the Catholics—and I might add the Catholics cannot tell their story without us. Such tellings will not be easy or without conflict, but Christians do not need to fear conflict since we know our unity is a gift from God.

Some may think this sermon too particular and perhaps too "personal." Few readers of this will know the Johns, Davids, Adams, Sarahs of which I speak. Yet it is in the unavoidability of the telling of such lives that McClendon has taught us we discover our own lives, our own story. Moreover just to the extent such lives exist—and exist for one another—we know God's church, God's society, is real and capable of standing against the powers.

A Resurrected Life

This last sermon is even more personal than "Our Many Stories and the Unity We Seek." On December 31, 1992 my father died. I was in Egypt. I knew, as I had known for years, I was to preach at his funeral. On January 8, 1993 we celebrated my father's life at Pleasant Mound Methodist Church in Dallas, Texas—the church he had built. I chose the scripture.

Christ's Gentle Man

Revelation 7: 9-17
Matthew 5: 1-12

My father was a good, kind, simple, gentle man. He did not try to be gentle for there was no meanness in him. He was not tempted to hatred, envy, or resentment. He was kind and gentle, possessing each virtue with a simplicity that comes only to those that are good through and through. It was simply his gift to be gentle, a gift which he gave unreservedly to those of us fortunate enough to be his family and friends.

That his gentleness was so effortless helps us better understand Jesus' beatitudes. Too often those characteristics—the poor in spirit, those that mourn, the meek, those who hunger and thirst for righteousness, the pure in heart, the peacemakers, and the persecuted—are turned into ideals we must strive to attain. As ideals they can become formulas for power rather than descriptions of the kind of people characteristic of the new age brought by Christ. For the beatitudes are not general recommendations for just anyone but, rather, describe those who have been washed by the blood of the Lamb. It is they who will hunger and thirst no more, having had their lives transformed by Christ's cross and resurrection.

Thus Jesus does not tell us that we should try to be poor in spirit, or meek, or peacemakers. He simply says many that are called into his Kingdom will find themselves so constituted. We cannot try to be meek and/or gentle in order to become a disciple of this gentle Jesus; but in learning to be his disciples some of us will discover that we have been made gentle. Jesus' gentleness is nowhere more apparent than in his submission to the cross; and even there he wished no harm to his persecutors. But it is no less apparent in his willingness to be touched by the sick and troubled, to be with the social outcast and the powerless, and in his time of agony to share a meal with his disciples—a meal that has now become the feast of the new age.

Part of our difficulty with the beatitudes is that some of the descriptions seem problematic to us—in particular, we do not honor the meek. To be meek or gentle is, we think, to lack ambition and drive. Gentleness at most is reserved for those aspects of our lives we associate with the personal; but it cannot survive the rough and tumble life of "the world." Yet Jesus is clear that his kingdom is constituted by those who are meek and gentle—those who have learned to live without protection. For gentleness is given to those who have learned that God will not have God's kingdom triumph through the violence of the world. No, that triumph came through the meekness of a cross.

It is surely fitting and right that on the death of my father we celebrate all his gentle presence meant in our lives. It is fitting and right that we mourn the loss of that presence. Yet he would be the first to remind us that his life should be celebrated and mourned just to the extent we remember that his gentleness was a gift made possible by Christ. For the great good news of this day is that my father's life only made sense, that his life was only possible, because our gentle savior could not be defeated by the powers of hate and violence. My father's life is only intelligible insofar as we see in his gentleness the gentleness of our Lord.

For example, in one of the climactic moments of my father's life, when he was honored for supervising the building of Pleasant Mound Methodist Church, the first words he said were: "I would like to say that I am only human, the one we should be thanking is Almighty God. He is the one that gave it to us. Words will not let me express myself." He thanked Don Ragsdale, the construction committee, and Don Wallace, who "did the best electrical job he had ever overseen." He thanked all the Christian business firms, whom he had been doing business with over the years, who gave material at cost. He closed by saying he had already received all the thanks necessary: "I just thank God and praise God for it."

Simple but eloquent words, they but embody the simple eloquence of his gentle life. His life was like the beauty he taught me to see in a solid brick wall whose bed joints were uniform and whose head joints true. For the simple gentleness of my father was that which comes to those honed by a craft that gives them a sense of the superior good. My father was incapable of laying brick rough just as he was incapable of being cruel. It literally hurt him to look at badly done brick work just as it hurt him to see cruelty.

Like his gentleness his sense of craft was also out of step with the spirit of the times. The world wanted work done quickly and cheaply. The world wanted shortcuts. The world wanted him to build houses of brick so soft they would melt from watering the yard. He was incapable of such work so he was not rewarded as the world knows reward. Yet he lived secure in the knowledge that he never built a house with a "hog in the wall"—that is with one side of a wall more coarse than the other.

For example, there is a rock building back in the woods outside Mena, Arkansas that my father and mother built. Few people will ever see that building, though it is one of the most stunning rock jobs I have ever seen. My father and mother could not have built it otherwise, for to do so would have offended my father's sensibility. For to lay rock well you must see each rock individually yet in relation to what may be the next rock to be laid. To see each rock requires a humility founded on the love of the particular that so characterized my father's life.

Perhaps nowhere was that better seen than when one walked with my father through the woods. For my father never saw "nature" in the abstract, but rather he saw this tree or plant, this stream or river, this sky against these particular clouds. As one whose whole life had been in the construction of buildings he seemed to prefer those aspects of our existence that we could not make. Thus he would talk endlessly, and he seldom talked endlessly, about what a wonderful ash tree this was or the wonder that a post oak leaf was—each so different from the others. He, after all, found the holly tree hidden in the woods at our home in Chapel Hill, a tree that I had walked by countless times but had never seen.

I think the wonder he possessed was what made him so fond of children. He did not see children as but potential adults. Rather he enjoyed their wonder at what an extraordinary rock they had found because he too thought the rock, common though it was, extraordinary. If they liked the rock enough to share their discovery with him it was extraordinary. Children loved my father, I think, because they sensed in him the gentle wonder that unfortunately many of us lose in the name of being "grown-up." He loved to teach us to fish or hammer a nail and he could do it with all the patience such teaching required—though I have to say I think teaching me to lay brick tested that patience to its limits.

Jesus' gentle life was challenged by the fractious and contentious character of his own people, the power of Rome, and the incomprehension of his followers. My father's gentleness in many ways had a more serious challenge—namely, Texas. Texans have not been a people known for their meekness or gentleness. We are a flinty people formed as we are by a dry wind that blows across a hard land. We are not known for our humility, but for our bluster.

My father was a Texan and he had some bluster to him. Like all Texans he liked to brag—particularly around carpenters. Yet try as he would to be a Texan, his gentleness prevailed. You could feel it in the stories he told of riding his horse to school each day as a young boy. He loved school but even more he tenderly loved that horse. It was that same love I suspect that made Bobby, the bobtail cat that walked out of the Arkansas woods, choose my father as her companion in life. My father accepted that choice as inevitable because he and Bobby seemed to understand one another in a manner that made the rest of us "outsiders."

I suspect such tenderness also had much to do with one of my fathers major failings as a Texan—a failing I might add that none of us ever explicitly acknowledged. For if the truth be known, though trained as he was from a early age to be a hunter, he was a terrible shot. My hunch is that his deficiency in this respect did not derive from lack of skill, but rather had more to do with his love of animals. One of my earliest memories was his deferring to a neighbor the shooting of a dog that was suspected of being mad. His gentleness simply would not let him assume the role of hero. Even mother was sometimes frustrated by this as she could not understand how he could miss the ducks that had landed on their tank in Arkansas. I suspect he just could not bring himself to kill birds, numerous as they are, whose beauty he so admired. Of course armadillos rooting up his azaleas was quite a different matter.

Perhaps a more determinative challenge to my father's gentleness derived from the fact that Texas, at least the Texas in which he was raised, was also "the South." He inherited the habits that separated blacks from whites. Yet those habits could never flourish in his soul. That his gentleness prevailed even here I think had much to do with the unavoidability of the comradeship forged from the crucible of unbelievable hard work. The years he worked with Mr. Henry and George Harper meant he could never believe their goodness should be ignored on the basis of their color. He, like so many of us, lacked the practices to know how the community formed through hard work could be carried forward in other aspects of our lives, but he also knew the sadness with which we must live in the absence of such practices.

The work that he loved, the work that wreaked havoc on his body, was also a challenge to his gentleness. One side of his hands was worn smooth by the millions of times he held the rough material he laid. The other side of his hands had been made as hard and coarse as the mortar that results when lime and cement are combined. The hardness of the material and the hardness of the work can make bricklayers "hard men." "The job" is no place for the faint of heart or for those of refined speech or taste.

Yet even there my father remained my gentle father. Working as hard as the men he paid, dealing fairly with their weaknesses and strengths, enjoying the "characters,"—the Clarence Boduskys, the Jesse Womacks, the Tiptons, Bearhunter, Bobby and of course, my uncles, George, Rufus, Dick, Tommy, and Bill. He loved and was loved in a world embarrassed to acknowledge that love was even present. Hard men will cry unashamedly when they hear that "Mr. Coffee" is dead because they know they will not see his like again on "the job."

No one knows the gentleness that characterized this man's life more than my mother. She knows that in spite of the tiredness that often gripped his life he never failed to have time for any of us. He never thought that in doing so he was sacrificing his own interest as his love for us was his interest. The tender love my mother and father embodied in their marriage reached out and gave me a brother. That they did so is not surprising since their love was one in which there was no fear of the stranger.

That my father's life was constituted by such gentleness must surely be the reason that God chose to give him such a gentle death. He lived peacefully and he died peacefully. Of course his dying does not feel gentle for us who loved him. We rightly feel a loss, knowing that such gentle souls are all too rare. How are we to live without him?

But the great good news is that he has joined the other saints of God's kingdom gathered around the throne. He is among those who now worship God continually sheltered as they are by the one who alone is worthy of worship. He has joined the great communion of saints, that same communion that we enjoy through God's great gift of this meal of gentleness. For in this meal we are made part of God's life and thus share our lives with one another. So we come filled with sadness, yet rejoicing that God, through lives like my father, continues to make present Christ's gentle kingdom.

Ending with this sermon brings us to where McClendon begins—with lives.[15] For if lives like Dag Hammarskjold, Martin

Luther King, Jr., Clarence Jordan, Charles Ives, Sarah and Jonathan Edwards, Dietrich Bonhoeffer, Dorothy Day,[16] Coffee Martin Hauerwas, and James William McClendon do not exist then what we Christians practice cannot be true. The attempt to do theology as if such lives did not need to exist is now at an end. God has forced us to see that there is no "foundation" more sure than the existence of such lives. Moreover, just as these lives are witnesses, so McClendon has taught us, our theology is futile unless it too is governed by the witness of such lives.

A Concluding Word on Method

Many will find this essay confusing. Will this form or way of doing theology pass muster in the academy? It is so idiosyncratic. Assertions are piled on assertions, but no clear argument or method is apparent. How can one be expected to learn how to do theology in such a mode?

The answer to the last question is simple—through practice. Though I lack the skills of a McClendon—a master craftsman—I have tried to imitate here his "method." For in truth there can be no "method" for theology in a world without foundation. All we can do is follow at a distance.

CHAPTER 8

Narrative Theology and the Religious Affections

Richard B. Steele

In this paper, I shall argue that Christian theology, when written from a narrativist and non-foundationalist perspective, can and should account for the role that religious emotions play in the life of Jesus' disciples. That is, such a theology must be able and willing to show how the authoritative narratives that the Christian church tells, and the congruent rituals, customs, and disciplines that it observes, not only inculcate a highly distinctive set of doctrinal convictions and promote a highly distinctive set of moral virtues, but also elicit an equally distinctive set of religious emotions. Unlike some of the other essays in this volume, mine will not attack foundationalism directly. But I shall, toward the end of the essay, attack something that George Lindbeck calls "experiential-expressivism,"[1] a popular modern theory of religion that takes a keen interest in the religious emotions. I contend that experiential-expressivism is akin to foundationalism, and that we who, in our effort to develop a narrative theology, feel compelled to reject the one, must also reject the other. On the other hand, I believe that while we must reject the experiential-expressivist theory of religious emotion, we must not ignore the crucial place of emotions in robust Christian faith; rather, we must account for it by principles consistent with our own methodology.

Structurally, this essay is divided into five numbered sections, each headed by its own thesis statement. Taken individually, these five theses, as well as the arguments used to support them, are deeply indebted to the work of many other theologians, philosophers, and moralists. This will be evident from the notes. It bears mentioning, however, that chief among those who have shaped my thinking are Professor McClendon himself and some of *his* chief sources, particularly Jonathan Edwards and various "postmodern" Anglo-American analytic philosophers.[2] My aim has simply been to establish the hitherto unnoticed connections between analytic philosophy's theory of the emotions and narrative theology's theory of character formation. I shall try to show: (1) what human emotions are; (2) how they are shaped by the communities to which we belong and by the authoritative narratives and distinctive practices of those communities; (3) how sincere commitment to any particular community affects our emotions; (4) what those effects are when the community to which we are most cordially committed is the Church of Jesus Christ; and (5) how the emotions experienced and cultivated by Christians differ substantially from those of members of other religious communities.

♦　　♦　　♦

(1) Human emotions typically display the following features: (a) They entail judgments of people, objects, events, or situations in which we have some personal interest. (b) They have reasons for being, not just causes. (c) They are—or at least they indicate—perduring features of our character, and are not just brief episodes in our stream of consciousness. (d) They may or may not have physiological symptoms, but usually do motivate us to act—or restrain us from acting—in certain ways. (e) They themselves (and not simply the actions they may motivate) are susceptible of moral appraisal.

I shall attempt to demonstrate this complex thesis by analyzing the grammar of emotion-words in our "ordinary language."[3] I shall say very little, except by way of illustration, about the aetiology or morphology of particular emotions, or about related psychological phenomena such as feelings, sentiments, moods, attitudes, and passions. However, the distinctive features of emotions will emerge with greater clarity if we contrast the language of emotions with that of, say, feelings.[4]

Properly speaking, feelings refer to episodes in our stream of consciousness and sensations in our bodies. Hence we can often determine the exact time and place of their occurrence. For example, a doctor will ask where a patient feels pain and how long it has hurt. Feelings are typically, though not necessarily, caused by circumstances beyond our control. You feel an itch on your nose one summer evening from a mosquito bite, or a qualm in your stomach when, on the day after your tenure review, the dean calls you a bit too solemnly into her office. You cannot, properly speaking, "intend" to feel a feeling, although you can intentionally do things that will cause or alleviate certain feelings in yourself, such as turning up the thermostat to get warm, or taking a drink to slake your thirst.

Emotions, in contrast to feelings, register our judgments, construals, or appraisals of objects in which we have some personal interest.[5] This is shown by the fact that emotion-words in common speech are generally transitive. That is, they take objects and are often modified by prepositional phrases. One may be anxious *about* an interview, angry *over* an insult, confident *under* attack, embarrassed *by* lipstick on the collar, or contemptuous *of* women who wear mink coats to church. The point is that emotions are targeted at objects. They indicate how one stands related to the world, how one assesses, construes, or regards objective realities. So one must make a judgment in order to *have* an emotion, whereas one need not make a judgment in order to *feel* a feeling. Hence, emotions should not be confused with feelings.

Of course, emotions can often be felt. Moreover, the intensity with which an emotion is felt is a fairly accurate, though by no means infallible, index of the degree of personal interest or concern one has in its object. For example, the grief I felt at my mother's funeral was exquisite. She had suffered so long, and had died so young, and her death had left such a terrible void in my heart! On the other hand, I once attended the funeral of the sister-in-law of a friend of mine. I went to the service out of sympathy for my friend, but having never met the deceased, I neither felt nor showed much emotion. When we *do* feel our emotions, they too, like feelings and bodily sensations, become episodes in our stream of consciousness.

Furthermore, some emotions, like all feelings, can have dramatic physiological symptoms. For example, anger over an insult is manifest in a scowl on the face, an edge to the voice, a clenching of teeth and fists, and a jump in blood pressure. Yet the emotion of anger is more than its accompanying feelings and symptoms: it includes a harsh judgment upon the offending party and perhaps fantasies of retaliation. And because some emotions do resemble feelings insofar as they seem to last for a measurable span of time and produce dramatic physiological manifestations, we must acknowledge that the line between those psychological phenomena we classify as emotions and those we classify as feelings is blurry.

Nevertheless, the conceptual distinction between these two classes holds good. For whereas we often speak of "feeling an emotion," we never speak of "emoting a feeling." Nor do we need to *feel* an emotion in order to *have* one. Emotions are not simply incidents in our stream of consciousness, although they sometimes are, but aspects or indices of our character. We cannot always locate them in specific parts of our body or measure how long they last. Where in your body do you feel your fondness for mystery novels or your envy over the lucrative grant that a rival scholar was recently awarded? And how many hours a day do you feel them? These questions are unanswerable because such emotions have no bodily symptoms at all. Rather, they motivate us to act. You might spend two hours venting your envy by writing a bitter review of your rival's work, or trying to remove the reason for your envy by rewriting your own proposal for next year's competition. Yet your envy itself is not two hours in duration; it lasts even when you are quite unconscious of it—say, when you are immersed in a Sherlock Holmes story. Put down the novel and think of your lucky rival again, and your envy comes right back! Or rather, it was there all along, dormant. For an emotion is not just something you *undergo*. It is part of who you *are*.

Another telling difference between feelings and emotions is that the former have *causes*, whereas the latter have *reasons*. Suppose I wake up in the middle of the night to use the toilet. It's dark, I'm groggy, and I stub my toe on the bathroom door. The impact *causes* pain—a feeling. But it does not cause—it only *occasions*—an emotion. Indeed, it might occasion any of several emotions. I might be violently angry at the door for being in my way, or mildly alarmed that I have so frequently forgotten to switch on the night light in recent weeks, or wryly amused over the bit of slapstick which I have just played out. The particular emotion which this situation actually elicits from me depends on many factors, not all of which are under my control. If I have already been awakened three times by a sick child, I am more apt to curse the door than to laugh at my faux pas. Nor am I necessarily conscious of all the possible emotional responses that I might make, much less alert enough at that moment to make a deliberate choice among them. Still, it would be true to say that anger at the door would be the least "reasonable" of the three possible responses listed above, since doors cannot be guilty of malice, whereas my memory might really be slipping, and my nocturnal antics might well be funny if they didn't hurt so.

It is important to note, therefore, that the unreasonableness of my anger at the bathroom door is not due to the inherent irrationality of emotions, but to the faultiness of my appraisal of the situation. For emotions are not necessarily irrational, nor are people always irrational by virtue of having emotions.[6] Rather, people are irrational when the judgments upon which their emotions depend are mistaken, or because the intensity of their interest in the objects of their emotions is for some reason out of due proportion to the true or proper relationship in which they stand toward those objects.[7] Consider my earlier example of the intense grief I felt—and felt free to express in tears—at my mother's funeral. There was nothing "irrational" about it. Indeed, it would have been loutish if I had felt no grief on such an occasion, or if I had felt too inhibited to express it by weeping. Yet that does not imply that I deliberately "decided" to feel and show my grief. Rather, it implies that our typical standards of rational activity may be too dominated by the paradigm of decision-making.[8] There is a fittingness, an appropriateness, and even a kind of moral beauty about those emotions which truly and spontaneously express the relationship we have with other persons or the interest we have in events and objects—providing, of course, that our personal relationships and interests are themselves morally praiseworthy.[9] Similarly, an inappropriate display of emotion is morally repulsive and/or psychologically aberrant. It would have been hypocritical or pathological for me to have blubbered uncontrollably at the funeral of my friend's sister-in-law. For one kind of hypocrisy involves the deliberate manufacture of the typical physical symptoms of emotions in situations where the emotions themselves are not sincerely felt, just as one kind of neurosis involves the eruption of emotions which are not appropriate to the situations that elicit them.

It follows that we are, to some extent, responsible for our emotions.[10] We must constantly be checking their aptness and intensity, and sometimes correcting them. It is seldom morally significant to say of someone that he feels his feelings. Itches and tickles just happen to him: they arouse neither pride nor guilt in him, and they incur neither praise nor blame from others.[11] His emotions, on the other hand, are good indices of his character and are susceptible, in varying degrees, to moral evaluation. Suppose he has been unemployed for three months and is then unexpectedly invited for a job interview. If he admits to feeling anxious about this, most of us would deem it quite natural, that is, perfectly reasonable in view of the inherent awkwardness of job interviews and the immense personal significance of the outcome. But now suppose that after the interview he learns that, due to the company's affirmative action program, the job has been awarded to a member of a "protected community." We would not blame him for being disappointed about not being hired, and, in view of the circumstances, we might even tolerate a few snide and politically incorrect comments from him about the lucky candidate. But if his resentment turns into a perpetual, seething malice toward persons of color, and drives him to join a White supremacist hate group, I think we would have grounds for censuring him—not just because the policies and activities of such groups are so reprehensible, but because his emotions are severely disordered and his character has grown vicious and corrupt.

In summary: human emotions entail judgments of objects; they have reasons for being, not just causes; they are perduring features and/or revealing indices of our character, not just passing episodes in our stream of consciousness; they may, but need not, have physiological symptoms, but usually do motivate us to or restrain us from action; and they are, in widely varying degrees, susceptible of moral appraisal. It follows that whatever shapes our judgments of the objects of our interest will also shape our emotions, and hence our character and behavior; and that the more something shapes our judgments, the more it will shape our emotions, character, and behavior.

Our next task will be to draw this account of human emotion, so heavily dependent upon postmodern analytic philosophy, into connection with what many contemporary epistemologists and narrative theologians are saying about how our lives are shaped by the communities to which we belong, the stories we tell, and the customary practices we engage in. Let us begin by positing as our second thesis:

(2) The authoritative narratives and customary practices of the various communities to which we belong are among the many factors which shape our judgments— and therefore our emotions.

This assumes that all human communities possess a set of normative stories that its members tell and retell, as well as a congruent set of conventions, rituals, and practices that its members observe with some regularity and devotion. Indeed, the fact that any human community can identify itself as such depends on the constant reiteration of its particular stories of origin and historical continuity, the faithful observance of its distinctive customs and disciplines, and the maintenance of its characteristic institutions. (For example, we Methodists, to preserve our identity *as* Methodists, must always be reciting the stories of John Wesley, singing Wesleyan hymns, celebrating covenant services, and organizing class meetings, revivals, and annual conferences.) Most readers of this volume, I presume, will be familiar with the rich body of literature by Professor McClendon and others that has tried to show this.[12] What I wish to make clear is that the authoritative narratives and customary practices of a particular community not only give that community its self-conscious identity, but also help to shape its convictions about "the good, the true, and the beautiful," to determine the virtues it expects its members to display, to shape the judgments it makes about new problems and situations that arise in its ongoing history, and hence to elicit a distinctive and specifiable set of emotions which "fit" with all this.

A vivid illustration of my point is provided by David Hume. He once compared similar incidents in the lives of Brasidas, a Spartan general during the Peloponnesian War, and Robert Bellarmine, a post-Tridentine Catholic controversialist.

> Brasidas seized a mouse, and being bit by it, let it go. "There is nothing so contemptible," said he, "but what may be safe, if it has but courage to defend itself." Bellarmine patiently and humbly allowed the fleas and other odious vermin to prey upon him. "We shall have heaven," said he, "to reward us for our sufferings: But these poor creatures have nothing but the enjoyment of the present life." Such difference is there between a Greek hero and a Christian saint.[13]

Now the situations confronting these two men were strikingly similar, as were their consequent actions. But their convictions, virtues, judgments, and emotions were quite different, at least partly because the narrative framework within which they lived, and the customs and disciplines which they practiced as members of their respective communities, also differed.

Consider Brasidas: He was certainly an exemplary Spartan soldier, renowned both for his courage in battle and for his brilliance as a military strategist and tactician. Yet he was unusual among his people in also possessing considerable personal charm, diplomatic finesse, and oratorical skill.[14] Now one of the defining moments in the Spartan tradition was the Battle of Thermopylae in 480 B.C.E., when a squad of three hundred Spartans, commanded by their king, Leonidas, defended a narrow mountain pass for ten days against a vast expeditionary force of Persians under the Great King, Xerxes I.[15] Eventually the invaders overwhelmed the Greeks and slew them almost to a man—but not before Xerxes had lost thousands of his soldiers and two of his own brothers, and had thrice been seen leaping in terror from the throne on which he sat observing the battle. Now the skill, courage, and humor of the Spartans at Thermopylae, in contrast to the treachery, cowardice, and brutality of the "barbarians," became legendary. So it is no surprise that when, in 422, Brasidas had to lead another small band of Spartans against a much larger (but not very prudently commanded) enemy, he sought to inspire them by appealing to their "Peloponnesian character."[16] Nor is it any surprise that when he, a Greek who blended the virtues of Leonidas of Sparta and Pericles of Athens, unwittingly found himself in much the same position as Xerxes of Persia, i.e., a giant bitten in self-defense by a feisty little mouse, he felt considerable amusement and admiration. Indeed, those are precisely the emotions that such a man in such a situation *would* feel, because they are psychologically congruent with the virtues he practiced as a Spartan solider and logically consistent with the stories of his people.

Now consider Cardinal Bellarmine, one of the leading figures of the Catholic Reformation. He was an eloquent preacher, an erudite scholar, an effective controversialist, and a skillful prelate.[17] His greatest literary work was a three-volume refutation of Protestantism, written early in his career, which stood for two centuries as an impregnable bulwark of the Roman cause. Late in life he was appointed to the Holy Office and had the dubious honor of helping to prosecute Galileo for heresy. Yet Bellarmine was by no means an uncritical papalist or a proponent of a rigid, heartless orthodoxy. The proceedings against Galileo revealed his esteem for the scientist's learning,[18] and his own theological principles "admitted the possibility that scientific discoveries could change the understanding of Scripture."[19] Moreover, one of his own works, which denied that the pope had direct temporal authority over the Christian world, was almost placed on the *Index of Books*.[20] And despite his staunch opposition to the Reformation, he was not above suggesting that the fate awaiting sincere Protestants who died in heresy would be similar to that of Catholic catechumens who died before baptism.[21] It is clear, therefore, that Robert Bellarmine was not just another ultramontane "organization man," but a sincere disciple of Jesus, who had interiorized the Christian virtues of faith, hope, and love, and who had a tolerant and generous attitude toward his opponents. For that very reason, it seems fitting that when he was infested with parasites, his response was neither one of irritation and annoyance (as it might be for lesser saints), nor one of admiration and amusement (as it was for Brasidas the Greek hero), but one of patience and compassion. The community to which he had devoted his life (the Church), the authoritative story upon which that community is

171

based (the story of Jesus' passion, death, and resurrection), and the practices which make that community what it is (sacraments which imply the goodness of creation and ascetical disciplines which teach the conquest of the flesh by the Spirit) all bade him to construe his fleas as "poor creatures." Indeed, the point is precisely that because Bellarmine did *not*, like that genteel skeptic, David Hume, regard fleas *as* "odious vermin," he neither felt the emotion (annoyance) nor performed the action (bathing or swatting) which such a judgment would elicit.[22] One taught to yearn for heaven learns how to endure irritations.

We are now in a position to propose a further thesis:

(3) The more committed one is to any particular community, the more attentively one will heed its narratives and the more diligently one will practice its customs. And the more one does that, the more forcefully those narratives and customs will shape one's judgments and emotions.

My wording here is very deliberate, for while I do want to insist that the "narratives and customs" of a given community shape its members' judgments and emotions, I do not want to imply that all of them feel exactly the same emotions toward the same objects, any more than they all think or act alike. That would be egregious over-simplification. Innumerable factors unique to each individual shape his or her cognitions, volitions, and emotions. Moreover, most people are members of many communities—family, gender, class, race, nationality, and so forth—each with its own stories and practices. Indeed, one of the distinctive problems of modernity is precisely that the number of communities to which each of us belongs, willy-nilly, has increased to such a degree that it is often difficult for us to decide which of these has the strongest claim upon our allegiance. For those who embrace modernity, it seems deplorably narrow-minded for individuals to identify themselves so thoroughly with one particular community as to allow *its* narratives and practices to assume normativity in their lives.[23] But for those who see modernity as a tangle of competing communities, with overlapping memberships and often mutually incompatible stories and practices,[24] commitment to some *one* of them may well be an act of robust self-definition and unusual moral courage.

This is precisely why the story of Brasidas and Bellarmine is so illuminating. It demonstrates what happens when people wholeheartedly commit themselves to a particular community and allow themselves to be formed by its stories and practices. They become, in Hume's words, its "saints" and "heroes," that is, the prime exemplars of its virtues, the chief interpreters of its ideals and convictions, and often the leaders of its decision-making bodies. But even if they possess no formal political power, a community's saints and heroes are rightly deemed its "authorities," because the story of their lives becomes an integral part of the governing narrative of the group as a whole, or at least a powerful witness to the truthfulness and worthiness of the ideals enshrined in the community's arch-narrative. Of equal importance, however, is the fact that they have a "feel" for the truth and worth of their tradition, an affective appreciation for its values, a simple and often childlike delight in its customs, a relish for its stories, and a personal experience of the joys and sorrows, the trials and temptations, distinctive to its particular way of life. This, too, they are uniquely able to communicate to others. Witness the impact of Bernard of Clairvaux, Francis of Assisi, and John Wesley on the Church.

Applying what we have said about Thesis No. 3 to members of the Christian community in particular, we can now say:

(4) When the community to which one is most cordially committed is the Church of Jesus Christ, its authoritative narratives (i.e., the Bible and the Christian tradition) and its customary practices (e.g., baptism and eucharist) gradually come to shape one's judgments and emotions more forcefully than other factors in one's life.

We have seen in the case of Bellarmine that unswerving allegiance to the Church, contemplative attention to its paradigmatic stories, rigorous proclamation of its teachings, and (we may presume) faithful participation in its sacraments, spiritual disciplines, and ascetical practices not only shaped his theological convictions and personal habits, but also his innermost "heart," that is, his way of construing the world.[25] Such integration of character is or ought to be the goal of all Christians, who are obliged by Scripture not only to hold certain beliefs and reject others, and to perform certain deeds and renounce others, but also to cultivate certain emotions and repent of others. Note all the emotion-words in this string of Pauline imperatives.

> Love in all sincerity, loathing evil and clinging to the good. Let love for our fellowship breed warmth of mutual affection. With unflagging energy, in ardor of spirit, serve the Lord. Let hope keep you joyful. . . . Call down blessings on your persecutors—blessings, not curses. With the joyful be joyful, and mourn with the mourners. Care as much about each other as about yourselves. Don't be haughty, self-important or vengeful.[26]

Here, some emotions are obligatory and others prohibited. Our entire nature, including its affective component, is to be transformed by the gospel. Sorrow (for our sins), gratitude (for our blessings), meekness (when calumniated), forbearance (when injured) temperance (when tempted), and courage (when threatened) are all praiseworthy emotions or virtues—traits of character—which necessarily include a finely nuanced emotional component. Edwards called them "gracious affections," believing them to be constitutive elements of sincere Christian faith.

But it is not the case that Scripture simply *stipulates* which emotions ought to characterize Christian faith. It also *displays* them in its "saints and heroes," and *elicits* them from its faithful readers.[27] And precisely here we may observe the shrewd psychological insight of the biblical authors. They apparently understood that one cannot simply tell people to *feel* thus and so, as one can sometimes tell people to *do* this or that. If one wants them to cultivate a particular emotion, one must shape the judgments which are entailed in that emotion, and more importantly, one must excite their *interest* in the object of that emotion. As Professor McClendon has brilliantly demonstrated, narrative is the literary device that Scripture employs to accomplish these ends. And a supremely effective device it is, for it invites and enables the readers of Scripture to make *its* story *their* story, to see the events recorded on the sacred page as events in their own personal history, to identify the characters in the Book as fellow members of the same ongoing community of faith, and to imitate the practices and share the experiences of their ancestors in their own day and age.[28]

Thus religious emotions, and particularly Christian emotions, embody the same features as all emotions. They entail judgments of objects of our interest, they have reasons for being, they are (or indicate) perduring features of our character, they motivate us to action, and they are susceptible of moral appraisal. What distinguishes the religious emotions of Christians from other kinds of emotions (and, as we shall see in the following section, from the religious emotions of members of other religious communities) is that they are displayed in and elicited by the normative story of Scripture, and tested for authenticity by the Church. Their object is the righteous and loving God revealed in Jesus Christ; their reason for being is the open invitation for all people to come unto him; their perdurance is seen in the life of ardent devotion; their behavioral manifestations are discipleship, service, and mission; and the criteria for their appraisal are set by the Church which is called and enabled to test the spirits.[29] We may conclude, therefore, that:

(5) The particular religious emotions which a Christian experiences are not simply happenstance episodes in his or her private stream of consciousness. Nor are they identical with the religious emotions experienced by members of other religious communities. Rather, they are essential components, along with doctrinal convictions and moral virtues, of his or her faith.

It should be clear by now that our emotions—religious and otherwise—are shaped by the communities to which we belong, the stories we revere and try to imitate, and the disciplines we practice with greater or lesser diligence. This view stands opposed to two other theories of emotion which are popular today.

The first view sees emotions as value-neutral, tradition-independent, conviction-free bits of experience which just "happen" to us. They are episodes in our stream of consciousness, not features of our character. There seem to me to be at least three reasons commonly adduced to support this view, which I will enumerate and refute *seriatim*:

(A) We know by experience that we cannot simply "will" ourselves to feel or not to feel a given emotion at a given moment. We often seem to be in the grip of our emotions rather than in control of them. This may be true, but it is beside the point. I am not denying that emotions often come to us unbidden, only that they come to us apart from judgments. And the more considered our judgments of those objects, the more fitting our emotions. Shark sightings at beaches sometimes excite panic in swimmers, and appeals by lifeguards to "stay calm" are useless. But that is because what most people know about sharks comes from horror movies instead of National Geographic films. An experienced marine biologist does not need to "control her emotions" at the sight of a shark. For the emotions that she feels in the presence of these great predators—wonder, admiration, scientific curiosity—are *already* controlled, as it were, by her superior judgment of the dangers and opportunities of the situation.

(B) We tend to take those emotions which behave most like feelings as our paradigm of how all emotions work. That is, we fixate on those emotions which are episodic rather than perduring, which are felt intensely when felt at all, which seem to be caused by factors beyond our voluntary control, and which have obvious physiological manifestations. These include fear ("panic attacks") hilarity ("gales of laughter"), rage ("temper tantrums"), joy ("each ecstatic instant" [Emily Dickinson]), and grief ("'Twas sad by fits, by starts was wild" [William Collins]). But as we have seen, not all emotions behave this way. Why should a swimmer's fear of sharks be a better example of an emotion than, say, a soldier's admiration for feisty mice? And in any case, even those emotions which do closely resemble feelings are still shaped by our judgments (right or wrong) of their objects, and therefore differ materially from feelings. Closer attention to the grammatical differences between the language of emotions and the languages of feelings, sentiments, impulses, instincts, sensations, etc. is called for, as I have tried to show in the foregoing. Failure to attend to the psychological wisdom imbedded in our ordinary language leads to confusion about the very phenomena we are trying to describe.

(C) We tend to see ourselves as the subjects or victims of passions which lurk beneath the surface of consciousness. These dark psychic forces exist in each of us, regardless of the communities to which we belong, the stories we tell, and the "outward" practices we engage in. And they are quite immune to our own efforts and those of society as a whole to control. But as Professor McClendon has shown, in a brief but penetrating discussion of this theory, the very person who originally developed it, Sigmund Freud, tried to explain how the passions work by reference to "another cluster of narratives—the stories of the developing sexual child, of the oedipal struggle, of the emancipated or illusion-free individual or the sexually liberated society—stories that carry their own substantial interpretive freight. . . ."[30] But if passions are inexplicable apart from stories, then our way of actually experiencing the world, which is supposed to be governed by our passions, must be dependent in some way on stories as well. And if stories are finally indispensable, then the real question becomes: Which story best accounts for our actual experiences, or rather, shapes our experiences in such a way that we learn to live as wisely and well as possible?

George Lindbeck has isolated another view of human emotion, and specifically of religious emotion, which many people hold today. He dubs this "experiential-expressivism," and contends that those theoreticians of religion who adopt it

> locate ultimately significant contact with whatever is finally important to religion in the prereflective experiential depths of the self and regard the public or outer features of religion as expressive and evocative objectifications (i.e., nondiscursive symbols) of internal experience.[31]

This approach thus begins with the assumption that ultimate truth is somehow "within" us, regardless of our heritage or creed, waiting to be discovered and expressed. Accordingly, it is staunchly anti-dogmatic and subjectivistic. Consider how William James, whom we shall take as our representative experiential-expressivist,[32] defined religion:

> [T]he feelings, acts, and experiences of individual men in their solitude, so far as they apprehend themselves to stand in relation to whatever they may consider the divine. Since the relation may be either moral, physical, or ritual, it is evident that out of religion in the sense in which we take it, theologies, philosophies, and ecclesiastical organizations may secondarily grow.[33]

It follows that the things which give a particular religion its distinctive character, such as its authoritative scriptures, liturgical customs, ascetic disciplines, and creedal norms are but symbolic expressions of some kernel of spiritual truth which it shares with other religions. But if the "truth" is universal, while the symbolic expressions are particular, even parochial, then the task of theology is to isolate the truth *in* the symbols, or rather to interpret the "meaning" *of* the symbols. This task is accomplished by the discovery of the underlying "foundations" upon which all religions rest, the universal principles, structures, or depth experiences which they all share.

But this task is vitiated by the following paradox: Any attempt to state the shared underlying meaning of all religions must avoid the use of the particular conceptual scheme and vocabulary of any of them; otherwise, it would implicitly and arbitrarily elevate that religion to a hermeneutical preeminence which, *ex hypothesi*, it cannot have. On the other hand, any attempt to state religious "meanings" in a non-religious or meta-religious language would be, by definition, a failure, since the very act of trying to *state* religious meanings at all, in any conceptuality or terminology whatsoever, would make that discourse implicitly and essentially religious. In short, religious meaning cannot be distilled from religious language or conveyed apart from it. But if that is so, and if every religious language is forged by a community which avows a particular set of beliefs and values, and performs a particular set of rituals and disciplines, then to speak religiously at all is to speak from within some particular tradition. One cannot presuppose, just because one could never state, some core of religious "meaning" capable of being isolated from the specific beliefs and customs which bear it. Thus Lindbeck concludes that there can be no

> inner experience of God common to all human beings and all religions because . . . the experiences that religions evoke and mold are as varied as the interpretive schemes they embody. Adherents of different religions do not diversely thematize the same experience; rather they have different experiences. Buddhist compassion, Christian love, and—if I may cite a quasi-religious phenomenon— French revolutionary *fraternité* are not diverse modifications of a single fundamental human awareness, emotion, attitude, or sentiment, but are radically . . . distinct ways of experiencing and being oriented toward self, neighbor, and cosmos.[34]

On the surface, it might seem that foundationalists and experiential-expressivists are looking for different things, the former for some body of absolute and incontestable truth, the latter for some universally shared "inner experience" of the divine. Still, there is a discernible similarity in the animating assumptions of foundationalist philosophies and experiential-expressivist approaches to religion, namely, that for people to apprehend the Ultimate, they must somehow escape, or at least transcend, the particular community of discourse to which they belong. Loyal acceptance of the official doctrines of that community, ready obedience to its authorities, and regular participation in its rituals are viewed as potential impediments to people's perception of that truth which supposedly stands high above it, or lurks hidden within it.

It seems clear, therefore, that those of us who feel bidden to reject foundationalism have an equal stake in rejecting experiential-expressivism.[35] But the mere fact that experiential-expressivism, with its flawed theory of religious emotion, cannot be acceptable to narrativist, nonfoundational theologians is no reason for us to harbor suspicions against religious emotion as such. It only means that we must show how our theory of religion gives a better explanation of how the affective component of religious faith stands related to the cognitive and volitional components. That is, we must demonstrate how a community's theological convictions, moral virtues, liturgical practices, ecclesiastical arrangements, spiritual disciplines—and religious emotions—are all bound to the stories it tells. I hope that this essay has made a start in that direction.

Community, Narrative, and an Ecological Doctrine of Creation: Creation and Ecology Beyond Modern Atheism

Elizabeth Barnes

Introduction

Much is being said today about ecology and Christian responsibility in light of environmental concerns expressed around the globe. Various thinkers of differing perspectives, who nonetheless share many of the same concerns, are now attempting to address ecological issues. Some of those thinkers are discussing community and some narrative, and some are discussing both in relation to the overarching subject of ecology and theological and ethical relevance and responsibility. Among those who have given sustained attention to this subject are Rosemary Radford Ruether in her book *Gaia and God: An Ecofeminist Theology of Earth Healing*[1] and Herman Daly and John B. Cobb in their book *For The Common Good: Redirecting the Economy toward Community, the Environment, and a Sustainable Future.*[2] In this essay, I intend to assess both of those proposals in light of James Wm. McClendon's narrative perspective and method and the differing presuppositions they represent. I shall analyze the understanding of community and narrative and suggested implications for ecological theology and ethics in the work of Ruether and Daly and Cobb and demonstrate that, despite their wishes otherwise, foundationalist assumptions limit the functioning of both community and narrative in the shaping of ecological Christian doctrine and an ecological doctrine of creation. McClendon's work, conversely, points the way forward precisely through the matrices of narrative and community to faithful creation teaching. Because his eschatological theology is, at the same time, narrative-and-community-centered theology unbound, and thus unlimited, by Enlightenment presuppositions requiring scientific or philosophical foundations as reliable ground on which to stand, McClendon offers to developing ecological reflection apposite critique and correction and valuable suggestions for constructive work yet to be done.

McClendon's Proposal for an Ecological Doctrine of Creation

Shaping an ecological doctrine of creation is the work of the church. McClendon's baptist theology, because it centers in the community of the church, offers fertile resources for the ongoing development of such a doctrine. His early pioneering work, *Biography as Theology: How Life Stories Can Remake Today's Theology,*[3] the first volume of his systematic theology, *Ethics,*[4] and the second volume, *Doctrine,*[5] together identify and describe both community and narrative in terms that begin and enable further the working out of an ecological doctrine of creation. McClendon's manner is to go straightaway to the biblical narrative(s), following a method of attending to biblical "pictures" which is characteristic of the baptist methodology and narrative approach he has shaped over the last twenty years. No philosophical or scientific foundations frame the parameters within which his work is allowed to proceed. While he is informed by scientific studies and the contributions of scholars in other disciplines and expresses gratitude for them, McClendon limits his task to the specific work he identifies as his. "I propose only to examine in the best light available the biblical 'pictures' of creation now available to the church, to relate these to the ongoing creative work of God (and of God's creatures), and finally to explore the connections between creation, salvation, and last things. . . ."[6] This characteristic lack of theological hubris defines McClendon's approach and work from beginning to end and allows an eschatological perspective that is, despite its broad scope, modest and focused. More importantly, it allows a perspective free of universalistic pretension dictated by Enlightenment foundationalism which assumes the role of telling everybody's story instead of the specific narrative of one's own faith community.

McClendon begins his doctrine of creation with the eschatological "picture" of the goal of creation, the heavenly vision in Revelation 4. His reason for doing so is two-fold: first, to orient notions about creation in the lived story and struggle of the people of faith; and second, to focus on *trust* as the generative context within which creation comes to consciousness and is believed. McClendon emphasizes "the defiant, active faith that shaped the understanding of God in Israel and early Christianity. This faith grew, not from cosmogonic speculation either scientific or mythological, but from the cry of trust that would not acknowledge any God but God."[7] He names five features which he believes are imperative to a Christian doctrine of creation: (1) "God is the origin and source of all else. God is Alpha." (2) "Creation is . . . God's ongoing blessing . . . intrinsically good." (3) "The creative divine rule is . . . under constant attack . . . challenged by worldly powers and worldly understandings." (4) "God's rule is both displayed and enhanced by the creation." (5) "Creation has a terminus or goal, and that goal lies in God."[8] Each of these is challenged both within the church and outside it. McClendon explicitly tags contemporary scientism which takes many forms, one significant aspect of which is the displacement of God as origin of all else. Other challenges take the form of anthropocentric focusing on the human species to the diminishment of other species and the consequent loss of the character of creation as blessing "with its tone of joy and delight." A genuinely "Christ-shaped ecological doctrine of creation" will evoke this delight in creation which does not "deny that the human creature has a distinctive place among the creatures." In fact, McClendon believes, "a fully ecological doctrine can alone appreciate that place."[9]

McClendon both begins and develops his doctrinal work *within* the community of faith and its practices of worship and discipleship. Technical and theoretical questions are not considered in a space apart, whether that be the physical space of an academic study or the theoretical space of scientific rationalism or abstract theological reflection. McClendon examines God's role as Creator and God's presence in creation and the relatedness and symbiosis of all creatures as a member of the community of faith who reads the biblical story and interprets both it and the community's discipleship story in terms of the baptist vision and hermeneutic of "this is that." The short-hand phrase, "this is that," identifies an interpretive vision and method shaped by "a regular motif in biblical literature in which language about one set of events and circumstances is applied under divine guidance to another set of events and circumstances."[10] This community-centered, narrative-shaped method guides all McClendon's work, analytic and constructive. Therefore, the Bible's narrative and the community narrative he lives with other baptist and non-baptist Christians compose the generative matrix of his theology and ethics. For him, community is church community and narrative is biblical and church narrative. McClendon recognizes and values neighborhood communities, civic communities, national communities, and even, to whatever extent it can be sensibly expressed, cosmic community. The point is that Christian theology and Christian ethics arise out of *Christian community*. McClendon's early groundbreaking work, *Biography as Theology*, emphasized the reality of character-in-community and its meaning: that *Christian* character is shaped in *Christian community*. It logically follows that Christian theology and ethics are shaped in Christian community, the worshipping, witnessing life of the congregation of believers as they live out, and live out of, the Christian story.

A "Christ-shaped ecological doctrine of creation," will be born from the originative womb of the church's practices, as are all the church's true and truthful doctrines. Indeed, many of those practices themselves require correction and revision, and McClendon's systematic theology and other work have engaged that task. A "this is that" mode of interpretation and a practices methodology focused in biblical and church narrative and in discipleship community yield a substantively different ecological doctrine of creation from that offered by those who do not employ this narrative-and-community-centered method. One of its characteristics is an "ecological reading of the biblical creation pictures."

While McClendon, like other theologians with an ecological focus, also examines Near Eastern creation stories and specifically the Babylonian *Enuma Elish*, he does not then leave aside the Genesis stories for others regarded more useful for an ecological perspective. Rather, he holds the biblical 'pictures' alongside other 'pictures' to gain a richer composite image.

A primary image for McClendon is that of the potter and clay in Jeremiah 18:1–11. "What the potter can achieve depends in part on the clay on hand: Clay may be too soft to stand, or too stiff to work, or its substance ill suited to the hardening furnace's fire. Or it may be just right. A good potter makes what she can out of the clay, perhaps modifying its texture to improve results."[11] McClendon looks at various biblical 'pictures' *within his own context of the praise and prayer of the worshipping community of which he is a member.* This is exactly the point I labor to underscore. Here follows a singular example. From Jeremiah's narrative and the Genesis stories McClendon's attention shifts now to his (former and present) congregation's hymnsinging, that is, to its practices of praise and worship. A beloved old hymn evokes an insight connected to the stories in Genesis and Jeremiah. "Alongside the Creator's own creativity is the creative potential (or the want of it) displayed in the creature. A line in Adelaide Potter's gospel song, 'Mold me and make me/ After thy will, While I am waiting/ Yielded and still' expresses the surrender that is surely one moment of authentic creaturehood."[12] Now, the theologian's attention returns to the biblical narrative and interlaces narrative and hymn, thereby evoking new ecological insight:

> Yet Jeremiah's message from the potter's house suggests a further role for the clay:
> > You are the potter, I am the clay;
> > Make me the chalice, Of a new day.
> > Here then my power, Talent and skill;
> > Fire them for action, Creative Will.
> For our action, too, both our yielding and our overcoming, is creation. What we have yet to explore is the sense in which not only angelic or human creatures, but also animals, plants, and inorganic nature, including finally the smallest quanta of energy, constitute creation's web, each segment created yet creative, each in its part fashioning the cosmic whole.[13]

McClendon's insight at this last point is much like that of other ecological thinkers informed by current scientific research and theory. However, owing to the matrix rich with biblical and liturgical narrative from which his insight is born, McClendon's focus is multifaceted and evocative, engaging the reader in a similar interlacing of images and a similar evocation of truth. Adding 'pictures' from the Psalter to those from Genesis, Jeremiah, and his faith community's liturgical story, McClendon continues to expand and enrich his interpretative mosaic, trusting that faith pictures which have long comprised the story of the people of God are as relevant in an ecological age as they were in earlier days: "this is that."

The Psalter pictures a creating, nurturing God who mothers all creation. Agreeing with Ruether and others that an ecological doctrine of creation will also be one valuing the motherhood of God, McClendon turns to Psalm 131:2, observing that "The psalmist is 'calm and quiet like a weaned child clinging to its mother' (131:2)—and that mother, in the Psalm's figure, is JHWH."[14]

Ruether makes much of early humankind's worship of the Mother Goddess and suggests that both more irenic and ecologically inclusive and healthful social organization was the result. That may well be factual. However, in her indictment of Jewish and Christian religious perspectives as the Father God supplanted the Great Mother, she neglects rich resources in scripture which other feminist perspectives have treated more appreciatively. As McClendon compiles and arranges the biblical narratives and the 'pictures' they offer, he observes that, while "Scripture was quite restrained on God's originative fatherhood," close reading of the Bible shows that, though references and allusions to God as creative Mother are infrequent, when they do appear, they are less restrained, confident in praise and gratitude to God. He notes the explicit mothering, birthing imagery in the following 'picture' from Deuteronomy: "You were unmindful of the Rock that bore you; you forgot the God who gave you birth" (32:18) . . . " Looking elsewhere in the Pentateuch, McClendon notes a more nuanced and suggestive 'picture' from Numbers in which a somewhat exasperated Moses speaks rhetorically, asking "God about his [Moses'] responsibility to his countrymen: '*Am I* their mother? *Have I* brought them into the world, and am called on to carry them in *my* arms, like a *nurse* with a baby?' (Num. 11:12a) The implication is that it was JHWH, not Moses, who 'brought them into the world' and is therefore responsible for ungrateful Israel." As God is Israel's Mother, God is also Mother of all the creation: "God's creative mothering is not confined to human offspring."[15] McClendon points out that Job offers a picture of God as both Father and Mother of all, of rain, dew, ice, and frost; God is Mother and Father who originates all creation, organic and inorganic. With information from Phylis Trible, McClendon develops this image from Job and, holding it beside yet another from Isaiah, shows that scripture's primary metaphor for expressing the costly pain of creation is God's motherhood. " . . . God speaks through Isaiah of Babylon to describe both originative and renewed creation (Isa. 42:5–25)."[16]

> Long have I restrained myself,
>> I kept silence and held myself in check,
> now I groan like a woman in labor,
>> panting and gasping.
> I shall lay waste mountain and hill
>> and shrivel up all their herbage.
> I shall change rivers into desert wastes
>> and dry up every pool. (Isa. 42:14f)

Here McClendon identifies converging themes, the travail of birth for both mother and child, on the one hand, and for both God and nature, including human nature, on the other.

As McClendon does different things with the motherhood of God from that which Ruether does with that profound insight, he also does different things with the great body of scientific discovery available to the church now. Informed by scientific data, he affirms "a growing awareness that our species is continuous with nature. We are part and parcel of the universe, and live in symbiosis with other living things and in mutual dependence upon the earth . . . Dust we are; like earth our floating home in space, our selves are composed of ancient star dust."[17] Conversant with the findings of cosmological science, he recognizes, " . . . the science of cosmology draws upon data from astronomy and high-energy particle physics to reconstruct a cosmos of dynamic, open emergence."[18] Interlacing that information with Christian faith's primary resources from its community's own lived narrative of worship and discipleship and the biblical narratives which shape

Christian community itself, McClendon moves to questions and reflections which scientific cosmology is not interested to ask and consider. As he sees it, cosmological science's "current content is friendly to the proposal that God's method in ongoing creation was interactive from the first amid interactive primitive particles, long before there were living cells or animals to form cooperative intentions." Indeed, cosmological science's mathematics of space might even be helpful, McClendon suggests, for reconceiving the Christian doctrine of heaven.[19] Drawing also from the biological sciences, McClendon considers the implications of evolutionary biology's openendedness. In a statement worthy to gladden any ecologist's heart, he writes a thought of sterling beauty:

> . . . investigating an ocean floor or jungle or forest or desert, one cannot predict what variations will take form in its ecological web, what new forms will emerge, and how these will creatively alter the symbiotic system they help constitute so as to enable still new emergents—new creative possibilities.[20]

Finally, with biblical narrative and discipleship community as his anti-foundationalist hermeneutical and methodological matrix, McClendon connects creation, salvation, and consummation by adding to the composite mosaic of 'pictures' from the Old Testament other pictorial narratives from the New. He looks first at the letter to the Romans. Here he notes a "surprising" turn in which Romans 8 "opens for us three topics, God's travail (implied), creation's travail (explicit), and the future of creation with God."[21] McClendon follows closely the progression of Paul's thought, possible only if one takes the biblical narrative seriously enough to deem it important for present ecological understanding and guidance, as McClendon does. At this place, he does what few thinkers have yet done: he suggests that ecological faithfulness and salvation are tied together in one knot. Commenting on Romans 8:17b-25, McClendon writes:

> Creation's suffering (here Paul reflects Isaiah 42:14ff.) is the labor of a woman giving birth; God's labor pains (thus Isaiah) are those of creation (thus Paul), and the two, God's and the world's, are mediated, brought together, by the labor pains of the Christian fellowship, who in company with their Master suffered and were sustained by God who is Spirit: 'through our inarticulate groans the Spirit himself is pleading for us, and God . . . knows what the

Spirit means' (18:26f.). Paul crowns this explanation with a summary that reiterates our present theme: 'in everything, as we know, [God] co-operates (*sunergei*, 'synergizes') for good with those who love God and are called according to his purpose' (8:28).[22]

Synergy, interaction, symbiosis, interconnection—all these terms express the meaning of Romans 8:28, McClendon interprets. Reading with ecological data interlaced with the biblical story, McClendon sees what the mathematical cosmologist sees and more. Creation is "work in progress" done by God, humanity, and creation; it is divine-human-creation synergy. This, McClendon claims, is the inner meaning of symbiosis, interaction. It is also the meaning of Romans 8.

McClendon pushes forward to the question of *why* creation? His context of inquiry as theologian and ethicist and his status as member of a faith community of worship and discipleship raise this question. To answer it, he returns to the eschatological vision of Revelation 4 and 5 with which he began. Emphasizing still the "pictorial nature of our 'protological' and eschatological knowledge," he explains his discovery:

> The pictorial symbolism of Revelation 5 implies that creation's goal will be found in history, and concretely in the story of Israel and Jesus. It implies that the wanted answer is not found apart from but exactly in connection with the paradigmatic suffering of the 'Lamb slain.' It announces that, thanks to that Lamb, creation will find its way to the 'praise and honor, glory and might' of its one Ruler (5:13).[23]

This is where considering nature—creation and ecology—in the context of biblical story and the faith community's narrative of worship and discipleship makes the biggest difference. *Here is where theology without foundationalistic underpinnings of scientism or philosophical metaphysics makes the biggest difference. The question of ecology has to do, in the last analysis, with the goal of nature.* Much ecological theology shaped by foundationalist methodologies and presuppositions flounders in the attempt to name a goal for the ecosystem; much else identifies that goal in inadequate terms. McClendon shows that an eschatological vision alone can disclose nature's meaning and goal. Creation's destiny, like humanity's, is at the heart of the matter.

To make this announcement is to suggest the inadequacy of other ways of determining creation's destiny. . . . The point of creation is known through Israel's story and known most clearly in its climax at the cross.[24]

Creation's meaning, like that of humankind, travels, McClendon insists, along the "vector" leading to the throne of God. Basing our reflection on McClendon's insights, we can say that ecological theology without foundations will begin with this "last things first" theme found in biblical narrative and expressed concretely in the worship and discipleship of the Christian community. A "Christ-shaped ecological doctrine of creation," McClendon shows, is at the same time narrative-shaped and community-shaped in just this way, and for exactly *this* reason, it is eschatologically oriented and focused. So being, it connects creation to salvation and consummation, displaying creation as an "arena of promise whose destiny lies in its relation to what lasts and what comes last and to the new that comes in Christ."[25]

Ruether's Theology of Earth Healing

With McClendon's constructive proposal before us, let us turn to the ecological proposal of Rosemary Radford Ruether. Ruether states in her introduction to *Gaia and God: An Ecofeminist Theology of Earth Healing* that she intends to "sift through the legacy of the Christian and Western cultural heritage to find usable ideas that might nourish a healed relation to each other and to the earth."[26] She explains her juxtaposition of the terms *Gaia* and *God* as reflective of the reality that "all the issues that I wish to explore finally pose the question of the relationship between the living planet, earth, and the concept of God as it has been shaped in the Western religious traditions."[27] *Gaia*, the name of the Greek Earth Goddess, signifies for her, as it does for many others, the religious vision needed for an ecological spirituality. She is aware that other feminists believe that the transcendent male God of Judaism and Christianity needs to be supplanted by the immanent female goddess Gaia, but Ruether believes that merely replacing the one with the other fails to deal adequately with what she terms the "god-problem." I might insert here that much contemporary theology concerns itself with this modern "god-problem", betraying its Enlightenment preoccupation with foundationalist questions of where to find a rational stratum upon which "god" can stand. Ruether's anxious investigation in *Gaia and God* joins that modern quest. I intend to show that working, as Ruether does, from a "god-problem" focus is a foundationalist assumption that vitiates much of what Ruether and others with similar perspectives and intentions hope to accomplish.

Ruether proceeds to construct her proposal by naming two strands in the Christian heritage which hold "glimpses" for the religious vision of earth healing needed today; the covenantal and sacramental traditions. While both are flawed, she states, they each offer important resources for the vision humanity needs now to appropriate and nurture. Although she cites ecological value in the Genesis creation narratives, Ruether is honest about her reservations about turning in the direction she has identified. Patently ambivalent, she reiterates still her claim that the covenantal and sacramental traditions have "profoundly valuable themes for ecological spirituality and practice."[28]

Ruether's reason for turning to the church's biblical and ecclesiastical story, however, seems finally not so much to be recovery of valuable themes in the covenantal and sacramental traditions as "luring" Christians to whom these are important into ecological responsibility. She writes, " . . . the vast majority of the more than one billion Christians of the world can be lured into an ecological consciousness only if they see that it grows in some ways from the soil in which they are planted."[29] Ruether is exactly on target as far as she goes, but she fails to take her insight far enough, both for Christians and for her own theological project. This is one place where her "god-problem" perspective intrudes, preventing her from seeing that Christians do not simply need to see that ecological faithfulness "grows in some ways" from their own soil. Rather, they need to recognize that living the Christian narrative within the community of faith can mean living an earth healing ethic and developing and modeling for modern culture an ecological spirituality and religious vision with power to transform both the church's own errors and its complicity in earth destruction and Western secular culture's destructive world view and practices as well. Ruether's ambivalence and skepticism, along with her theological foundationalism, prevent her from following through on a Christian theology of earth healing adequate to the church's need. She fashions an ecofeminist view, but her foundationalistic presuppositions and doubts about the recoverable resources in Christianity thwart her full intention. Most significantly, she does not set forth the possibilities inherent in *the Christian community's faithful living of the best of its story*; again, her theological perspective and method prevent her from doing so. Instead, rather than focusing on the ongoing narrative of the Hebrew-Christian faith community and those same traditions she has named as valuable, Ruether focuses *outside* the community of faith and its liturgical and discipleship practices with their possibilities for ecojustice and spotlights instead the broader, cultural context where "new forms of gender parity" might be structured.[30] Although she evidently wishes to put community at the center of her proposal, the role of the community of faith is not clear; indeed, it is barely apparent at all. While Ruether orients her theology in a kind of community, it is the total biotic community rather than the faith community and its life of worship and discipleship which centers her theological investigation and construction.

Similar problems beset Ruether's treatment of story. Instead of focusing on the church's story, Ruether's "ecofeminist theocosmology" turns almost exclusively toward the story science offers for understanding the nature of reality and the place of all in it. She enumerates and concentrates on three premises shaped according to the foundational rational pattern underlying reality and holding it together. They are, she asserts, "the transience of selves, the living interdependency of all things, and the value of the personal in communion."[31] Ruether expounds on the elemental components of transience and interdependency and calls for "new psalms and meditations" expressing kinship with the cosmos. The "personal in communion" she clarifies by showing that, for her, plants and animals are persons, participating with humans in personal communion.[32]

Developing her thesis, Ruether leaves aside the traditional Jewish-Christian covenantal and sacramental perspectives with which she purposed to begin and celebrates instead the modern scientific story of the "matrix of energy of the universe," curiously identifying it with "a heart that knows us even as we are known."[33] In her final chapter, the covenantal and sacramental traditions appear only as two "voices of divinity from nature," the first establishing "norms of ecological relations" and "organized systems" for realizing those norms, and the second infusing the "heart," supplying the "motivating desire for biophilic living."[34] Still, Ruether does not show what those norms are and how they function in "organized systems." Nor does she clarify how the sacramental tradition motivates the heart for "biophilic living." Significantly, the covenantal and sacramental traditions now are voices "from nature" rather than voices from biblical story and ecclesiastical history.

In a concluding litany in praise of community, Ruether focuses last on the need for "building communities of celebration and resistance." Here she names the need for conversion, insisting that the transformation now needed calls for "real 'conversion,' a *metanoia*, or change of heart and consciousness."[35] In addressing how this change will occur, Ruether names the churches in a list of "pilot projects of ecological living" including schools, homes, farms, and local businesses. But because "most of our institutional forums of worship are tied to alienated, patriarchal consciousness," and "their worship is literally 'deadly,' although some are open to partial transformation," Ruether does not regard the churches as hopeful sources of new consciousness and conversion required for earth healing.[36]

At various places Ruether appeals to biblical notions like "a new creation already present." Such references seem somewhat artificial, since they are the language of alienated churches which, in her view, are no longer functional for the new task ahead. Ruether employs Christian language and ideas wherever she deems them helpful and convincing; yet those linguistic symbols and ideas are clearly uprooted from their soil in the ongoing Jewish-Christian narrative of worship and discipleship. In turn, although she talks about the need for metanoia, a change of heart, and resultant "committed love," Ruether fails to identify the originative power and motivating energy for that committed love except as it comes from the "wellspring of creativity" synonymous with the energy of the universe itself. Community functions for Ruether, but it is clearly not the community of the worshipping, witnessing, discipleship church.

Daly and Cobb's Theology for a Just, Sustainable Future

Herman Daly and John Cobb focus on economics for community in *For The Common Good: Redirecting the Economy toward Community, the Environment, and a Sustainable Future*. Their concern is the disintegration of community and the need to find a way to restore it. An economist and a theologian, they are both Protestant Christians, informed by the process metaphysics of Whitehead. Linking their task and vision to that defined by the World Council of Churches, the authors specify their responsibility as providing an image of economic theory and practice that is just, participatory, and sustainable.[37] They further define their task and vision as a religious one demanding "clarification of the needed religious world view" adequate to "offer hope for change at a deep religious level."[38] Such change in religious perspective will occur in community, they believe, and religious change and economics for community will happen together. Daly and Cobb are concerned to replace the radically individualistic view of *Homo economicus* in classical economics with a communitarian view of the economic person as person-in-community. Like Ruether, they envision a society constructed as a community of communities, organized in local village communities and reversing the modern trend toward sprawling, blighted urban centers. Like Ruether, too, Daly and Cobb see that such a paradigm shift will emerge out of a conversion, a change of heart, and the "committed love" strong enough to birth and nurse it. They orient the source of this love in religion, although they, too, again like Ruether, are ambivalent and suspicious about the chances that religious groups, including their own Christian Protestantism, will supply the religious vision and commitment needed for the present day.[39]

Analyzing the biospheric perspective of "deep ecologists" Arne Naess and George Sessions, the influential vision of Aldo Leopold, and J. Baird Callicott's similar view, Daly and Cobb conclude that these perspectives do not go far enough. This is the case because the respect for other living creatures, and even love for the biotic community, which these ecologists call for and regard as the motivational power demanded for an ecological vision are rootless as far as they image the vision. According to Daly and Cobb, their proposals leave aside the ethical question of *why* humans should love and respect the biotic community. Likewise, the ethical-religious reasons for *enjoining* love and respect for the ecosystem are not identified. Daly and Cobb challenge the most common reason given, namely, that interconnection throughout the universe of organic and inorganic beings itself enjoins and inspires love and respect. They do not see convincing evidence that either intentional appeals to feelings of kinship, or consciousness-raising about interdependence have great effect in changing people's perspective. Additionally, they question the focus on the cosmos which cosmocentric ecologists adopt. Lack of clarity about what that cosmic "whole" involves and who the members of its "community" are presents problems. Pressing their critique, Daly and Cobb flag the tendency in cosmocentric perspectives to diminish the gravity of the suffering of living creatures.

Turning toward their own biblical tradition in the attempt to correct these problems, Daly and Cobb point to the Jewish-Christian prophetic tradition and direct its warning against idolatry toward certain of their contemporaries. Although their approach is not a polemical one, they do not hesitate to name as idolatrous some biocentric and geocentric forms of thinking. Therefore, they explicitly distinguish their view as contrary to these, believing that those forms of biospheric thought posit ultimacy elsewhere than God. Commending their own theistic, prophetic view and stance, Daly and Cobb claim its superior potential for the hard work ahead. They explicitly name the cosmic "whole" grounding all else as the God of the prophetic tradition, believing that this prophetic theism alone is strong enough to lead beyond the anthropocentrism of modern culture and its rejection of ultimacy and to support belief which "elicits committedness and directs commitment."[40] Here, Daly and Cobb speak most directly to a question they raise early: what is sufficient to inspire a vision and claim the energy of people and communities? Mere recognition of interdependency is not enough, they repeat. Rather, commitment and channeling of commitment are central. Many holding a biocentric or geocentric view broaden the scope of commitment as inclusively as possible, Daly and Cobb observe, referring to those who follow James Lovelock's lead and espouse a commitment to Gaia as that broadly inclusive "encompassing unity." Ruether, as we have seen, is among this number. Daly and Cobb argue that, while such perspectives share similarities with theocentrism, significant differences particularize their foci such that "philosophical and theological positions in their precise details direct commitment in divergent ways." It is exactly at the point of these precise details and their direction of commitment that the prophetic critique is salient, they insist.[41]

While Daly and Cobb's proposal is an advance over Ruether's, the community of the church is as little considered in their process theism as in Ruether's Gaian ecofeminism. Rather, for Daly and Cobb, believers in God are merely those who hold a theistic perspective. They fail to recognize that their view betrays itself upon close analysis to be a liberal, individualistic, Enlightenment-shaped foundationalism. Their critique of nontheistic biocentrism and geocentrism is germane but does not go far enough and is short-circuited by its own limitations. The Christian prophetic critique which they hope to level does not issue from its nurturing and centering source, namely, the Judaic-Christian narrative of God's dealings with Israel, Jesus, and the church and its location in the community of worship and discipleship for whom the God of the prophetic tradition is central. Finally, it is apparent that Daly and Cobb are limited by the process metaphysics which shapes their view, and by its foundationalistic presuppositions. Consequently, they are thereby prevented from carrying through with the prophetic perspective they seek to embrace and offer. The same is true for their wish to orient their perspective and proposal in community. The worshipping, witnessing, and working community of the faithful is not the center of their ecological prophecy and religious vision. Community for them, as for those whom they critique, is something broader, "more inclusive"; if it is not biocentric or geocentric, then it is at least religio-socio-centric. Church is not explicitly ingredient to community in Daly and Cobb's theo-socio-centric proposal. Whatever they have gained by turning toward a theistic, prophetic vision they have diminished by not turning far enough in their chosen direction.

Conclusion: Creation and Ecology
Beyond Modern Atheism

McClendon addresses the challenge of modern atheism in his chapter on "The Identity of God" in *Doctrine*.[42] While the statements which follow are not an implied reference to those ecologists whose proposals I have critiqued in this essay, let me say here that considerable ecological thought is emerging out of modern atheism. Will its roots be sufficient to sustain it? Although the question is an interesting one, the church's task is neither to reject atheistic ecological proposals nor to rescue them. Indeed, Christian and non-theistic views share some of the same concerns and hope to initiate some of the same restorative ecojustice actions. Still, modern atheism's threat to the church lies in the not-always-conscious assimilation of its thought and methods into theology's own presuppositional ideas and practices. McClendon addresses this problem relative to the doctrine of God. Here, too, I propose, is where the ecological perspectives critiqued in this essay are vulnerable to infiltration by this modern and pervasive threat.

Referring to the legacy bestowed by the nineteenth century's rejection of the "God-hypothesis," McClendon notes that "there arose a confusing simultaneity between the silent awe that waits upon the Unbounded One and the silence of confusion congealing into indifference. . . . This incoherent double silence has touched the theology of the day."[43] It behooves the community of faith, McClendon asserts, "to purify and strengthen its awareness of God. Then atheism will itself have served a providential purpose, as God turns evil into good."[44]

Reflecting further on this modern dilemma, McClendon asks whether process theology might illumine a way forward. While certain contributions of value have been offered by process thought, he acknowledges, those are outweighed by the foundationalism of Whiteheadian metaphysics comprised by four "basic counters." They are: process itself, creativity, the eternal objects, and actual occasions. However, an "overriding" fault in process theology graver than its reliance on the "basic counters" named is its "failure to direct its adherents back to Scripture's story of God—to the *Lord* of the prophets and the Father of Jesus, to the risen Lord Jesus Christ, and to the Lord who as Spirit gathers believers in pentecostal power."[45] Here, too, reposes the overriding fault of Daly and Cobb's own form of process theology and of Ruether's ecofeminism. Though Ruether begins by appealing to the convenantal and sacramental traditions in scripture, she transposes those traditions away from scripture *to* nature and neglects to employ them in any way that matters. Daly and Cobb's effort to situate their proposal in the biblical prophetic tradition suffers a like fate. Finally, these thinkers direct their readers' attention elsewhere than the Bible's narrative of God and God's story with Israel, Jesus, and the church.

Here, the close relationship between community and narrative is seen more vividly. McClendon affirms faith community as indispensable context for knowledge about God and God's story with us. But his insights prod me to add that not just process thinkers and others scientifically oriented have diverted their own and our attention away from the scriptural narrative and the faith community's lived narrative with God. Even our revered fore-bears like Thomas Aquinas and Anselm of Canterbury, I submit, diverted the church's attention to distracting philosophical con-structs like the classical arguments for the existence of God, which they largely authored, rather than focusing on the biblical narra-tive and the worshipping community's faith story. In fact, diver-sion from the biblical story and attention focused elsewhere may well be the primary source of Christianity's unintended but im-plicit collusion with modern atheism. I press this point more strongly than McClendon, but he, too, asks, " . . . to what extent have the very God-concepts Christianity has transmitted from its many-valued past gestated and nursed the atheism of the pre-sent?"[46]

In summary, diversion, distraction, and denial—these unholy three—and their progression from the former to the latter have merged and confused the "silence of awe" and the "silence of atheism." Christian theologians have *diverted* from the biblical story to other stories which function as philosophical foundations upon which their theological proposals are constructed. In so doing, they have *distracted* themselves and us from the biblical narrative and, finally, have effectually *denied* the biblical story and God's story with Israel, Jesus, and the church.

With McClendon's insights informing us, *I propose further that diversion, distraction, and denial, in turn, summarily function to oust God from any genuine connection to humankind and the creation.* The implications for ecological theology and an ecological doctrine of creation are dire. However, as I have attempted to show, McClen-don's baptist theology offers to ecological thought, as to Christian theology and ethics generally, a way out of this noxious impasse. No "basic counters" circumscribe his community-and-narrative-centered theology, hamstringing it in the manner of foundation-alist theologies absorbed with the modern "god-problem." Ruether's ecofeminist theology of earth healing rests on a foundation of "basic counters" consisting of the triad of transience of selves, interdependence, and the value of the personal in communion. Consequently, the covenantal and sacramental biblical traditions named as her center fade and evaporate, displaced by the "basic counters" themselves. God the problem remains a problem. Similarly, Daly and Cobb's process construction rests on the Whiteheadian philosophical foundation of process, creativity, eternal objects, and actual occasions. Whatever can be said ecologically and theologically is allowed or disallowed by those "basic counters."

James McClendon's orientation, on the other hand, is in the biblical story of God's true and trustworthy relations with Israel, Jesus, the church, and the creation, and in the community narrative lived in worship, witness, work, and discipleship. Redirecting and returning attention to the scriptures and to the faith community's story of faithful living, McClendon directs attention, thereby, to the ecological resources within that rich narrative and community tradition. He concludes his chapter on creation so:

> [Of the chapter] Its task was made harder by the three hundred year old tendency to assign the full understanding of nature to natural science alone, to dissociate God from the world (the absence of God theme), and to focus creation thought only upon the human creature. . . . This chapter's version of Christian creation teaching . . . is incomplete and some may find it unpersuasive. *It will have done its work, though, if it points a way ahead for Christian theology—work to be done by many hands rather than work completed already. Perhaps what is said here may free some for that work.* In any case, the chapter has sought to celebrate creation as it is.[47]

Rejecting philosophical and rationalistic foundations, scientific or theological, McClendon points a way along the path of narrative and community, avoiding modern tendencies of diversion, distraction, and denial. The numerous hands engaged in the work of shaping an ecological doctrine of creation can profitably follow that way.

Narrative Justice as Reiteration

Glen H. Stassen

My theme is justice. My question is how to find an adequate non-foundational, narrative definition of justice that can guide us in a critical way.

The Struggle Against Injustice: Narrative of Our Time

In his biographical chapter on "The Religion of Martin Luther King, Jr.," James McClendon writes of the religious experience that enabled King to become the champion of justice that he was:

> In their spirituals, Blacks did not merely cry out and conspire for justice, though they did that; they did not merely invoke another realm where justice *shall* prevail, though they did that, too. Rather, Blacks discovered that God was with them and they with God already, discovered God in themselves and thereby their own humanity. It has been suggested that human dignity is an essential of Black religion. . . . [This helps us understand] the surprisingly low level of racial prejudice in Negro pulpits and pews. Whites were welcome to attend those churches and even to speak, although the same courtesy was not reciprocally extended by Whites to Blacks.[1]

As McClendon suggests, Martin Luther King's struggle for justice drew much of its strength from the biblical images of the Exodus that gave him a sense of participating in *God's* struggle for justice: "King understands his work under the image of the Exodus; he is leading his people on a new crossing of the Red Sea; he is a Moses who goes to the mountaintop, but who is not privileged to enter with his people into the promised land.[2]

Similarly, McClendon tells how Clarence Jordan's boyhood awareness of the injustice of the segregation system

> struck Clarence with special horror one summer night when he heard terrible groans coming from the nearby chain-gang camp, and realized that a Black prisoner he knew, Ed Russell, was being tortured in the stretcher—the stretcher being a Georgia version of the ancient rack—used in disciplining convicts. What added irony was the boy's knowledge that the administering torturer was the same Warden McDonald who only hours earlier had been lustily singing "Love Lifted Me" in the Baptist revival choir. So by the time he graduated from high school at sixteen, Clarence had decided to become a scientific farmer who would help poor farmers make a better life. Some of these would be Whites, but Blacks were at the very bottom; therefore he would especially help them.[3]

In his *Ethics*, McClendon describes Dietrich Bonhoeffer's experience, in his first year of teaching in the university, of Hitler's injustice against Jews: "on April 1, 1933, Hitler proclaimed a national boycott of Jewish shops in Germany. Brown-shirted gangs roamed the streets, beating up Jews and other victims. The immediate problem for Christians was the infection of the church itself with Nazis and Nazi sympathizers in the clergy."[4] Bonhoeffer spoke clearly as no other theologian did, seeking to lead the church to engage in a struggle against such injustice to Jews:

> The church as church—the Confessing Church—was to be the community that would by its nonviolent action "speak 'for the dumb,' the innocent victims of Nazi criminality."[5]

And in his chapter on Dorothy Day he describes Dorothy's own experience of "the misery of poverty" when her father had no job and her family had no decent apartment. She had the job of taking her baby brother on long strolls in a baby carriage. She would go through slum districts where she could "watch the slatternly women and the unkempt children" of poverty, and could dream of someday doing something herself "toward making 'a new earth wherein justice dwelleth'."[6]

The story of our times is to a large extent the narrative of the struggle against injustice:

- the unimaginable injustice of the Nazis against Jews, and others.
- the struggle of the civil rights movement against segregation and discrimination and for freedom and human rights.
- the echo of that struggle by women and various minorities.
- the struggle of the former colonies for self-determination, independence, and economic viability.
- the struggle against the injustice of the Vietnam War and Watergate.
- the struggle of the people of Latin America, Eastern Europe, the Philippines, and South Africa for freedom, justice, and human rights.
- The struggle of poor children in an affluent society to be raised and educated, and to find families, jobs, and hope, so they can be rescued from a violent, drug-infested subculture of despair.

It has been not only struggle, in the sense of an unpleasant, conflict-filled, lonely, Sysyphusian uphill push against a heavy bolder that then rolls back down to the bottom. The biblical narrative tells of God's pillar of cloud and fire, God's promise to go with us and lead us out of injustice into community, and of the meaningful joy of participating in God's delivering grace. Justice will roll down like a river, and we shall swim in it with joy. The poor will be summoned in to the banquet, and we shall feast together with the king. After the dark night of despair, participating in the dawn of a new sunbeam of justice has given profound meaning to many of us. It is a theme in McClendon's writings that speaks to many, and that invites us all to take our part in the drama.

True, there are other stories of our time as well. But surely the struggle against injustice and for new communities of justice has been profoundly important for very many of us. And it should be. Justice is central to the biblical narrative. The Hebrew and Greek words for justice (*tsedeqah, mishpat, dikē, dikaiosunē*) occur 1,060 times in the Bible. The central revelatory event in the Old Testament is the story of the deliverance of an oppressed group of slaves from the domination of an authoritarian Pharaoh to the

Promised Land of covenant justice. The central revelatory event of the New Testament is the story of the escalating conflict between Jesus and the Jewish and Roman authorities whose injustice he criticizes, and who respond not by repenting but by conspiring together to execute him unjustly by the Roman Empire's method of state terrorism. I count 51 instances in the synoptic gospels (not counting parallels) when Jesus criticizes the authorities for their injustice. Many of the same passages indicate their response: a growing determination to get rid of Jesus. It is their commitment to injustice and refusal to repent that drives them to nail him to that cross. The struggle against injustice is a central narrative of our time, and of the Bible.

The Hole Where Justice Belongs

By contrast, McClendon writes of Ralph Waldo Emerson. Descended from Neoplatonism, European romanticism, and the Swedish rationalistic mystic, Swedenborg, Emerson's Transcendentalism was an even more acid dissolver of particularity, concreteness, and community than Kant's Enlightenment rationalism. Its understanding of God and the Over-soul was universal and abstract, "as near empty of content as the severe abstractions of a Zen master or the meditative goals of a medieval contemplative." Although Emerson used Christian terminology such as God, Jesus, Spirit, Soul, etc., McClendon points to his

> early and enduring rejection of the Scriptures and the historic church alike. Perhaps this rejection best reflected itself in Emerson's general disinterest in the vital moral issues that racked America in his day—slavery and its aftermath, the Civil War, women's liberation struggles, the coming battles for social justice in an industrial society—issues in which the churches, whatever side they took, were deeply involved. The Over-soul, though, was detached from all that.[7]

This would seem to be the very opposite of what narrative ethics stands for, the very epitome of what we are trying to correct. Yet something strange is happening to us. From H. Richard Niebuhr, to "the Yale School," to the narrative ethicists, I cannot find a critical understanding of justice that guides us in relating to the vital moral issues of justice and injustice that rack America in our day. It is as if we were above all that.

I can find indications that justice is an important virtue. I find statements of the importance of the conviction of justice in McClendon's biographical studies and in his studies of the biblical understanding of the Rule of God and the Atonement. I know that we are on the same side of almost every issue I can think of. I can find a moving essay about justice for the mentally retarded in Hauerwas, which I have intensely special reasons and loyalties for identifying with and celebrating. I have great appreciation for the many contributions of both. I identify with them for many reasons and for many loyalties, so much so that I hesitate, and hesitate again, to raise such a critical question. But I do not find in this vast body of literature, from H. Richard Niebuhr to us, a critical delineation of justice that guides us in criticizing or correcting injustice, or struggling for justice, in relation to the powers and authorities of our time.

That avoidance can lead to Emersonian detachment from the narrative of our time, in spite of our best intentions to the contrary. It can create a vacuum in our own community convictions that will be filled only too gladly by twisted ideologies. It can cause naive defenselessness against those societal influences that shape our characters, as McClendon has written. It can blind us to the narrative of what God is doing in our time, so we miss the whole story. It can play into the hands of those interests that want our injustices hidden from sight.[8]

How can we fill this hole?

Perhaps we can begin by looking again at the story of how we got here. We may notice four factors in our story that have kept us from filling the hole.

1. There is rebellion in our story. Narrative ethics is a revolt against the Enlightenment ethics of abstract universals (a revolt in which I participate.)[9] In McClendon's case, it is a revolt more particularly against the utilitarian situationism of Joseph Fletcher and the Christian realism of Reinhold Niebuhr.[10] Fletcher and Niebuhr were both hampered by their assumption that ethical norms come in the form of a rational principle of utility or an absolute ideal of pure, unselfish, nonresistant love. And they saw history as not much open to God's action. In these ways they had inherited the Enlightenment bias against particularity and community, theology and prophetic eschatology within history.

The problem is that leading philosophical definitions of justice by John Rawls, Jürgen Habermas, and disciples of Kant or Mill, all work in an Enlightenment mode. They claim a universal foundation for their definitions of justice. So narrative ethicists reject their definitions of justice. What is needed is "justice without foundations"—a delineation of justice derived not from Enlightenment universal rationalism, nor from nineteenth-century utilitarianism or idealism, but from a narrative tradition in which we can belong, one that at the same time exhibits respect for other traditions.

A particular feature of our story may be that H. Richard Niebuhr, who is in several ways the grandfather of us all, saw justice as his brother's turf. The one time he ventured onto brother Reinhold's turf in print, he got attacked and painfully injured.[11] In that amazing family, there was brotherly rivalry, and Richard was the shyer brother. He may have decided, consciously or unconsciously, to stay away from his brother's turf thenceforth. Reinhold's misconstrual of Richard's position was rooted in his Enlightenment-influenced rejection of Richard's insistence on God's active and knowable sovereignty within history.[12] Now, a generation or two later, it may be time for us to reintegrate a repressed part of our history—Reinhold's concern with justice, along with a narrative insistence on God's action within history. Until we do, we shall not be whole.

2. Along with rebellion against the Enlightenment our history contains the wish to recover theology. The Enlightenment denigrated theology and reduced ethics to thin universal principles. We wanted to recover the ability to speak theologically. But that may have led us to work at what strikes the ordinary Christian as a fairly high-powered level of abstraction. Narrative ethics inherited much of the style of contextual ethics, disparaging rules and principles and preferring to plumb the depths of profound theological beliefs. We may not have always succeeded in being profound, but we have often succeeded in not being concrete and definite. We have not always been clear where we come out on concrete issues of life in our time, and we have seemed diffuse. This was the opposite of our intention. The very point of the recovery of narrative was to recover the concrete and particular, and overthrow the tyranny of the abstract and universal. Yet our preference for profound theology and antipathy against legalism may have led us to see a concrete definition of justice as something less than profound, something untheological, something too practical. Lacking a clear definition of justice, we lacked an essential ingredient for consistent character, and became that much less concrete.

3. Narrative ethics has stressed character and virtues—a long overdue emphasis. Some might say this emphasis means we are individualistic. It makes us reluctant to articulate convictions about justice that would criticize the institutional powers and the interested ideologies and paint the fairer alternative clearly enough so it could be envisioned. Narrative ethics is not about social action, but about character. Yet that is wrong. McClendon insists that selves are shaped by society, and therefore we need a theory with which to address society so we can interact critically with its shaping forces. "Nor does character ethics foster a whimsical and privatistic approach to morality. . . . We might do better to refer to the ethics of character-in-community, thus acknowledging the reference of character to the human setting which fosters and recognizes it." Communities have "characteristic beliefs," shared convictions, and these shape persons. "We recognize the 'characteristic' laws of English-speaking communities, or the 'characteristic' ethos of a Spanish village, in part because we sense in each case the presence of deep-seated communal beliefs about what is right, what is fitting, what makes for the common good. Such normative beliefs are the convictions of these communities. Individuals, while they may dissent from this or that common conviction . . . , nevertheless are shaped by the need to agree or to dissent, and so their own convictions are formed in interaction with the community's."[13] Narrative has a social setting; this is one of the three strands of narrative ethics.[14] A character that cannot point out what is wrong with an unjust institution or a deceptive ideology is a weak character, likely to be blown about by every passing ideological wind or institutional interest. Narrative ethics, correctly understood, does not hide behind the concept of character and refuse to criticize the very forces and institutions that do so much to shape our character and the character of their victims.

4. Perhaps one other factor in our story is the extensive influence of Alasdair MacIntyre as the philosopher upon whom many narrative ethicists depend. Odd though it seems, in all of his writings, MacIntyre has not yet articulated a delineation of the meaning of justice. He has defended traditional reasoning at great length, but has not given us a critical theory of justice that could guide us in the struggles of our time. His thought functions as an attack on the Enlightenment and a defense of Aristotelian tradition, but it does not function to criticize injustice or describe a more just alternative. His focus is on epistemology as based on a tradition rather than on rationalism, and not on the understanding of justice and its concrete meaning in our historical situation. Ironically, this is a focus on foundations—on getting the foundation right—on finding a traditional rather than a rationalistic foundation. The Enlightenment still works its revenge, in a mirror-image kind of way.

Furthermore, MacIntyre seems to believe that standing in an Aristotelian and Thomistic tradition makes Hebraic tradition foreign to him. He writes at length about Homer, Plato, Aristotle, and the Greek side of the Middle Ages, but never about Moses, Amos, Isaiah, Jesus, and the Hebrew side of our heritage. He claims it is not his tradition.[15] Thus the biblical concern for justice drops out. Its absence creates a large hole. Overdependence on MacIntyre's philosophy can create a pernicious omission, a surprising hole, for a Christian ethicist who claims to reflect biblical faith. We need a supplement to MacIntyre—perhaps not a philosopher but a social theorist or political philosopher—who has extensive sensitivity to the biblical tradition. It must be a theorist who works narratively, with great respect for the thickness of the ethics of communities and particular traditions, rather than obeisance to the thinness of the ethics of universalist and rationalist foundationalism.

Filling the Hole: Michael Walzer's Reiterative Justice

These criteria describe Michael Walzer's reiterative justice. In fact, I believe Walzer's narrative approach to a historically and pluralistically contextual definition of justice is much needed for our time of transition, global interweaving, and struggle to be delivered from oppressive domination. Something like his sophisticated method for overcoming the Enlightenment bias against

208

community, particularity, shared understandings, historically rich narratives, religious beliefs, and values is crucial if we are to live together in a way that affirms ethnic and religious minorities, and if we are to have community that is not emptied of rich tradition. Walzer's elegant delineation of the meaning of justice is receiving increasing notice from a diverse group of ethicists.[16]

Because Walzer's method is radically particularistic, it can do justice to particular religious communities and traditions and the local color of their rich, historically situated conceptions of the good, rather than reducing everything particular and historical to the thin gruel of a detached and abstract principle. Walzer's first book, *The Revolution of the Saints* (1965) was a study of the Puritan revolution, showing how religious understandings of the good self and the just state were the root of radical politics. His *Just and Unjust Wars* "looks back to that religious tradition within which Western politics and morality were first given shape" for several key insights (1977, xiv). *Spheres of Justice* (1983) looks at several religious communities for wisdom and insight. *Exodus and Revolution* (1985) is a narrative study of the meanings and uses of the biblical Exodus in the history of political theory and social change. *Company of Critics* (1988) argues (via biography, as McClendon does in *Biography as Theology*) that authentic social critics get their leverage for criticizing the injustice of a society, not from a detached and universal perspective, but from their identification with the shared understandings of the society and its internal tensions. A forthcoming book will study the political ethics of the biblical prophets.

Walzer writes in a tradition that combines these communitarian strengths with critical focus on the injustice of domination, exclusion and inequality—a focus dangerously missing from many communitarian theories. Therefore Iris Marion Young identifies with Walzer's criticism of methods of detached rationality, and praises him for basing his definition of justice on opposition to domination. She refers frequently to Walzer to support her own arguments.[17] Similarly, Susan Moller Okin says *Spheres of Justice* "is exceptional" among mainstream contemporary theories of justice in its helpful attention to injustice in the family, and to women and gender.[18] Walzer's definition of justice "is opposed to pervasive inequality and dominance. It has the potential to be a valuable tool for feminist criticism." "From its largely nonsexist language to its insistence that the family constitutes a significant 'sphere of justice' and its specific references to power imbalances between the sexes and discrimination, Walzer's theory stands out in contrast to most moral and political philosophers' continued indifference to feminist issues."

A crucial step in Walzer's method is *reiteration*. Reiteration is a narrative step that replaces the Enlightenment demand for universal foundations. In his essay on Martin Buber, for example, he says:

> We understand others by reiterating our self-understanding. . . .
> "We know that . . . we have genuine national unity and a real nationalist movement; why should we assume that these do not exist among the Arabs? . . . " We must try to see the world from the perspective of the other. It is important to stress, however, that this is the very opposite of another commonplace, which enjoins us to step back from every particular perspective, to detach ourselves, to take a God's eye view of the world. The first mode, stepping into rather than stepping back from, is the more modest enterprise.[19]

Reiteration functions both to get us to walk in the shoes of another community, and also to confirm truths we see in our community when others reiterate them. Walzer hopes other societies will reiterate something like the Exodus experience—"an exemplary event, always available for re-enactment by new protagonists working, as it were, from revised scripts."[20] His book, *Exodus and Revolution*, is the story of such reiteration.

Applying the concept of reiteration to *Company of Critics*, we notice that each authentic critic Walzer studies not only identifies with her or his society, as Walzer argues, but also has a reiterative identification with a second or third community—often a marginalized community within the larger society. These communities sharpen their critical perspective and give them courage and strength of conviction. The greatest fear for a critic is to be left totally alone.[21] Reiteration in other communities provides a sense of community support.

Martin Buber, Walzer points out, was grounded in Jewish community in Israel and their need to survive, but also affirmed the right of Palestinians to have a national community and to survive—based on his method of reiteration and I-Thou dialogue.

Walzer dedicates the book to "my friends in Jerusalem." In so doing he indicates both that he will not criticize Israel from the outside, *and* that he identifies with Buber's reiterative politics toward Palestinians.

Albert Camus, similarly, exemplifies an anti-absolutist politics that "depends not on critical distance but on critical connection. And so it invites us once again to doubt the standard view of the social critic as someone who breaks loose from his particular loyalties and views his own society from the outside—from an ideal point, as it were, equidistant from all societies. This is a role Camus explicitly rejected." Speaking for himself, Walzer comments, "The task of the social critic is precisely to touch the conscience. . . . You can't do that from a stance of turning your back; you have to do that as an insider."[22] And I would like to add that Camus also practiced reiteration, identifying in many of his stories with indigenous Algerians.

Foucault, on the other hand, lacks "any stable reference to moral ideas or any sustained commitment to people or institutions by which outcomes might be measured. . . . His detachment makes for disability; when critical distance stretches into infinity, the critical enterprise collapses."[23] He is committed to rejecting the notion of basic rights and the distinction between guilt and innocence, so he has no principled way to distinguish between the Gulag Archipelago and our ordinary variety of discipline.[24] Walzer concludes:

No state, regime, leader, party, movement, or central committee commands [the critic's] unquestioning loyalty. Ideally, the critic is a masterless man, a masterless woman, who refuses to pay homage to the powers-that-be. Critical distance is established by this refusal, and no further refusals are necessary for the sake of criticism.[25]

Walzer himself identifies with overlapping communities: the Western tradition of democratic rights; Jewish immigrant grandparents, Jewish kibbutzim, and Israel; social democracy; intellectuals; the anti-Vietnam-War movement; American society, which is not the same as the government; people oppressed. When he writes of "deep interpretation of shared understandings," he does not mean simply the shared opinions on a momentary issue held in a society; he usually means underlying community convictions that are reiterated in other historically particular ways in several of these overlapping communities. (Walzer's narrative hermeneutic of "shared understandings" as the basis for his definition of justice closely resembles McClendon's consistent attention to "convictions" and "community convictions" throughout his writings.) Thus Walzer has the strength of communitarian narrative without excluding narrative truth in other communities. In fact, the core of his community narrative itself demands respect for all others. He is a participative communitarian rather than an integrative communitarian; democratically inclusive rather than organically exclusive.[26]

In *Spheres of Justice* his method is hermeneutical, "deep interpretation" of the shared understandings in the community. He includes the perspectives of a medieval Jewish community, ancient Athens, a worker-owned garbage company in San Francisco, guest workers in Germany, the Trobriand Islander community in the Pacific, workers in the Pullman factory, an Israeli Kibbutz, the Aztecs, women assigned the "shit work" in household, hotel, and hospital, and many others. But at the same time he is trying to identify with widespread convictions in the tradition of western political philosophy, and often of the United States. He wants to be heard. He is seeking to persuade his readers to support, and participate in, social change, and thus helps us see what convictions we do hold that can persuade us to support a more helpful understanding of justice than our unconsidered opinions. He writes as an engaged member. He is interpreting "our" shared understanding.

Concrete Particularity Overcomes Domination

The meta-narrative that forms the context for Walzer's understanding of justice is a narrative of domination, and of pilgrimage out of domination. He introduces his book, *Exodus and Revolution*, as "a history of the idea of deliverance from suffering and oppression: this-worldly redemption, liberation, revolution. . . . Why is this story so endlessly reinvented [reiterated]? That is what I have tried to explain."[27] And after telling the twenty-century story, he concludes [in summary form]:

1. Wherever you live, it is probably Egypt.
2. There is a better place, a promised land.
3. The way to there is through the wilderness.
4. There is no way to get from here to there except by joining together and marching.[28]

The narrative can be seen in his first book, a study of the Puritan Revolution that moved from the Egypt of the divine right of kings and their imposition of state religion to democracy and religious liberty. It is the narrative of pilgrimage out of the dominance of the Vietnam War (in his books, *Obligations* and *Just and Unjust Wars*), and out of the other forms of domination that are the story of our times. *Spheres of Justice*, his major definition of justice, begins with a statement of intention: "My purpose in this book is to describe a society where no social good serves or can serve as a means of domination." The aim is "a society free from domination . . . : no more bowing and scraping, fawning and toadying; no more fearful trembling; no more high-and-mightiness; no more masters, no more slaves." "I want to argue that we should focus on the reduction of dominance."[29] He means that wealth should not dominate religion, politics or health care: people should be made priests because they follow the way of God, not because they have money; people should be made Senator because they serve justice not because they have money or can get it; people should get medical care because they are sick, not because they have money. People should get money because they do something useful, or need it, not because they belong to the right religion or the right race. People should do hard work because they share in responsibility and get rewarded, not because of their gender or ethnic membership. People should get education because they can learn, and do some good with it, not because of who their parents are.

This is what Walzer calls complex equality. It is not necessary that everyone should have equal amounts of everything. To achieve that would require infinite and continuous governmental intervention. What is necessary is that one kind of good (money, religion, medical care, love) should not be able to dominate other kinds of goods to which they are not appropriate.

THEOLOGY WITHOUT FOUNDATIONS

It is poetically fitting that Walzer first got his key insight of complex equality from Blaise Pascal, who blazed the trail for much that we are arguing in this book (as per Terrence Tilley's work in chapter three above). Walzer says "The argument for complex equality has been beautifully put by Pascal in one of his *Pensees.*" He quotes Pascal:

> The nature of tyranny is to desire power over the whole world and outside its own sphere. . . .
> *Tyranny:* The following statements, therefore, are false and tyrannical: "Because I am handsome, so I should command respect." "I am strong, therefore men should love me. . . ." "I am . . . et cetera."
> Tyranny is the wish to obtain by one means what can only be had by another. We owe different duties to different qualities: love is the proper response to charm, fear to strength, and belief to learning.[30]

So Walzer defines eleven spheres according to the nature of the social good that determines each: membership in community, security and welfare, money and commodities, professional office, hard work (i.e., dirty work), free time, education, family and love, divine grace, recognition, political power. It is our shared understanding, our community conviction, that power in one of these spheres should not enable one to dominate the other spheres. Each set of social goods should come to us by different criteria. He then examines various actual practices and discussions in narrative form in order to interpret what criteria our convictions, as embodied in our practices and discussions, support as a fair way to shape power in each sphere. The result is an enticingly concrete understanding of justice, historically rooted in practices and real discussion, and pluralistically defined. Walzer gets wonderfully specific. Unlike almost all other male philosophers of justice, he works out just understandings for gender relations for families, and Susan Moller Okin commends him delightedly for it. He tells marvelously insightful stories of a collectively owned and managed Italian-American garbage company in San Francisco; workers in a factory, town, homes, shops, and police force—all of which were owned by the Pullman Company; Stalin's Stakhanovites; George Orwell's schooldays; the list goes on and on in a Babbette's Feast of narrative richness. The need for concreteness in our understanding of justice is one of our criteria that I identified above. I know of no other writer who comes close to Walzer in concreteness or richness.

Walzer is not claiming that there are precisely eleven spheres and no more. We notice a sphere when we notice a set of social goods that should come to people by different criteria than the criteria that govern other spheres. Someone may propose a twelfth or a thirteenth. Other societies will have other spheres. They depend on each particular society's concept of the social meaning of the particular good under discussion. This creates two kinds of pluralism: different societies differ; and within each society, the criteria differ in each sphere. Surely this should provide enough particularity, concreteness, diversity, community-difference, and richness to delight the most anti-Enlightenment narrativist! It is based on respect for the different community understandings of social goods held by different communities.

And it has another advantage, hitherto not noticed as far as I know. We have long been bedeviled by the rigid two-realms doctrine according to which the ethics of Jesus applies to the private sphere, while the ethics of some other lord, revealed to reason, applies to the public sphere, each sphere walled off from the other. Lutheran scholars fight this understanding of Luther, and baptist ethicists fight this understanding of racial and economic justice. Others engage in their particular battles against a double-standard ethic that creates an autonomous, secular sphere where the church knows not what to say, and creates an uncertain church that either hides its head in its own private sandbox or decides to join the secular sphere, leaving its own gospel behind and selling its soul to "social issues and secular ethics." Analogously, feminist theorists like Seyla Benhabib, Nancy Fraser, Susan Moller Okin, and Beverly Harrison criticize liberal ideology's separation of profession, politics, and the public from *Kinder, Kirche,* and *Kuche.* The result is to shield gender relations in the family and the church from standards of justice, and to shun women from full participation in the public sphere. It causes multiple, complex distortions of reality.

Yet there is a lingering, often inarticulate sense that there is indeed some difference—not an essentialist, ontological difference, but a shared, particularist sense—that one relates a bit differently to one's lawyer than one does to one's lover. There is a difference between criminal law and civil law, and a difference between law and grace. The state should not interfere in religious liberty, and should respect the right to privacy. Walzer's enumeration of eleven or more spheres recognizes that there is this difference between spheres. But Walzer corrects the idea that there are two rigid spheres; there are a multiple number according to the social goods and their meanings in the particular society. This undermines the dualism that has caused so many problems. And more important, it rightly sees that criteria of justice apply to all spheres. Even though the specific rules of justice are particular to each sphere, justice is still important in families, religious communities, factories, and schools. The criteria are adapted according to the social function of the social goods that identify the sphere. This overcomes the dualism while recognizing the pluralism. It is not abstract, universal, and thin, but concrete, particular, and rich.

Narrative-Communitarian Justice
with Concrete Reiterative Content

Several philosophers have criticized Walzer's understanding of justice in *Spheres* for not having foundations, that is, for being based only on the shared understanding of a community. How then can it criticize the injustice embedded in that shared understanding? I believe they can be shown to be wrong.[31] But for now and here, I want to travel in the direction of the content of justice rather than theories of knowing and validating.

The content question is whether Walzer has a reiterative understanding of justice that guides his interpretation of the concrete meaning of justice in the different spheres and in different societies. Also at stake is whether this can help us be more articulate about our understanding of narrative justice.

One deep conviction underlying his definition of justice in all spheres and across different communities is his explicit and fundamental opposition to domination. This is the main point of his theory. It provides powerful leverage against a merely relativist or conventionalist understanding.

It leads to his major, original proposal of "complex equality": *An essential feature of justice is that power in one sphere of life should not allow people to dominate other spheres.* Furthermore, his interpretation of the substantive meaning of justice in different spheres pivots not only on a community's concepts of the meaning of social goods, but also on three underlying rights. These have not been widely noticed in interpretations of Walzer's understanding of justice, but they underlie his various writings. They provide strong unity and critical perspective for Walzer's thought. These three underlying rights are grounded not in abstract reason, but in particular historical experience. They are validated by their ability to make sense of our particular considered judgments. Each right has a negative and a positive dimension:

1. *Life*: there is the right *not to be robbed of life*—killed, starved, tortured, or denied shelter or health care. Walzer often calls this the right to protection or security. There is also the positive right to the *goods of life*—resources for developing one's interests and capabilities, for seeking social usefulness, wealth, creativity, meaning, happiness. Walzer calls this welfare, life plan, developing the "interests and capacities of individuals," or pursuing a "reasonable and humane conduct of life."[32] Its particular content varies with individuals' interests and capabilities, and with societies' values and resources. Hence a substantive account of distributive justice requires attention both to the positive right to the goods of life, and to shared conceptions of social goods, which vary from society to society. This is a communitarian understanding of a liberal right.

2. *Liberty*: there is the right *not to be robbed of basic personal liberties*. Accordingly, there is the positive right *to participate in decision-making and value-creating* in one's community. The right of participation is central throughout Walzer's writings. It, too, is both individual and communal: it is essential to human self-respect, and its substantive content varies according to the communities one belongs to and the kinds of decisions they make and values they shape.

3. *Community*: there is the right of *membership*, the right not to be excluded or deprived of community. This requires that one's community be able to survive and be respected. Therefore "particular historical communities" have a positive *communal right to preserve their "ways of life"*[33] *and shared understandings*. A community's shared understanding is like an individual's consent: it

must be respected. Thus Walzer concludes his book with a universal communitarian principle:

> One characteristic above all is central to my argument. We are (all of us) culture-producing creatures; we make and inhabit meaningful worlds. . . . We do justice to actual men and women by respecting their particular creations. . . . Justice is rooted in the distinct understandings of places, honors, jobs, things of all sorts, that constitute a shared way of life. To override those understandings is (always) to act unjustly. . . .
>
> There is a certain attitude of mind that underlies the theory of justice and that ought to be strengthened by the experience of complex equality: we can think of it as a decent respect for those . . . deeper opinions that are the reflections in individual minds, shaped also by individual thought, of the social meanings that constitute our common life. . . . Every form of dominance is therefore an act of disrespect.[34]

Read in isolation, as an absolute rather than a *prima facie* obligation, this statement could be taken as pure communitarianism; as if we should not criticize the shared understanding of a community that justifies slavery or wife abuse. This is why we must be clear that there are *three* sets of rights plus a basic opposition to domination. These rights can conflict. When a society's practice violates one of the rights, Walzer calls us to the praxis of social criticism and social change—interpreting different communities' particular understandings respectfully, and criticizing them.

These three sets of rights rest on self-respect and mutual respect, or human dignity. Walzer repeatedly returns to the fundamental point that a person who cannot or does not participate in decision-making is deprived of self-respect. And the concluding paragraph of the book comes to rest on its basic ground of meaning: "Mutual respect and a shared self-respect are the deep strengths of complex equality, and together they are the source of its possible endurance."

What would be the virtues that correspond with this understanding of justice? The answer could be interestingly suggestive. Basic would be the virtues of **inclusive respect and opposition to domination**. Corresponding to the negative and positive rights to life would be the virtues of **active nonviolence and caring nurture**. Corresponding to the rights to liberty would be **active**

nonauthoritarianism and public participation. Corresponding to the rights to community would be **nondiscriminating hospitality and community spirit**. These differ from the virtues of a more hierarchical tradition, or of a greedier and more violent culture. Perhaps we are ready to move from a time of increasing violence to active nonviolence, not only as has been modeled for us in the civil rights movement and in the toppling of dictatorial governments by nonviolent direct action, but in dismantling nuclear weapons and guns on the streets and in the home. And as Mahatma Gandhi and Martin Luther King symbolize active nonviolence, so in our time we are developing a tradition of active nonauthoritarianism in the sense of shared governance and opposition to domination and the deprivation of liberty. Perhaps nonauthoritarianism can take on a meaning analogous to nonviolence, not merely as passive resistance but active initiative; not only as oppositional but also as directly creating the alternative of mutually shared servanthood-authority. Perhaps we are also ready to move a bit from a time of self-indulgence and greed to public participation. Perhaps we are ready to move a step or two from an acquisitive culture to the kind of caring nurture that can move people now lacking in hope to developing a life plan and taking steps in the direction of that plan. Perhaps we are ready to take a new step toward ethnic and religious inclusiveness—a dream yet unfulfilled.

The Narrative of Reaction Against the Enlightenment

I have a deeply felt concern. In non-foundational narrative ethics we are making a major correction of the universal rationalism that we associate with the Enlightenment. I share in urging that correction. I make no brief for Enlightenment foundationalism. But I worry deeply if the movement for narrative theology and ethics should define itself in a reactionary way, reacting against all that the Enlightenment and classical liberalism stand for. As an ethic or a social theory, reaction is dangerous. The Enlightenment acknowledged some truths that are not its exclusive possession, and that should not be rejected now just because they were seen as true then. They are true now as well, on other grounds than those the Enlightenment built.

In *The Politics of Cultural Despair*,[35] the highly respected intellectual historian Fritz Stern studies the communitarian reaction of three influential German cultural critics against liberalism, the Enlightenment, and western urban culture:

> As moralists and as guardians of what they thought was an ancient tradition, they attacked the progress of modernity—the growing power of liberalism and secularism. They enumerated the discontents of Germany's industrial civilization and warned against the loss of faith, of unity, of "values"....
>
> Their one desire was for a new faith, a new community of believers, a world with fixed standards and no doubts, a new national religion that would bind all Germans together. All this, liberalism denied. Hence, they hated liberalism, blamed it for making outcasts of them.... All the vast and undesirable changes in the lives and feelings of Western man they blamed on liberalism [and the Enlightenment].... They ignored—or maligned—the ideal aspirations of liberalism, its dedication to freedom, the hospitality to science, the rational, humane, tolerant view of man."

They discouraged political involvement, and encouraged the cultivation of inwardness. They contributed mightily to the growth of a politics of cultural despair, and unintentionally prepared German culture to be receptive to the anti-liberal communitarian thrust of Nazi ideology.

In our time of transition, undisciplined resentments can develop dangerous force. We have been taught to feel extensive cynicism about politics. We need an ethic that takes communitarianism seriously, but does not lead us into reactionary discarding of basic human rights and democratic participation. Walzer provides that ethic. The concern I express, and the appreciation for Walzer's corrective, is what Benhabib (above) points to when she warns that integrative-homogeneous-romantic communitarians threaten the priority of liberty, and argues instead for participative-pluralist communitarians like Walzer.

Okin[36] contrasts Walzer's helpfulness with "the pervasive elitism" and "pervasive sexism" of Alasdair MacIntyre's form of communitarianism. She says MacIntyre grounds rationality in an Aristotelian [and organic] tradition that is "deeply infused with patriarchalism," that believes in natural hierarchy rather than equality among persons, and that excludes women, slaves, farmers, artisans, merchants, and ordinary male members of the underclass—or parents or children—from the virtues. Unlike Walzer, she says, MacIntyre has not confronted "the problem of domination that resides in any tradition-based theory of justice." Furthermore, MacIntyre fails to provide an ethical standard by which to judge the justice of social structures and correct the domination. One could reply that MacIntyre means to identify with a Catholic tradition that strongly emphasizes human rights and human dignity and has powerful resources for correcting many of these problems.[37] Yet if MacIntyre ever mentions the human rights dimension of the Catholic tradition, it is well hidden, as is any developed definition of justice that does the critical work Okin is calling for. One can read 2000 pages of MacIntyre, including a 450-page book entitled *Whose Justice . . .*, without finding a definition of justice that serves the function of social analysis and social criticism. Therefore his talk about justice often serves a defensive rather than a social-critical function. I believe he is working on a correction of this point at the time of my writing, and I look forward to it.

Similarly, Gloria Albrecht sharply criticizes Stanley Hauerwas, who relies heavily on MacIntyre.[38] To answer her effectively, Hauerwas needs to embrace our pluralistic historical context with a participatory rather than organic-integrative-homogeneous communitarianism. He needs a social theory that exposes the domination in our historical context, and an understanding of justice that guides the struggle to which the biblical narratives call us in our present situatedness. Otherwise, Albrecht argues, he will perceive otherness as his enemy, as fragmentation; and will obscure the material societal practices that shape our character under the fog of a false consciousness of apolitical isolation. I believe this is not Hauerwas's intention, and that his own writing is growing. I believe he can provide a stronger defense, and contribute more effectively to the struggle for justice, by supplementing his reliance on MacIntyre with Walzer.

Some of these criticisms surely miss the intentions of MacIntyre and Hauerwas. But my own narrative is so deeply influenced by the events of which Fritz Stern writes, and those of which James McClendon wrote (referred to in the introduction to this essay), that I worry about how narrative ethics may function in our churches and culture if we lack the kind of definition of justice that Walzer provides, or appear to devalue it.

I join with those who celebrate the worldwide convergence on human rights as the key to justice, a convergence supported by most church groups, as well as many third-world and former communist-bloc nations seeking freedom. Why not adopt a definition of justice that includes a strong affirmation of human rights? In fact, we would not have to "adopt" it; the struggle for human rights is already our story. It is the story of those whose biographies McClendon studied, especially Martin Luther King and Dietrich Bonhoeffer. Both King and Bonhoeffer defined justice in terms of human rights, as the strongest public ethic with which to free people from Naziism and segregation.

The objection against a human rights ethic is that human rights are a product of the Enlightenment. But that is a false reading of our history. Human rights are a product of the baptist wing of the Puritan Reformation in England, the very tradition that James McClendon has taught us to begin respecting. They were first articulated by Richard Overton in 1645, a half-century before the Enlightenment began.[39] Overton was an Anabaptist and a General Baptist, teaming up with a Congregationalist, thus representing three parts of the tradition from which McClendon is teaching us to learn. Overton developed the concept on biblical and experiential grounds in the struggle for religious liberty, and wrote narratively—with great persuasive power and interest. He is widely recognized as the best writer of the Leveller movement, largely because of his narrative style of argument. Human rights also have a prehistory in a long Catholic tradition, as David Hollenbach has shown.

Furthermore, human rights have entered our experience not because we read John Locke or Thomas Jefferson, but because of our participation in the drama of the struggle for justice that has been so formative for us in the latter half of the twentieth century. The story of our times has been the struggle to stop the injustice of the Nazis, the struggle of the civil rights movement against racism, the struggle of women and various minorities, the struggle of the former colonies for self-determination and economic viability, the struggle of the people of Latin America, Eastern Europe, the Philippines, and South Africa, and the struggle of poor children in our affluent society. These have all taken human rights as their watchword. Added to these is one more struggle: the struggle of churches to get free of those interests and ideologies that opposed these hard-fought battles for justice. The forces of reaction that opposed these efforts to achieve justice have tried in various ways to infiltrate the churches and to tear down the banner of human rights. Human rights have their narrative context not in the Enlightenment, but in the efforts of oppressed people to achieve their human dignity against the opposition of powerful forces. If we set narrative ethics against human rights because of our opposition to the Enlightenment, we are in great danger of playing a role written for us by the forces of oppression and backlash.

Walzer's Reiterative Justice
Fits McClendon's Narrative Ethics

We have already seen many ways in which Michael Walzer's understanding of justice fits James McClendon's non-foundational theology and ethics. Three more could be added:

First, a special contribution of McClendon is his insight that "three strands are necessary to a truly biblical, a truly Christian morality." They correspond to God as Creator, Covenantor/Reconciler, and Holy Spirit:

1. We are creatures, embodied selves in a natural environment, bodies that are part of the natural order, responding to our Creator.

2. We are members of a society, interacting with our neighbors, part of a social world that is constituted by the corporate nature of Christian existence, the church, and thereby by our participation in human society, responding to God who covenants, legislates, commands, governs, and reconciles.

3. We are witnesses to the new and changed life of walking in the resurrection of Jesus Christ, part of the kingdom of God, the "new world," responding to the presence of the Spirit who makes all new.[40]

The three strands correspond to three important dimensions of narrative or drama: natural environment and personal embodiment, social setting, and development of plot into what is new.[41]

We may also see them, with Dietrich Bonhoeffer, as Incarnation, Crucifixion, and Resurrection.

These three strands correct fears that narrative ethics might become fanciful fairy tale, myth, disembodied storytelling, a ghettoized introspective church disconnected from environment and social setting, or a moralism focused on individual virtues to the neglect of environmental or social justice. Thus McClendon suggests "Gnosticism neglected the . . . body strand, Protestant individualism the social strand, and Catholic legalism . . . the revisionary resurrection strand."[42] Justice is crucial to McClendon's narrative theology, if it is to be a three-strand narrative.

Walzer pays attention to all three strands:

Bodily needs: Walzer emphasizes the need for community, security and welfare. He also takes special note of the fact that somebody has to do the dirty work to deal with the bodily needs of babies, of the sick, and society's garbage. Walzer shows insightful sensitivity to ways we shovel these responsibilities off to women and minorities, and shows creative alternatives that have in fact worked well in families, kibbutzim, and garbage companies. Beyond this, McClendon's first strand suggests that Walzer should add a twelfth sphere for environmental protection and conservation.

Social needs: Walzer is brilliant on our need for membership in community, and of course his whole project concerns social justice. He pays consistent attention to different forms of power and domination as well, and offers an imaginative corrective based on shared understandings or convictions deeply embedded in our society.

Making things new: Walzer's understanding of justice arises out of his own experience in the civil rights movement, the anti-Vietnam war movement, and a lifetime of work as a social critic interested in an ethics and politics that do not merely criticize from an abstract and self-righteous distance, but that can play their role in guiding us out of Egypt, through the wilderness, into a community of greater covenant justice—which will then still need its social critics and prophets. He has much wisdom to offer in his practical book for social change movements, *Political Action*, and in his critical book, *Radical Principles*.[43] The centrality of the metanarrative of the Exodus and the early study of the Puritan Revolution symbolize the hope in his thought.

There is a *second* way in which Walzer's justice fits McClendon's ethics. Many of us are grateful to McClendon for putting us in touch with the heritage of the small "b," widely inclusive, baptist tradition, with its basic shared understanding that the biblical narratives *are us*. "The vision can be expressed as a hermeneutical motto, which is shared awareness of *the present Christian community as the primitive community and the eschatological community*."[44] The first step in developing a narrative understanding of justice needs to be biblical study of the meaning of justice in our metanarrative. That is not my task here; I have tried to work on it elsewhere.[45] I want to commend the biblical work done by Stephen Mott and Bruce Birch.[46] Biblical justice means deliverance from alienation and oppression into a community with *shalom*, for which the norm is the character of Yahweh revealed in the Exodus, delivering those oppressed by the Pharaoh's tyranny into a new community free of domination and faithful in community practices that enable the poor to find food, and clothing, and shelter.

The next step is to find a contemporary theorist of justice who is compatible with biblical narratives of justice, and who is insightful about justice and injustice in our society. For many reasons that should by now be apparent, I believe Michael Walzer's understanding of justice offers the help we need. His project has roots in a tradition that predates the Enlightenment: the Jewish tradition of justice, reiteration, and Talmudic interpretation, and its younger cousin, the Puritan Revolution's tradition of democracy and human rights. It is a living tradition in contemporary form.

Third, James Wm. McClendon, as I know him, fits that tradition, fits Walzer's definition of justice, embodies it in all three strands. The fit is *just right*.

Non-Foundationalism Without Relativism

CHAPTER 11

Living in Another World as One Response to Relativism

Mark Nation

Any attempt to speak without speaking any particular language is not more hopeless than the attempt to have a religion that shall be no religion in particular. . . . Thus every living and healthy religion has a marked idiosyncrasy. Its power consists in its special and surprising message and in the bias which that revelation gives to life. The vistas it opens and the mysteries it propounds are another world to live in; and another world to live in—whether we expect ever to pass wholly over into it or no—is what we mean by having a religion.

Santayana[1]

Christianity turns upon the character of Christ. But that character must continually find fresh exemplars if it is not to be consigned to the realm of mere antiquarian lore.

James Wm. McClendon, Jr.[2]

Introduction

Rev. Fred Phelps. Every liberal's nightmare, Rev. Phelps apparently has been making the talk-show circuit. He has been, as one talk-show recently announced, mounting a "Crusade Against Homosexuals." His message is quite simple: "God hates fags." It becomes clear as one listens to Rev. Phelps that he is convinced that virtually everyone in the audience is bound for hell. Thus in the midst of his rudeness, name-calling, and various expletives, he offers the second part of his simple, straight-forward message: "Turn or burn."

It is also clear almost immediately whom the audience has empathy for on this talk-show: it is not Rev. Phelps. And as one listens to the passionate statements made by members of the audience and panel to Rev. Phelps, one notes that there are two conflicting messages given. The one most frequently stated is some version of "to each his or her own. You have your opinions or lifestyle and I (or they) have mine (or theirs). What right do you have to judge mine (or theirs)?" But, of course, what is implied is that Rev. Phelps's opinions are wrong; thus the person arguing that one opinion is as good as another doesn't really believe that. A more sophisticated version of a critique of Rev. Phelps might suggest that he may legitimately hold his religious convictions, but should keep them to himself (or, perhaps, within his own fundamentalist community). That is to say, convictions are for our private lives; the public realm should be ruled by a tolerance that cannot accommodate competing religious convictions.

Rev. Phelps is simply the latest incarnation of what is perceived as a moral absolutism that strikes fear in the hearts of all who are opposed to violent inquisitions, witch burnings, religious wars, and the bashing—literal and otherwise—of homosexuals. I was reminded of this the other day when an ex-Catholic was trotting out the hackneyed line that she worried when someone did something in the name of God "because you know how much terror has been perpetrated in the name of God." Those of us who hope we live our lives in the name of God know the concern is overstated, but, nonetheless, contains enough truth that we feel the sting of the accusations.[3]

But something occurred to me recently as I reflected on the "absolutism" represented by Rev. Phelps. There is a difference in the nature of the worries about absolutism and relativism.[4] The worry about absolutism for the average person is not primarily a theoretical or intellectual worry, a worry about something called absolutism or objectivism. Rather it is a worry that is related most of all to power and coercion. Rev. Phelps, so it is believed, is simply a more vulgar expression of the convictions of many religious folk out there. Such a perspective would indicate that it is not far from the positions of the religious right or the Roman Catholic Church to updated versions of religious wars and the persecution of dissenters.

On the other hand, even among those not trained in philosophy the worry over relativism is usually expressed, however inadequately, as an intellectual, theoretical, and emotional worry. It is a worry that maybe it *is* the case that any conviction or moral practice is as good as any other. Unlike the worry about absolutism this worry seems, on the surface, not to be provoked by some external threat. What could it mean for someone to force his relativism on me? And, yet, of course, as with the concern about absolutism, the concern about relativism is related to the world in which we live. Though there are philosophical issues related to both concerns, I would argue that some of the key issues for both relate to the world(s) in which we live. In point of fact, what I will argue is that it is inappropriate to drive a wedge between the world in which we live and the philosophical issues involved. But more on that later. Now let us turn to an exploration of how we got to the point of experiencing what Peter Berger has described as "the vertigo of relativity induced by modernization."[5]

Coming to "Relativism"

As early as the Fourth Century B.C.E. Plato responded to the teaching of Protagoras that "The human is the measure of all things"[6] partially through offering theories about metaphysics and what is still not an uncommon distinction between (mere) belief or opinion and (certain) knowledge. It is not at all clear that either person understood their differences to be a debate about something labelled "relativism." Now that we do perceive a problem with that label we, however, see antecedents in debates such as theirs. But the problem designated by the term "relativism" is actually a much more recent one.

Patrick Gardiner argues that our concern with "relativism" stems largely from modern German philosophy.[7] Gardiner argues that it was, ironically, the idealist Immanuel Kant who provided the seed for our modern understanding of conceptual schemes. For it was Kant who stressed "the active role performed by the mind in relating and organizing the sensory data and determining

231

the forms under which they were presented."[8] Kant claimed, and Gardiner affirms, that this shift from an understanding of the objectivity of knowledge effected a "Copernican revolution" in philosophy.

> Just as in the sphere of astronomy the apparent movement of the sun and stars had been shown to be explicable by reference to the situation of the terrestrial observer, so at the level of epistemology certain pervasive features of the experienced world, previously treated as if they were embedded in external reality, could in fact be shown to have a purely subjective source in the constitution of the human intellect.[9]

But more than Kant, the critic and contemporary of Kant, J. G. Herder, seems a precursor of others who would provide the intellectual categories for what is sometimes called relativism. Going beyond Kant, Herder claimed that knowledge and reasoning were socially derived.

> It was impossible, Herder argued, to separate the notion of man as a rational being from the conception of man as a user of language. We do not first think and then learn to speak; the two capacities arise and evolve as aspects of a single unitary process, so that to assert that man is a rational animal is tantamount to affirming that he is a 'creature of language'. But a particular language is itself a social phenomenon, constituting an indispensable tie between the members of a given community and associating them through a fine and often scarcely perceptible network of shared assumptions and conventions. . . .[10]

Herder was one of the influences on Hegel and Hegel on Marx. Marx, among other things, taught many people to see knowledge as socially constructed. Marx, Nietzsche, and Freud, according to Paul Ricoeur, taught us, in general, to use a hermeneutics of suspicion about the correspondence of our knowledge and reasoning with any objective reality.

It may be the case that Kant, Herder, and their intellectual successors gave us some of the intellectual tools to realize that there is a mental and social construction of reality. However, there are at least two other dimensions of the situation I want to mention. The first is the way in which a number of what are now called postmodern philosophers have come to believe that the certainty, the intellectual foundations proposed by thinkers like Descartes and Locke are not certain at all. This recent move was begun especially by the writings of W. V. O. Quine and the later writings of Ludwig Wittgenstein. The questioning has continued through the work of such individuals as Thomas Kuhn, James Smith and James Wm. McClendon, Jr., Richard Rorty, and Jeffrey Stout. The second is our sociological situation, which some also describe as postmodern. It is this second dimension and one overlapping element of the first that are the focus of this essay.

Peter L. Berger, the noted sociologist of knowledge, helps us begin to understand some of the relevant elements of our current social world.[11] Berger has stated that "modern consciousness entails a movement from fate to choice."[12] What has happened, especially in the twentieth century, is that various technologies have made us conscious of the fact that many things in our lives, including convictions and moral practices, are matters of choice. Before the advent of great mobility and mass communication choice played a much smaller role in people's lives. From the moment they were born people were socialized into stable families and societies, roles, convictions, and moral practices. These were all experienced as fate rather than choice.

This socialization provides what Berger calls "plausibility structures."[13] The socialization we experience shapes our consciousness in such a way that we find some things plausible and some things not, depending upon the ethos of the social structures. And, of course, if our social structures are solid, unchanging, and unchallenged then we will hold to our convictions and moral practices as not only plausible but, for all intents and purposes, as objective.

What has happened in the twentieth century is that we have had an explosion of new technologies, especially as they relate to mobility and communication. Therefore almost nothing in our lives is experienced as fate or unchangeable. Practically everything, including our convictions and moral practices, are experienced as matters of personal choice.[14] As Peter Berger has put it:

> In premodern situations there is a world of religious certainty, occasionally ruptured by heretical deviations. By contrast, the modern situation is a world of religious uncertainty, occasionally staved off by more or less precarious constructions of religious affirmation. Indeed, one could put this change even more sharply:

For premodern man, heresy [i.e., literally, the taking of a choice] is a possibility—usually a rather remote one; for modern man, heresy typically becomes a necessity. Or again, modernity creates a new situation in which picking and choosing becomes an imperative.[15]

What was once fate is now choice, a world full of choices. The world is now seen as " . . . a great relativizing caldron."[16]

Many of us have had the experience of entering college and encountering people from other cultures or other religions, or taking our first anthropology or sociology course and experiencing there a sense of discomfort, of moral and intellectual vertigo. What Berger, and more recently Kenneth Gergen, argue is that we are now awash in a sea of such experiences. Because of the commonness of mobility and the explosion of the technologies of communication and information we are, on the one side, bereft of a solid community, and on the other inundated with alternative visions of reality. This is what Kenneth Gergen describes as "the technologies of social saturation," technologies

central to the contemporary erasure of individual self. . . . There is a populating of the self, reflecting the infusion of partial identities through social saturation. And there is the onset of a multiphrenic condition, in which one begins to experience the vertigo of unlimited multiplicity.[17]

Gergen goes on to give one example of the way in which the technologies of saturation have raised questions about objective truth.

A century ago most scholars confined their activities to their local communities and a handful of correspondents. As travel grew easier, learned societies proliferated. As long as membership in them was circumscribed, the kind of agreement necessary to achieve a sense of objectivity was relatively easy to achieve. However, with air travel, mass publication of journals, international conferences, low-priced long-distance phones, and electronic mail, communal insularity became increasingly difficult to maintain. All that was "avowed fact" in one locale became food for criticism and replacement in another. It became no more a question of "the facts," but "whose facts?" Broad opposition breeds doubt.[18]

This doubt often gets played out in terms that sound to many like a dangerous relativism. I am sure that Allan Bloom is right that "almost every student entering the university believes, or says he believes, that truth is relative."[19] It would also not surprise me to learn that students have some general sense that

> the study of history and of culture teaches that all the world was mad in the past; men always thought they were right, and that led to wars, persecutions, slavery, xenophobia, racism, and chauvinism. The point is not to correct the mistakes and really be right; rather it is not to think you are right at all.[20]

How are we to respond to the perceived problem of relativism on the one side and the perceived problem of coercion and oppressiveness (moral absolutism) on the other? In the limited parameters of this essay let me respond with a few reflections and the telling of a story.

An Intellectual Problem?

Given that our predicament of relativism is not merely or even mostly an intellectual problem, then it seems likely that any adequate response would also need to be more than simply philosophical reflection. Nonetheless, given that a part of our problem is intellectual confusion, we will need to offer some hints on why it is that convictions and moral practices are not matters of indifference (which is what some people mean by relative). This section offers only a small sampling of the kind of thing that needs to be said.

It is important to help some people see that any absolute claim for relativism is self-refuting, since the claim for relativism is, of course, also relativized.[21] A second, related, point is to suggest that those who imagine themselves to be thoroughgoing relativists have merely granted the status of absolute to some standard of which they are less than conscious. Stanley Fish has expressed it this way:

> [W]hile relativism is a position one can entertain, it is not a position one can occupy. No one can be a relativist, because no one can achieve the distance from his own beliefs and assumptions which would result in their being no more authoritative for him than the beliefs and assumptions he himself used to hold. The fear that in a world of indifferently authorized norms and values the individual is without a basis for action is groundless because no one is indifferent to the norms and values that enable his consciousness.[22]

I think Fish is absolutely right. But just because one cannot "occupy" relativism does not mean that the entertaining of the position cannot have quite a grip on what one believes or the way one lives and reflects on living.

What Berger and Gergen have helped us to see is that what we earlier imagined to be objectivity can now be seen to be what it was, viz. a relative consensus about certain matters. The consensus was solid enough that the opinions could be claimed as knowledge, even objective knowledge. Then this "objective knowledge" received institutionalized sanction. As philosopher Richard Rorty has pointed out, we have confused this institutionalized sanction with a Cartesian understanding of objectivity.

> But such institutional backups for beliefs take the form of bureaucrats and policemen, not of "rules of language" and "criteria of rationality." To think otherwise is the Cartesian fallacy of seeing axioms where there are only shared habits, of viewing statements which summarize such practices as if they reported constraints enforcing such practices.[23]

Of course Rorty's point is similar to the famous (or infamous) statement of Nietzsche:

> What, then is truth? A mobile army of metaphors, metonyms, and anthropomorphisms—in short, a sum of human relations, which have been enhanced, transposed, and embellished poetically and rhetorically, and which after long use seem firm, canonical, and obligatory to a people. . . .[24]

Nietzsche goes on to refer to truths as illusions. However, it is not necessary to embrace Nietzsche's acerbity to realize the truth of his claim that truth is understood and underwritten or undercut socially. Richard Rorty has put it this way:

> For pragmatists, the desire for objectivity is not the desire to escape the limitations of one's community, but simply the desire for as much intersubjective agreement as possible, the desire to extend the reference of "us" as far as we can. Insofar as pragmatists make a distinction between knowledge and opinion, it is simply the distinction between topics on which such agreement is relatively easy to get and topics on which agreement is relatively hard to get.[25]

I am not sure that I want to adopt the label pragmatist, but I agree with Rorty's point. And as a Christian why not? I do not believe

God or truth is reducible to human community(ies). But as a Christian I do not believe God or truth can be known any more fundamentally than in the contingent history of God with the ancient people of Israel, with the man named Jesus, and with the people who gathered in the name of Jesus as recorded in Christian Scriptures. And furthermore I believe that the task of discerning truth for today happens most fundamentally among a people who read the Scriptures, gather to worship this God, and seek to be faithful to the God who is worshipped. Since I believe this truth is Good News I also want to expand the community of those who see it as true.

What Berger, Gergen, and Rorty help us to see is that the primary response the church needs to make to this modern problem is not philosophical, at least not in any narrow sense.[26] It is, rather, to live the truth, to be the people of God. If we as Christians experience a "vertigo of relativity" it is because we do not take our life together seriously enough. As Stanley Hauerwas has put it, "the truth demands truthfulness."[27]

Why would I claim this as the primary response? The answer lies in the way in which I understand the problem, conjoined with various theological commitments to which I hold. Having already described the former, let me enumerate some of the latter.

The first is a simple assertion, yet with profound consequences.

> The church precedes the world epistemologically. We know more fully from Jesus Christ and in the context of the confessed faith than we know in other ways. . . . The church precedes the world as well axiologically, in that the lordship of Christ is the center which must guide critical value choices, so that we may be called to subordinate or even to reject those values which contradict Jesus.[28]

Given this claim and the notion of plausibility structures what is needed should be obvious. As Stanley Hauerwas has put it, "the great problem of modernity for the church is how we are to survive as disciplined communities in democratic societies."[29] We must take more seriously than we often have the need to socialize those within our churches.[30] This begins, of course, by people within the church simply living the faith they confess. But such living must be accompanied by the education and socialization of children in homes and churches. It entails the teaching and disciplining of adults within the church.[31]

Someone might respond that what I have just said in the last part of the last paragraph is obvious. In a sense it is. Of course the church has always engaged in teaching and to some degree in socializing. I am simply suggesting that given the increasingly pluralistic nature of our society we must take even more seriously the deliberate socialization of our people, the passing on of our traditions.[32] Further, I am specifically suggesting that this is a substantive response to the experienced vertigo of relativity.

Correlative to the conviction that the church is the primary place where we learn what reality is and, therefore, what we should believe and how we should behave, is the conviction that we should commend our convictions to others. Since we believe the Gospel of Jesus Christ is true then we want to invite others to join us in the community that seeks to live by this truth. And since this Jesus calls upon his followers to live nonviolently we commend our convictions nonviolently.[33] Theologically this is warranted by the claim that Jesus is Lord.[34] This alone ought to make it imperative. However, it is difficult not to be conscious of the fact that in today's world people (understandably) worry about the Rev. Phelps's. One of the reasons why many have difficulty hearing the Gospel is because the Church has too often been violent; i.e., it has not always practiced nonviolence when it was *only* required by our Lord!

As I said earlier, the true response to relativism today is the living of the convictions we claim are true. So, let us look at an extended illustration of a church that lived truthfully and then ask what we can learn from it. The account that follows is about André Trocmé and the parish that he pastored during World War II in the village of Le Chambon.[35]

Living Truthfully: A Story

Magda and André Trocmé and their children arrived at the small, predominantly Protestant village of Le Chambon-Sur-Lignon in September of 1934 in order for André to be the new pastor. According to André, the village was dying when they arrived. He was concerned that this village of 3,000 inhabitants seemed devoid of meaning and purpose, symbolized by their nine month winters. They needed something more than their three month tourist season to give purpose and to express their life together as a village and a parish. André thought of several alternatives but finally decided on a private secondary school which would foster a spirit of internationalism and peace.

During their first few years at Le Chambon the Trocmés were involved primarily in the establishing of relationships. Two formal ways in which networks of relationships were established was through Bible studies and the school. Numerous people were involved in the thirteen youth groups André had organized to study the Bible. A number of people were involved in one way or another with the school that opened in 1938.

By 1939 most everyone in the village of Le Chambon had been touched by the fervor and excitement of André Trocmé. Through his sermons, the Bible study groups, and the school a new sense of purpose was injected into people's lives. But the excitement of Le Chambon was not a reflection of what was beginning to happen on the European scene. One month before the Trocmés arrival in Le Chambon Hitler became the Reich Führer of Germany. A little more than five years later, on September 3, 1939, France declared war on Germany. May 17, 1940 saw the German invasion of France, and a little more than a month later France surrendered, signing an armistice which gave the Germans control of three-fifths of French territory.

Le Chambon was part of "the unoccupied zone" and therefore ostensibly free and still under French domain. This unoccupied zone was governed by Marshall Pétain, with headquarters at Vichy. However, this government showed quite early that its policies would not differ significantly from German policies, particularly regarding the Jews.

Within two months after the establishment of the Vichy government a decree that had earlier prohibited slander and libel toward a group of people belonging to a particular race or religion was revoked, thus paving the way for legal sanction of anti-Semitic behavior. Nationalistic sentiments prevented some of the French from turning against French Jews. But, for many of the French people the 75,000 Jewish refugees residing in France were objects of hatred. And, in the end, most of these refugees would experience a painful death at the hands of those armed with anti-Semitism and hate.

It was within this atmosphere that the first Jewish refugee came to the Trocmés' door in the winter of 1940–1941. Magda naively assumed that the mayor would help her get the refugee the necessary papers so she would not have to fear being deported back to Germany. Magda quickly learned, however, that for many nationalism and self-interest were more important than helping refugees. Magda also learned, against her own inclinations, to disobey some authorities. She could not concede to the mayor's wishes that she send the refugee away.

But this act of disobedience, an act rooted in love for enemies as well as neighbors, was not the first or the last to be performed by the villagers of Le Chambon. They began in the fall of 1940 when an order came down that all schools were to have fascist-style salutes (with a stiff arm and palm down) every morning before classes. André saw this as an opportunity to resist both the Vichy and German governments. Soon, no one in the school was giving the salute. A similar incident of resistance occurred less than a year later when the mayor gave an order for the church bell to be rung to celebrate Pétain and the National Revolution he helped bring about in France.

These acts may seem insignificant. But they were concrete expressions of faithfulness to Christ as André Trocmé saw it (and as others in Le Chambon were coming to see). They both symbolized and precipitated what would become a life of resistance for the village of Le Chambon until 1944.

We should not think that resistance to the Vichy government was the primary concern of the Trocmés or the villagers. Indeed, first in their minds was helping those in need—in this case the Jewish refugees. For André it was simple. He " . . . could not bear to separate himself from Jesus by ignoring the precious quality of Human life that God had demonstrated in the birth, the life, and the crucifixion of His son."[36] André knew that Jesus had said to love one's neighbor and one's enemy. Edouard Theis, the man André chose to direct the school, said that André's favorite parts of the Bible were the Good Samaritan passage in Luke and the Sermon on the Mount. André's concerns, translated into sermons and action, had a transforming effect on the village of Le Chambon. A once dying village was transformed into a city of refuge for more than two thousand Jewish refugees.

The ways in which the people of Le Chambon hid Jews was really rather simple. For villagers living in more than a dozen boarding houses and even more private homes, the refugees simply became a part of their lives, sharing in the daily activities of Le Chambon—within the limits of secrecy. Because these villagers' lives were intertwined through faithful attendance at worship, Bible studies, and through the school, there existed a significant network of relationships. It was partly this network that obviated the capture of refugees on several occasions. Halfway through the occupation of France, after the Nazis also occupied Southern France, some information funnelled through this network came from mysterious callers warning of impending searches.

The mysterious callers were only one example of the help Le Chambon received from those outside. During the entire occupation, Le Chambon barely survived financially. Had it not been for such assistance as the $200 per month sent by the American Friends Service Committee their life would have been even harder. In addition to hiding refugees, André and his parish were also instrumental in helping many escape from France.

"If you stand firmly opposed to overwhelming destructive power, you expose yourself to destruction."[37] So it was that the resistance activity was not to be without cost to the villagers of Le Chambon, although it was certainly not as great as it could have been. According to André Trocmé's estimates, there were about 2500 refugees who came to Le Chambon, most of whom would undoubtedly have died had they been turned away.[38] Amateurs at saving lives that they were, nonetheless only a few of the parish at Le Chambon lost their lives. André Trocmé and two other leaders were imprisoned for approximately two months and released only a few days before everyone in their camp was executed. In the summer of 1942 there was a successful raid which resulted in the arrest of two Jews; it is likely that one was killed. Edouard Theis and André had to become refugees themselves for a few months to avoid being killed by the Gestapo. Daniel Trocmé, André's second cousin, was executed because of a successful raid on his boarding house. The killing of the village doctor, Roger Le

Forestier, and the accidental (?) death of the Trocmé's son, Jean-Pierre, could have been related to the hiding of the refugees. Nevertheless, Le Chambon was quite successful as a city of refuge for more than two thousand people in dire need.

Conclusion

What can we learn from the story of Le Chambon that might be helpful in thinking about relativism? The main thing to learn is also the most obvious: truth need not be relativized simply because others believe it is not truth. Everyone and everything outside the parish at Le Chambon were telling these people that Jewish refugees should not be helped. In fact, most would have encouraged active disdain for the refugees. This, as most saw it, was objectively moral. And yet despite the dominant opposing convictions, the people of this parish, at risk to life and limb, cared for these refugees consistently for several years.

Why did they live this way? Even before the refugees came to their village the parishioners had grown in their convictions and moral practices that neighbors and enemies were to be loved, that the stranger was to be welcomed. Their pastor, the school, the Bible studies, and their lives themselves all served to communicate that these convictions were true. Thus, when the refugees arrived it was an almost automatic response to reach out to them in love.

We ought not to miss two points. First, the issue in France was not one of relativism. Quite the contrary, it was one of competing sets of convictions. Hitler could hardly be accused of being a relativist. One does not order the extermination of eleven million people in concentration camps because one believes one conviction is as good as another. No, in France, as elsewhere in Europe, during World War II there were ample robust convictions to go around. Relativism was not an issue.

What was at issue was the question of who was right. The reigning "objective truth" said that the Chambonnais were wrong. But the Chambonnais were not so convinced. That was because the socialization of the community had already deeply convinced them of the truth of the convictions that neighbors and enemies were to be loved, strangers were to be welcomed.

242

And, of course, decades later almost everyone is convinced of the truth of at least some of their convictions. In fact their lives so beautifully displayed their convictions that their story has testified powerfully to millions. Further, it ought not to be missed that they had correlative convictions regarding God, Jesus, the Church, etc. that are at least rendered more credible by the truthfulness of their lives.[39]

One of the concerns that often accompanies the worry about relativism is the slippery slope toward nihilism. But why is it that many in Europe after World War II suffered some sense of nihilism? It is surely not because of some theory of relativism. Rather it is partly because of the horrors of World War II and the realization that those horrors were perpetrated in the name of truths held to be objective. What was devastating was the realization that what they held to be true was not only not true but was a "truth" forced on the world at the cost of some fifty to seventy million lives. The chief response to such nihilism is not to construct a less flabby theory regarding truth, it is rather to argue the Nazi "truth" was wrong then as well as now and to proclaim with lives and lips—as did Le Chambon—a rival truth. It was not some theory of truth that sustained the Chambonnais through or after the war but, rather, the living of the truth.

We as reflective Christians certainly ought to give appropriate attention to the intellectual questions involved in the current dilemma of relativism. However, as Christians we do not believe there is some philosophical foundation that is more fundamental than God revealed in Jesus Christ. In fact, we are concerned that Richard Rorty is right in his claim that philosophy has too often been

> [F]or the intellectuals, a substitute for religion. It was the area of culture where one touched bottom, where one found the vocabulary and the convictions which permitted one to explain and justify one's activity as an intellectual, and thus to discover the significance of one's life.[40]

We want our vocabulary, our convictions, our touching bottom, if you will, to happen within our convictional communities, the Church. Therefore, what we ought to attend to as much as anything is helping to shape Christian communities that in turn will shape the characters of our church members so that we will be a people who live lives reflecting the truths we claim to believe. It is in the living of faithful lives—lives of conviction, humility, openness, and nonviolence—that we commend the Christ whom we confess as Lord while simultaneously continuing to shape our own communities around this Lord rather than the competing convictions of our culture. It is in this way, moreover, that we learn to inhabit another world, the world of the Church, a world in which we believe that we come to learn the truth about ourselves, the world, and the Lord that created it all.

CHAPTER 12

Textual Relativism, Philosophy of Language, and the baptist Vision

Nancey Murphy

Introduction

It seems appropriate on the occasion of a *Festschrift* not only to review the accomplishments of the one so honored, but also to look ahead to see what benefits may yet be gained from his works. In *Understanding Religious Convictions*, James Wm. McClendon, Jr., and James M. Smith used the philosophy of language of J. L. Austin to solve problems in philosophy of religion that arose from misunderstandings about the nature of language.[1] In this paper I shall briefly describe and evaluate that achievement. In addition, I shall highlight a new problem for philosophers of religion that also arises from misunderstandings about language—and one that will be at least as devastating to Christian self-understanding if not answered. This is the problem of the instability of textual meaning—that is, relativism with regard to textual interpretation. These views have arisen as but one aspect of a general skeptical reaction to the demise of foundationalism in epistemology. I shall argue that a solution is already at hand in the works of none other than J. L. Austin and James Wm. McClendon.

McClendon's Use of Austin

In *Understanding Religious Convictions*, McClendon and Smith offered a proposal for understanding religious language that was based on Austin's speech-act theory. They situated their work in a line of succession from R. B. Braithwaite through Ian Ramsey. I propose to situate it on a somewhat broader map.

Modern Assumptions about Language

If we look at theories of language developed by philosophers in the modern period, the predominant view could be described as atomistic and referential (or representative). That is, complex utterances were to be understood by analyzing them into their simplest parts, and the meaning of the parts was to be accounted for in terms of reference. Thus, for John Locke, words referred to or represented ideas—*"words in their primary or immediate signification, stand for nothing but the ideas in the mind of him that uses them."*[2] Ideas, in turn, stood for things; simple ideas were "perfectly taken from the existence of things."[3] Simple ideas were compounded to form complex ideas; sentences represented the connections the mind makes between ideas. Locke's approach stands behind much modern philosophy of language.

Gottlob Frege (1848–1925) has been one of the most significant influences on modern philosophy of language. Frege was largely responsible for banishing "psychologism" from considerations of language—that is, for the rejection of views such as Locke's that understood language first in relation to mental contents.

Frege's famous distinction between *Sinn* (sense) and *Bedeutung* (reference) might have distracted modern philosophers from their preoccupation with reference, since Frege claimed that *sense* was the primary meaning of 'meaning.' However, he understood the sense of a word in terms of the contribution it makes to the truth of sentences, and the truth of sentences, for Frege, depended only on the *reference* of the words that make it up—so reference returned through the back door.

The logical atomists, Bertrand Russell, Ludwig Wittgenstein in his early work, and others, followed Frege in supposing that philosophy of language was to be done by devising formal artificial languages rather than by analyzing natural languages. These philosophers epitomize modern tendencies in philosophy of language: *atomic* sentences were to get their meaning by *representing* atomic facts. And it is just at this point that we can see most clearly a tie between modern theories of language and modern epistemology, since the atomic facts that ground the meaning of language were also to serve as the *foundation* for all knowledge. The verification theory of meaning was a hybrid proposition that served as a manifesto for the logical positivist version of empiricist foundationalism, as well as for the logical atomists' empiricist theory of meaning.

With this very clear expression of a referential approach to language came the recognition that whole realms of discourse, such as ethics and aesthetics, could not be treated in the same manner as factual discourse. This prompted the elaboration of a second theory of language—or, more precisely, the elaboration of a theory of *second-class* language. For example, A. J. Ayer, in his influential popularization of logical positivism, claimed that ethical judgments, having no factual meaning, serve merely to *express* the attitudes or moral sentiments of the speaker.[4] Hence we may call this the expressivist theory of language. In general, it stated that language that is not factually meaningful, if significant at all, merely expresses the attitudes, intentions, or emotions of the speaker.

Theological Consequences

So it is fair to say that modern philosophers presented two options for understanding religious language: to attempt to count it as factual language, but with its own sorts of referents, or to count it as expressivist in nature. Braithwaite, McClendon's and Smith's foil, had provided an expressivist account of religious language: when Christians say "God is love" they are really expressing their intentions to lead 'agapeistic' lives, an intention they fortify by telling inspirational stories about Jesus—which need not be true.

Many Christians, I imagine, would dismiss Braithwaite's theory out of hand, but it is interesting that some early modern theologians, writing a century before Braithwaite, had already provided their own expressivist accounts of religious language. Friedrich Schleiermacher, for instance, defined Christian doctrines as "accounts of Christian religious affections set forth in speech"; the Christian symbols were therefore to be evaluated in terms of their adequacy for expressing the Christian's inner awareness.[5]

In more conservative branches of the Christian tradition, propositional (referential) views of religious language abound. Here, however, the referents are supernatural rather than natural realities. These views have their own problems, one of which is to counter the charge that they overlook the element of self-involvement appropriate to all religious discourse.

I suggest that modern theories of language have thus proved detrimental to Christianity by offering two and only two accounts of the nature of language. Theologians and philosophers of religion have been forced to choose one or the other, and the forced option has helped to establish a gulf between conservative and liberal Christians. In addition, neither the propositional nor the expressivist theory has provided an adequate account of religious language.[6]

The Value of Austin

Against this background we can see the value of the Austinian account of religious language developed in *Understanding Religious Convictions*. Austin rejected the Fregean predilection for artificial languages, as well as the atomistic approach of his predecessors. For Austin, the meaning of an utterance is as much a function of the context within which it is used as it is of the words that make it up. Most important, however, was his move to shift attention from meaning as reference to meaning as use.[7] Or to put the matter more accurately, if language is used for more complex purposes than simply to describe facts, then we have to ask more complex questions about it than the question that had so long preoccupied philosophers—namely, how does language *mean*? Now it is necessary to ask more broadly how language functions and what counts as success in using it.

McClendon and Smith have summarized Austin's criteria for a "happy" speech act under four headings: (1) Preconditions—speaker and hearer must share a common language and be free from relevant impediments to communication. (2) Primary conditions—the speaker must issue a sentence in the common language that is a conventional way of performing that kind of speech act.

(3) Representative or descriptive conditions—the sentence must bear a relation to a state of affairs that is appropriate to that sort of speech act. (4) Affective or psychological conditions—the speaker must intend to perform the speech act by means of the sentence, and have the relevant attitudes or affects; the hearer must take the speaker to have the requisite intentions and affects (uptake).[8]

So, to take an example from *Understanding Religious Convictions*, for a speaker happily to *confess* that "God led Israel across the Sea of Reeds" the following conditions must be satisfied: (1) This sentence must be an understandable sentence in a shared language, and (2) of a recognized 'confessional' form. (3) There must have been a suitable state of affairs involving the people Israel, a sea, and an act of God. Finally, (4) the speaker must have intended the utterance as a confession of faith and must have a suitable attitude toward this event such as awed gratitude. The hearers must have taken the speech act as a confession of faith.

What I wish to emphasize about this account of religious language is the fact that in its light both the expressivist and referential theories of language can be seen to express partial truths, yet neither alone provides an adequate account of religious (or any other) language. To "state the facts" about God without an appropriate attitude toward God is surely to have failed to get the point of what one is saying. Yet confession of religious attitudes, detached from any factual content, is to confess nothing. Notice that different kinds of speech acts will require different kinds of relation to the real world: happily to confess that Jesus has come in the flesh requires a different state of affairs than happily to pray that he will come again. Here, *use* is the primary category for analyzing language; *appropriate reference and appropriate expression are subordinate factors in that the use determines what counts as appropriate reference and appropriate affect.*

Recent Developments

Since the publication of *Understanding Religious Convictions*, the most important advance in the understanding of religious language has come from the "Yale School." These authors, apparently unaware of the contributions of McClendon and Smith, have reached comparable conclusions about religious language, as a result of the influence of both Austin and Wittgenstein. For example, George Lindbeck has argued that to understand doctrinal change it is necessary to ask what *use* is made of doctrines within Christianity. Lindbeck emphasizes their regulative function: they prescribe and proscribe forms of first-order religious language and regulate its relation to communal practices.[9] Ronald Thiemann has argued that in order to understand the doctrine of revelation we must ask what the Scriptures, taken as revelation, *do*. He answers that their primary force is to narrate promises.[10] Neither Lindbeck's nor Thiemann's work presents a full-fledged account of religious language, but both, happily, reflect an awareness of the need for a theory of religious language that goes beyond both the referential and expressivist theories. Both reflect, as well, a recognition of the embeddedness of religious language within the shared life of a community, and the impossibility of understanding it without understanding the conventions and practices of that community—a Wittgensteinian point.

The Relativity of Textual Interpretation

If the issue of expressivism versus referentialism has created a gulf between liberal and conservative theologians, it has done so quietly—it has created failures to understand, but little direct conflict. However, I suspect that the issue of relativism with regard to textual interpretation will be more explosive. For years there has been a widespread recognition of interpretive relativity: recognition of various forms of historicism, of the hermeneutic circle, of contextual interpretations; none of this is new. What *is* new is a different attitude: whereas earlier thinkers saw these sources of relativity as something one ideally would want to overcome, some current literary theorists see it as neither possible nor desirable to attribute stable meanings to texts. Literary-critical terms with origins in post-Structuralism are becoming more and more prevalent in the vocabularies of both theologians and biblical scholars. But can the Christian intellectual world survive if deconstructionist and reader-response theses are taken with full seriousness? David Lehman describes deconstructionism as

> not merely postmodernist but preapocalyptic. It is a catastrophe theory inasmuch as it proceeds from the perception of an extreme linguistic instability that undermines the coherence of any state-

ment—a breakdown in our collective confidence in the power of words to communicate ideas and represent experience. It announces or implies that a rupture has occurred, an irreparable break with the past, and that nothing can ever be the same again.[11]

In this section I shall first trace some of the philosophical and literary roots of reader-response criticism and deconstructionism, and then argue on the basis of the Austinian theory of language that extremely relative conclusions regarding the meaning of texts are unwarranted.

Sources of Deconstructionism and Reader-Response Criticism

In order to analyze developments in literary theory, it will be helpful to have before us the dimensions or conditions for the successful use of language, as we have come to know them from the works of Austin and Wittgenstein, and McClendon and Smith. I would describe them as follows: First, let us distinguish between linguistic and social conventions. The former include grammar, in the most basic sense of the word, and proper word usage. Social conventions include proper forms for various speech acts, such as requests, prayers, promises. In Wittgensteinian terms, these conventions arise within *language games* and the *forms of life* with which they are associated—'grammar' in Wittgenstein's specialized sense. There is, again, the referential dimension—the relation between language and world. In addition, it is helpful to distinguish McClendon's and Smith's affective dimension into two categories, which I shall call expressivist conditions and uptake. Expressivist conditions include both the speaker's (writer's) intentions and appropriate accompanying attitudes and emotions. Uptake, as for Austin, is the hearer getting the point of what is being said (written).

This gives us a list of five dimensions or kinds of conditions for successful use of language:

1. linguistic conventions
2. social conventions
3. reference
4. expressivist conditions
5. uptake.

The writings of Ferdinand de Saussure (1857–1913), the founder of modern linguistics, are essential for understanding the works of contemporary literary theorists such as Jacques Derrida, Paul de Man, and Stanley Fish. Saussure distinguished between *langue*, the linguistic system, and *parole*, particular speech acts, and insisted that it is *langue* that the linguist must study. *Langue* stands over against individual speakers, who can choose to use the system on specific occasions, but cannot choose the system; the system limits what can be said.

A second Saussurian distinction is between diachronic and synchronic linguistics. Diachronic linguistics studies the changes in language over time, and is of less interest than synchronic linguistics, which studies the relations among signs at a given point in history. Saussure's synchronic linguistics presented a non-referential theory of signs wherein signs point only to other signs. The crucial way in which signs relate to one another is by means of difference: they are defined not by their positive content but negatively by the simultaneous presence of other signs in the system. That is, human sound capacities form a continuum; we break up the continuum in order to identify sounds as words: 'bat' versus 'cat' versus 'cot.' Thought, too, is a continuum, and the development of distinct ideas is dependent upon making linguistic distinctions. So, for example, 'red' is not to be understood by pointing to red things, but by the fact that it is limited by the presence in the language of 'orange' and 'violet.'

In the 1960s, Saussure's study of synchronic systems of difference was generalized to other fields, producing "Structuralist" approaches in anthropology, psychology, philosophy. Structuralism views all cultural phenomena as products of systems of signification, wherein it is the relations among the elements of the system, rather than the relations between the elements and 'reality' that produce meaning. All such systems are arbitrary, and there is no way of apprehending reality independently of them.

Similarly, Structuralist literary critics reject the idea that a literary text reflects a reality that is already given. They focus their attention on the text itself, as opposed to either the author's intent ("the intentional fallacy") or the effect on the reader ("the affective fallacy"). The key to a text is form: structures of sound, rhythm, rhyme, sequences of images, even ratios of passive to active verbs.

Deconstructionism

Both reader-response criticism and deconstructionism are reactions against Structuralist theories. Deconstructionists such as Paul de Man and Jacques Derrida reject the structuralist claim that structures are given in the texts. "'Form' itself turns out to be more an operative fiction, a product of the interpreter's rage for order, than anything vested in the literary work itself."[12]

Deconstructionists accept the Saussurian and Structuralist rejection of a referent external to the text.

> The word doesn't reflect or represent the world; the word contains the world and not the other way around. Therefore, texts are self-referential—they refer only to themselves, not to anything outside themselves. There is no such thing as the real world . . . all that's left is a succession of misleading signs, a parade of words beyond the power of humanity to control them.[13]

Deconstructionism also accepts (but intensifies) the Structuralist distinction between textual meaning and authorial intention. This was already suggested at the end of the preceding quotation: words are beyond the power of humanity to control them. Thus, "the author is dead." As the Structuralist theorist, Michel Foucault, says: the existentialist 'I' has been destroyed, translated into a 'one.' "It is not man who takes the place of God, but anonymous thinking, thinking without a subject."[14] Authors are unwitting mouthpieces for reigning ideologies. In fact, says Paul de Man, a text is as likely to conceal as to reveal the intentions of the author: literary criticism allows for two incompatible, mutually self-destructive points of view, and therefore puts an insurmountable obstacle in the way of any reading or understanding.[15]

The central preoccupation of deconstructionism is a reaction to Saussurian assumptions about the role of difference in language. To 'deconstruct' is to blur the distinction between two terms—binary opposites—especially in cases where one member of the pair is more highly valued than the other: primary/derivative, necessary/possible, present/absent. The point of this can be seen if we recall that it is just such differences, in Saussure's linguistics, that account for the meaning of terms. By blurring distinctions between terms, the deconstructionists aim to show that linguistic conventions, as understood in the Saussurian tradition, are inadequate to fix the meaning of a text.

Furthermore, the very practice of deconstructionism and the behavior of its adherents are meant to show that social conventions can be flouted. External reference is denied. The author's intentions are concealed. So we can see that by negating one by one the conditions mentioned above for successful communication, the deconstructionists are able to argue that any and every text inevitably undermines its own claims to a determinate meaning, and thus they end up by emphasizing the role of the reader in the production of meaning.

Reader-Response Criticism

Reader-response criticism rejects the Structuralists' rejection of the "affective fallacy" and agrees with deconstructionists in claiming that structure is in the eye of the beholder. Michael Vander Weele distinguishes three categories of reader-response critics: psychological, social, and intersubjective. The first category, including Norman Holland and David Bleich, emphasizes the variety of interpretations produced by different individual readers, and denies that meaning is tied to conventions. The social model (Stanley Fish and Jonathan Culler) emphasize the literary competence that comes from participation in and understanding of a cultural tradition of reading. Intersubjective theorists (Wolfgang Iser, Louise Marie Rosenblatt) stand between the other two types, and emphasize the transaction between unique individuals and social conventions.[16]

While Vander Weele categorizes Fish simply as a member of the social type, I believe a survey of his earlier and later works will serve to illustrate both poles of the spectrum of reader-response theories. Thus, I shall distinguish between the early Fish and the later Fish. While the early Fish is an ally of deconstructionism, the later Fish will turn out to be an ally of Austin and McClendon in their postmodern understandings of language.

Fish began by focusing on the question: What does this word (sentence, poem, play) do? In the sequence from writer to text to reader, meaning only 'happens' when the text has an effect on the reader:

[T]here is no direct relation between the meaning of a sentence (paragraph, novel, poem) and what its words mean. . . . It is the experience of an utterance . . . that *is* the meaning.[17]

The sort of effect the early Fish sought to understand can be illustrated by his analysis of the following sentence:

> That Judas perished by hanging himself, there is no certainty in Scripture: though in one place it seems to affirm it, and by a doubtful word hath given occasion to translate it; yet in another place, in a more punctual description, it maketh it improbable, and seems to overthrow it.[18]

Fish points out that the first clause is understood to be shorthand for "the *fact* that Judas perished by hanging himself." Thus the reader is set up to expect that the rest of the sentence will follow from this positive assertion, and thus "there is no . . . " ought to be followed by "doubt" rather than "certainty." The rest of the sentence, step by step, frustrates the expectation set up in the first clause, progressively disorienting the reader. So the sort of response with which Fish is concerned here is psychological: frustration, confusion, and the like.

However, the later Fish is concerned with genuine Austinian uptake. In "Is There a Text in This Class?" he concentrates on *understanding* texts, and emphasizes the shared *conventions* that make it possible for reader or listener to "get it."[19] Here his illustration is an anecdote:

> On the first day of the new semester a colleague at Johns Hopkins University was approached by a student who, as it turned out, had just taken a course from me. She put to him what I think you would agree is a perfectly straightforward question. "Is there a text in this class?" Responding with a confidence so perfect that he was unaware of it . . . , my colleague said, "Yes; it's the *Norton Anthology of Literature*," whereupon the trap (set not by the student but by the infinite capacity of language for being appropriated) was sprung: "No, no," she said, "I mean in this class do we believe in poems and things, or is it just us?"[20]

While Fish uses the anecdote to illustrate his claims regarding the "instability of the text" and the "unavailability of determinate meanings," he argues here, against the supposed implication that texts can mean anything we want, that the possibilities for different interpretations are in fact sharply limited by the practices and assumptions that make up the text's social context. In this case, it is the general rubric "first day of class" that makes the first meaning available; the second becomes available only within the narrower context of "Fish's victims." Both interpretations were a function of public and constituting norms of language and understanding.

So the later Fish still maintains that reader-response is what constitutes the meaning of the text, but argues for the necessity of *social conventions* to enable uptake, and recognizes as well that these same conventions enable the reader or listener to reach correct understanding of the writer's or speaker's *intention*, and of the intended *reference*. We could say that the later Fish's point is that neither linguistic conventions, nor referent, nor intention alone is sufficient to establish meaning. Social conventions must be considered as well.

Consequences of Post-Structuralism for Biblical Criticism

It will have been obvious all along that deconstructionist and psychological-type reader-response theories are fatal for any community that intends to take the Bible as authority for thought and practice, but it is worth noting how directly and explicitly these arguments cut against the most widely held understandings of the goals of biblical interpretation. First, word studies had already been called into question by the Structuralists on the basis of Saussure's concentration on synchronic rather than diachronic semantics: meanings of words change over time and cannot be known by means of their etymologies. But deconstruction pushes the point to the extreme by flouting synchronic conventions—by demolishing conventional associations and distinctions and creating new, idiosyncratic meanings. Recall, also, the early Fish's denial of a direct relation between the meaning of a sentence and what its words mean.

Second, some hermeneutic theories, beginning at least as early as in the work of Friedrich Schleiermacher, have sought the meaning of the text in the mind of the author. For Schleiermacher, the goal of interpretation was to enter imaginatively and sympathetically into the author's religious consciousness, re-living and re-thinking the author's thoughts and feelings. However, it is important to add that Schleiermacher did not see this as the sole hermeneutic task. More recently, E. D. Hirsch, Jr. has argued that the meaning of the text is to be understood *primarily* in terms of the author's will or intention.[21]

Yet many today would deny the possibility of recovering the author's intentions. The deconstructionists and early reader-response theorists join the New Critics and other post-Structuralists in asserting that the author's intentions are not available to the interpreter; deconstructionists would add that these intentions would be of no interest even if they were.

Finally, Hans Frei has claimed that lying behind historical-critical approaches to the Bible is the assumption that the meaning of a text is to be identified with the history behind the text.[22] Notice that this is a species of referential theory of language—the primary sense in which the texts have meaning is by virtue of their historical referents. But deconstructionists close off this avenue, also, with their claim that texts refer only to other texts. And, again, there is at least some truth here. Our access to the history behind the text is generally only by means of the text itself, and the critic's reconstruction is, after all, nothing but another text. There is no objective, independent reality against which the original text can be compared. Are not the deconstructionists right—we have not a text and a fixed historical referent, but rather two sets of texts, the biblical passages and the critics' interpretations?

So it would appear that if these post-Structuralist claims are true (or even if they are not true but nonetheless come to dominate the intellectual world) then study of the Bible will have no practical import, however interesting it may be to play with a variety of interpretations.

To many readers, deconstructionist claims will appear willfully perverse and deserving only to be ignored. But, as I have indicated, I think that there are at least partial truths here that present serious challenges to Bible readers; and because of these partial truths, a frontal attack on deconstructionism may not be successful. I suggest an indirect strategy; namely to unmask the *modern* assumptions upon which the deconstructionists' negative conclusions are based. I shall then shift to a ('postmodern') Austinian understanding of language and show that despite the fact that many deconstructionist criticisms of traditional theories of hermeneutics are valid, we are not thereby compelled to accept textual relativism. In doing so we shall find ourselves retracing the steps from the early to the later Fish.

Modern Assumptions behind Deconstructionism

The term 'postmodern' is so closely associated with deconstructionism that I now hesitate to use it for describing the works of philosophers such as Austin, who have decisively moved beyond modern assumptions. The irony is that deconstructionist arguments against stability of meaning all trade on modern assumptions about the nature of language; furthermore, to provide a refutation of this 'avant garde' literary movement we need only to *return* to the work Austin did nearly a half century ago. Modern assumptions are clearly evident in two of the positions described above: Texts have no external referent; if reference is the basis of all meaning, then texts have no fixed meaning. Texts conceal the author's intention; if (non-referential) language is significant in that it expresses the inner state of the speaker or writer, then, again, the texts must have no fixed meaning.

The deconstruction of Saussurian differences also betrays a modern mindset in that it is parallel to a mistake made by some modern epistemologists. Deconstructionists argue that the conventional meanings of any pair of terms can be deconstructed. In fact, all meaning is based on convention; any convention can be violated, as they show by producing thoroughly unconventional readings of texts. The point they seem to be missing, however, is that their unconventional interpretations are only intelligible against a background of conventions that they are not flouting in a given instance.

The parallel argument from epistemology is an argument for skepticism based on the fact that any belief can be called into question. However, it is now widely recognized that total skepticism does not follow from this fact, since one needs to assume the truth of many beliefs in order meaningfully to call other beliefs into question. René Descartes and his more skeptical followers were able to make this mistake because of their foundationalist model of knowledge. If the acceptability of one's entire system of beliefs depends upon a relatively small set of foundational beliefs, then the criticism of these few supposedly indubitable beliefs brings the whole system down.

The lesson to be learned from this episode in the history of epistemology is that negative conclusions regarding the part (dubitability of specific individual beliefs; meaning indeterminacy in particular instances) cannot automatically be generalized to the entire system. The argument by analogy from epistemology to theory of meaning goes through because in both cases there is something about the context that must be assumed in order to arrive at the negative conclusions in the first place; and this something blocks the generalization from part to whole. So in epistemology, one must assume the truth of some beliefs in order to generate reasonable doubts (e.g., Descartes must assume that there is such a thing as dreaming to get his skeptical argument off the ground); deconstructionist arguments for total indeterminacy of meaning make use of linguistic conventions that cannot simultaneously be called into question without defeating those very arguments. Thus, total indeterminacy of meaning does not follow from the fact that particular conventions can be ignored at particular times.

An Austinian Answer to Textual Indeterminacy

Let us now abandon the modern supposition that biblical texts must be understood in the first instance either as descriptions of historical events or as expressions of mental states of the authors, and consider them instead to be speech acts (or collections of speech acts). It has already been suggested by others that Austin's speech-act theory has valuable implications for hermeneutics.[23] My purpose here is a more specific one: I intend to use Austin's theory to demonstrate the fallacies in arguments, based on deconstructionism or early reader-response theories, for the claim that biblical texts have no fixed meaning.[24]

At this point we need to make a distinction. It is common to analyze the hermeneutic problem into two aspects: the first is the question of what the text meant in its original setting; the second is how to appropriate that meaning in our own very different historical setting. If the deconstructionists' arguments are valid, then the problem for biblical studies is not merely that of historical distance—it is the more radical problem that texts have no stable meaning even in their original setting. The focus of the present section is to answer this radical claim; the problem of historical distance will be taken up in the next section.

An Argument for Stability of Meaning

My argument here might be characterized as a transcendental one.[25] I begin with the assumption that the biblical texts (often, sometimes) served in the context of the early church to perform felicitous speech acts. If this was the case, then we can argue that the necessary conditions for happy speech acts (as described by Austin) *must have been* fulfilled. Then we will see what can be said about the deconstructionists' three attacks on the determinacy of meaning.

It is not unreasonable to assume the success or effectiveness or happiness of the New Testament texts (at least much of the time) in their original settings. In fact, one might describe the canonization process as that of choosing from among early Christian writings those that had been found useful and effective in a variety of Christian communities—canonicity as universal (or nearly universal) uptake.[26]

What criteria, then, would these texts need to have satisfied in those settings, and what are the consequences of their having done so for deconstructionist claims?

Conventional and Expressive Conditions

To presuppose the felicity of the speech act (or set of acts) that a text is meant to perform is to suppose that the author was successful in employing linguistic conventions in order to enact his intentions. Notice, first, that to assume that an author succeeded in expressing or enacting her intention by means of linguistic conventions is to assume that there *were* linguistic conventions. To note that a set of texts was preserved and circulated to a variety of communities over a span of years shows that those conventions were somewhat widespread and invariate over time.

Second, if we know what an author *did* through or by means of a text, and if we have no reason to suppose that the author was dishonest or incompetent in using the language, then we have public access to what the author intended. There is no hidden mental component—the intention or the meaning—to be sought beyond the speech act itself. So it is true in a sense that we can never recover the mind of the author—it is true in the trivial sense that we never have immediate access to anyone's thoughts but our own. But it is obviously false in another sense, since in the normal, "happy" state of affairs, people's speech acts are public enactments of their intentions.

So if the deconstructionist lament over the disappearance of the author is meant to point out that we have no access to the inner awareness of the author, it is true but uninteresting. It is only interesting if one believes that knowing the meaning requires access to private intentions, and that texts generally or always fail to enact the writer's intentions. But this latter claim amounts to saying that all texts fail to perform happy speech acts, and it is obviously false.

Now, it may appear that my argument here is circular—that is, to claim that the texts performed happy speech acts is simply to state in different words that the texts had stable meaning in their own day. To put it another way: does not the deconstructionist (and early reader-response) challenge raise exactly the suspicion that to everyone in the New Testament communities the texts may have meant something different—and I am simply assuming the contrary?

To see why the argument is not circular, we need to emphasize that getting the meaning—uptake—is no more a private matter than it is to have an intention. If uptake were a private "I get it!"[27] then it would be entirely possible for a whole church-full of readers to 'get' something different. But on the account of language here presented, getting the meaning is 'operationalized' as a communal (shared, intersubjective) response to the text—a living of its import rather than a mere hearing of it. The intrinsic relation between language and action, emphasized by both Austin and Wittgenstein, is crucially important here.[28] So conceived, it would have been a public matter whether the texts 'meant' the same to everyone. And in some cases, as shown in Paul's letters, the author could *and did* object when his writings had been taken wrongly.

The fact that there was controversy over the meaning of texts in New Testament times is no rebuttal of my claim; in fact, it supports it. The mistake made by deconstructionists, I have argued above, is to ignore the conventional aspect of language. The result is that no adequate criteria are left for judging any interpretation to be a *mistake*. If this *were* the case, then we would have what Wittgenstein calls "private language," and he has argued persuasively that such a thing is logically impossible.[29] So the fact that there were controversies, and that looking back we can recognize some interpretations as mistakes, provides grounds for a *reductio ad absurdum* of the deconstructionist position.

Referential Conditions

To presuppose the felicity of speech acts performed by New Testament texts is to suppose that appropriate referential or representative conditions obtained. Note that what constitutes *appropriate* referential conditions will depend on the kind of speech act in question. For example, consider Hans Frei's suggestions about the purpose of the Gospel narratives. Frei claimed that the *force* of the Gospel narratives is to provide identity descriptions—stories to render a character. Their purpose is to say: this risen Christ whom you know as present to you in worship is in fact Jesus of Nazareth, who was born ... taught ... suffered and died.[30]

The referential conditions for a speech act of this sort include the background condition (1) that the readers must have in fact known the presence of the risen Christ. The more immediate conditions that must be fulfilled for the success of the gospel stories as speech acts are: (2) The narrative must serve to identify one specific individual—and for this certain historical facts needed to be true—enough facts to distinguish Jesus from any other similar characters. We might include here the identity of his parents, his home town, the outlines of his public ministry, and the circumstances of his death. (3) The stories of his teaching and actions must be truly *characteristic* of him—that is, they must have presented an accurate portrait of his character. Notice that truth-*likeness* is at least as important here as objective historical accuracy. In fact, we can sometimes render a character more accurately by means of stories about what the person might have done than by recounting specific incidents.

Contrast the force of the Gospels, now, with Paul's preaching of the resurrection. Here Paul was addressing communities in which some still lived who had known Jesus. The force of Paul's speech acts is to proclaim that this well-known historical figure has been raised. The representative conditions here are re-ordered. As a background condition there must have been a historical Jesus known to those present by acquaintance or testimony, and this condition we can easily assume to have been fulfilled. The more immediate and interesting condition is that there must have been some peculiar event involving the body of that well-known figure that could reasonably have been described by the metaphorical term 'resurrection.' But since this event was not directly observable, the most that could be asked was that a sufficient number of hearers have access to enough evidence to be able reasonably to accept Paul's testimony.

So it is indeed true that today we have no access to the historical events 'behind the texts,' but in some cases the original hearers or readers did have such access, and we can infer a good deal about that history from their endorsement of the texts. But it is worth reiterating that the history is not to be equated with the meaning; nor is the reconstructed history in any sense *foundational* for deriving the meaning of the text. The order must be the reverse—first to understand what the text was *doing* in its original setting, then to ask what historical knowledge (some of) its readers must have had in order for it to succeed.

Summary

To sum up, if we assume that something like Austin's speech-act theory is an adequate account of language, then insofar as we have reason to believe that biblical texts performed happy speech acts in their original settings, exactly to that extent do we have reason to believe that the *conditions* for happiness were met. These conditions include (relatively) stable linguistic conventions, (approximate) fulfillment of a variety of relevant historical conditions, and close (enough) correspondence between what the authors intended to say and what they actually said.

The qualifications in parentheses provoke us to ask how stable the conventions must be, how close the correspondences? The only general answer that can be given is: close enough to work; the necessary degree of precision will depend on the particularities of each speech act. So while it may not be possible to argue for an absolute fixity of meaning, it is indeed possible to argue for the degree of stability required for practical purposes, and with a theory of meaning as *use*, practical purposes are exactly the ones that matter.

Historical Distance and the baptist Vision

I mentioned above that only half of the hermeneutic problem is solved if we can show that the texts had a (relatively) determinate meaning in their original contexts. The other half is to show that we have access to that meaning. Volumes have been written on how this historical distance is to be overcome—how our contemporary 'horizon' is to be fused with that of the text—in order to permit understanding in our own day. Yet a prior question is: what do we mean by 'understanding'?

In keeping with earlier proposals in this paper, I suggest that we consider the issue as a matter of uptake. So the first requirement for a community today to get the point of biblical speech acts is that it understand itself to be addressed by the texts. The second requirement is that the community now be in some sense *the same interpretive community* as that of the writer. Here the later Fish is helpful in his analysis of the relations between reading strategies and interpretive communities.

> Why should two or more readers ever agree . . . ? The answer . . .
> is to be found in a notion that has been implicit in my argument,
> the notion of *interpretive communities*. Interpretive communities are
> made up of those who share interpretive strategies. . . . This, then,
> is the explanation both for the stability of interpretation among
> different readers (they belong to the same community) and for the
> regularity with which a single reader will employ different inter-
> pretive strategies and thus make different texts (he belongs to
> different communities). It also explains why there are disagree-
> ments and why they can be debated in a principled way. . . . The
> notion of interpretive communities thus stands between an impos-
> sible ideal and the fear which leads so many to maintain it. The
> ideal is of perfect agreement and it would require texts to have a
> status independent of interpretation. The fear is of interpretive
> anarchy, but it would only be realized if interpretation (text mak-
> ing) were completely random.[31]

Thus, the community today must share interpretive strategies with the author and the original readers. How is this possible? Wittgenstein's account of the relation between interpretation of language and shared forms of life is relevant here; it suggests the importance of common activities and social conventions. The reading strategy and related understanding of church life described by McClendon as the "baptist vision" is peculiarly well-suited to meet these requirements.

The baptist Vision

In his (projected) three-volume systematic theology,[32] McClendon set out to capture the defining features of the tradition stemming from or similar to the anabaptist (or radical) reformation movement of the sixteenth century. This tradition includes a varied collection of church bodies, including Baptists (to the extent that they have not adopted Reformed ecclesiology and theology), Mennonites, Brethren, and some Pentecostals, Disciples, and intentional communities. Earlier writers had attempted to characterize this form of church life as 'biblicist,' but all churches would claim their own way as the (or a) biblical way. Consequently McClendon saw the need for an account of the particular relation in which baptists (translation of the German *Täufer*) stand to the texts. It was for this purpose that he developed his notion of the baptist vision. Such a vision should be "the guiding stimulus by which a people ... shape their life and thought.... [O]nce acknowledged for what it is, it should serve as the touchstone by which authentic baptist life is discovered and described, and also as the organizing principle around which a genuine baptist theology can take shape.[33]

McClendon's proposal can be expressed, he says, as a "hermeneutical motto," which is shared awareness of *the present Christian community as the primitive community and the eschatological community.* In other words: "the church now is the primitive church and the church on the day of judgment is the church now; the obedience and liberty of the followers of Jesus of Nazareth is *our* liberty, our obedience."[34]

McClendon claims that this is the common reading strategy found *within* Scripture. When Peter, on Pentecost, says: "this is that which has been spoken through the prophet Joel" (Acts 2:16) he is applying language about one set of events, addressed to one community, to another set of events, speaking it to another community in a later set of circumstances. McClendon quotes Davie Napier, who says:

> we have in the Old Testament no past which has not already been appropriated in the present, and so appropriated as to *be* in the

265

present, to *live* in the present. [The past] *was* past, but now *is*. . . .
As such it is not so much . . . merely memorialized as reexperi-
enced—created and lived again.[35]

So we have here a reading strategy that satisfies the first
requirement for Austinian uptake at this end of the historical
process. We might describe it as the present church's *determination*
to take the texts to be addressed to itself, despite awareness of
historical distance, so that the illocutionary force *then* is to be the
illocutionary force *now for us.*

The Church Now as the Primitive Church

The second requirement for uptake is that the church now be,
in some sense, the same interpretive community as the primitive
church, and McClendon's baptist vision makes provision for this
requirement as well. However, the baptist vision is no naive denial
of history. There are inevitable differences between then and now:
different customs, different cultures, even different world views,
categorial frameworks. What we must see, then, is the sense in
which *relevant* circumstances can be similar enough to allow for
uptake. We can investigate this requirement by considering,
again, the dimensions within which the conditions fall for a happy
speech act.

Conventions

From a speech-act perspective, translators and exegetes have
the same role to play as they do under the guidance of any
hermeneutic theory. Their job is to bring it about that author and
reader share a common language and to clue the contemporary
reader in on the linguistic conventions of the author's day.

But to learn a language—that is, to learn its 'grammar' in the
philosophical sense—is to learn a world view. Here we can see the
relevance of George Lindbeck's claim that texts *create a world.* To
understand biblical language is to enter sympathetically into that
world, just as one becomes *absorbed* in a good novel.[36] This reading
strategy is the opposite of that of modern interpreters, for whom
the goal was to bring the Bible into the modern world; to understand it by the lights of modern thought.

At least as important for entering the world of the Bible,
though, is taking up the *practices* of the primitive church. "I bid

three hearts" cannot succeed as a speech act if there is no bridge game in progress. Likewise, "Do this in remembrance of me" cannot succeed apart from the eucharistic context; Paul's pleas for orderly worship cannot succeed where there is no worship. So we can conclude that, in general, the speech acts of the Bible cannot succeed if the present church is not actively engaged in an attempt to recreate the practices, the forms of life, of the primitive church.

This may raise a question, though: Does not engagement in the practices of primitive Christianity presuppose that we already know the meaning of New Testament texts? Here we find a baptist version of the hermeneutic circle. Historical criticism helps to recover the practices of the early church in their own setting; attempting to live out those practices in our contemporary setting sensitizes us to new meanings in the texts. The New Testament churches were not perfect—they were struggling to become the Church. Insofar as we, too, are struggling to become the Church, we will be better able to hear what the texts are saying, and as a consequence better able in the future to 'perform the Scriptures.'

Referential Conditions

A third condition for understanding the speech acts of the Bible is knowledge of the original historical context, and here historical methodologies play their usual role.

However, even with attention to all of these conditions, under-standing, uptake, will usually not be perfect or complete. Yet the point of this discussion is that current readers can put themselves in better or worse positions to understand the biblical texts. While the solitary scholar will still have much to offer—especially for helping to bring about shared linguistic skills—to the extent that she is alienated from the practical life of the church, she will be in a disadvantaged position for uptake. Church bodies that do not insist on discipleship, or that see their forms of life as having legitimately evolved away from the practices of the early church, will likewise be disadvantaged.[37] They will have their own inter-pretive strategies, which, according to Fish, should be expected to yield different readings—and all the more is this the case for those outside of the Christian tradition altogether.

Conclusion

In our day there appears to be a more pressing need than ever for increased confidence in the usability of the biblical texts. Many take postmodern philosophical moves to be the *cause* of skepticism with regard to the Bible, skepticism with regard to truth claims, and now a radical skepticism about whether we can even know the meaning of the biblical texts. There is a deep irony in this suspicion, however. I would argue that what we have seen in modern history is the following: Modern philosophers first devised theories of knowledge and then related theories of language (meaning). As it turns out, foundationalist accounts of knowledge have not worked well for theologians; it has not been possible to reconstruct theological knowledge on the basis of the sort of indubitable foundations, either experiential or scriptural, that modern theories of knowledge seemed to require.[38] The result has been growing skepticism regarding theology's truth claims, and finally (for many) the relegation of theology to the expressivist domain, where the categories of truth and falsity do not even apply.

However, since the middle of this century, philosophers have begun calling modern assumptions about knowledge into question, and have worked to devise new accounts of the nature of knowledge, how it is justified, what we mean in calling a belief 'true.' Two factors have driven this change. First, foundationalist theories of knowledge continued to have internal problems, and after three hundred years of trying, philosophers have rightly begun to suspect that the problems are insoluble. Second, it has become more and more obvious that foundationalist theories do not adequately describe the acquisition or justification of our most highly respected bodies of knowledge, namely, the sciences. As Thomas Kuhn has pointed out, if science fails to fit our current theories of rationality, then we have a choice: we can either say that science is irrational, or we can conclude that the theories of rationality need to be changed. More and more, philosophers are opting for the latter.

Those who would claim that the new non-foundationalist (holist) theories of knowledge are the cause of relativism are making a mistake. Relativism arises for foundationalists when no single set of indubitable foundations can be found. The history of

modern epistemology and philosophy of science shows that pur-
ported foundations (1) turn out to depend on the supposed non-
foundational knowledge for acceptance, or (2) turn out not to be
indubitable, or (3) if they are indubitable turn out to be useless,
since there is no reliable way to argue from them to any interesting
conclusions. So it is the 'facts' of our epistemic predicament *along
with the assumption that there must be foundations* that produces
skepticism and relativism.

To foundationalists, holists sound like relativists because they
admit there are no foundations. Now, some holists are relativists,
but they need not be. The absence of foundations entails relativism
only if foundationalism is true. Holists deny the foundationalist
assumption, and many go on to provide non-relativist accounts of
knowledge.[39]

There is a parallel account to be given of developments in the
philosophy of language. Moderns developed theories of language
whereby language is meaningful only if it refers to an external,
'experienceable' reality (or, alternatively, if it expresses the intention of the author or speaker). But critics have shown that hermeneutic theories aiming at the recovery of historical referents or
authorial intentions run into grave difficulties. One might say that
these strategies have turned out not to reveal solid 'foundations'
for interpretation of texts. Post-structuralist literary critics have
shown, as well, that the literal sense of the words is an equally
unreliable 'foundation.' But the situation is parallel to that of
science and theories of rationality. If modern theories of meaning,
combined with the 'epistemic facts' regarding texts, leads to the
conclusion that no text has a fixed meaning, we have two options:
to stand by modern theories of language (as the deconstructionists
do, unwittingly) or to provide more adequate theories of language
and meaning. My claim in this paper is that Austin, and McClendon and Smith, and the later Fish have already supplied a more
adequate theory of language. All that remains is to exploit it
(further) for approaching problems of biblical interpretation.

So far I have spoken of theories of knowledge and theories of
language as though they merely describe our practices of knowl-
edge- and meaning-making. But of course, theory and practice
interact: philosophies of science shape scientific research and
reporting; theories of hermeneutics shape scholars' approaches to

the texts. If, following Austin, we say that meaning is found primarily in what the text *does*, this has consequences for our use of the texts, as scholars and as members of churches. *If the texts' ability to perform a definite speech act depends upon the existence of a community with shared conventions and proper dispositions, then textual stability is in large measure a function, not of theories of interpretation, but of how interpretive communities choose to live.*[40] An Austinian theory of language calls upon Christians to adopt the stance toward the texts that McClendon describes as the hermeneutic principle of the baptist vision: "This is that." The illocutionary force then is the illocutionary force for us here and now; the form of life of the church here and now is to be that of the primitive church. In this motto we find the missing piece of the contemporary hermeneutic puzzle.

EDUCATION WITHOUT FOUNDATIONS

Schooling for the Tournament of Narratives: Postmodernism and the Idea of the Christian College

Charles Scriven

We exist, James McClendon, Jr., remarks, "as in a tournament of narratives."[1] Whatever idea or possibility confronts us, the narratives we identify with shape how we think and feel and act. Narratives are bedrock for both personal and communal frame of mind—for insight, for attitude, for conduct.

These narratives are many—across the total human landscape, beyond counting. Frequently, like contenders in a tournament, they conflict with one another, one story feeding this loyalty or outlook and another that. The result is variety in human culture, often welcome and often winsome. But more than anyone would like the conflict of narratives feeds strife as well, including violent strife. Differences of faith, politics, morality, and custom occasion charm—and bloodshed.

Under these conditions, how ought the church to train its young adults for life and work? How can church-sponsored colleges faithfully address the "critical years" of post-adolescence when, as Sharon Parks writes, the emerging self is especially open to "life-transforming vision"?[2] Amid sweeping pluralism, what form should Christian higher education take?

The short answer, I will argue here, is that teaching and learning in the Christian setting, including the Christian college, should honor and reflect the church's narrative. In accordance with that narrative, Christian higher education should not only display (in its own way) the church's true identity, it should be a deliberate strategy for building and bracing the circle of disciples. In McClendon's metaphor, the Christian college should be a means of churchly struggle in the tournament of narratives.

To put it yet another way, what I will claim here is that Christian colleges, without embarrassment and without apology, should be *partisan*. The claim entails a challenge both to some key assumptions of modern liberalism and to certain excesses of the newer, postmodern thinking. Yet even though it runs counter to the commonplace, it is plausible. And at a time when standard assumptions about higher education seem increasingly doubtful, even destructive, the claim is important.

For the idea of partisan higher education, the severest clash is with modern liberalism. As the Enlightenment took hold, the liberal ideal grew into, and substantially remains, the conventional wisdom in the West. Although the Christian monastery, with its explicit (and partisan) Christian discipline, was the "taproot," as Parker Palmer says, of today's educational institutions,[3] under the influence of the Enlightenment it came to be a symbol of schooling misconceived. In the United States, for example, the first colleges and universities were sponsored by churches, and were immersed in the piety of these churches.[4] But as modern assumptions gained wider currency, the connection between higher learning and religious training began more and more to be seen as an obstacle for education, not an advantage. At his inauguration in 1869 Charles Eliot, the Harvard president who cut the last links between the university and its original Christian patrons, mocked the teaching that tries to instill some *particular* set of beliefs about what is good and true. That may be "logical and appropriate in a convent, or a seminary for priests," he said, but it is "intolerable" in universities.[5] Eliot perhaps gleaned his comparison from Cardinal Newman, who in *The Idea of the University* had declared more than a decade earlier that the university is neither a convent nor a seminary.[6] In any case, the misgivings about religious training in higher education were taking an ever-stronger hold. In 1904 DeWitt Hyde, who studied at Harvard while Eliot was there and soon afterward became the president of Bowdoin College, called the "narrowness" he associated with church colleges "utterly incompatible" with responsible higher education. "A church university," he declaimed, "is a contradiction in terms."[7]

Now, well toward the end of the twentieth century, these sentiments still predominate. Partisan education, especially in matters religious and moral, is seen widely to be, at best, narrow, and, at worst, bigoted and victimizing. Responsible teaching does not inculcate a particular point of view or set of virtues; it rather imparts knowledge and skills sufficient, as Mortimer Kadesh writes, to enable the self to criticize its "social milieu" and to "form" its being and "determine" its wants.[8] Even a teacher at a Southern Baptist college echoes the conventional understanding: "It's not my job as a professor to tell [students] what to think," the teacher told *The Chronicle of Higher Education* recently, "it's my job to *make* them think."[9]

In a tournament of narratives, the professor's remark sounds like a recipe for defeat. But what matters as much or more is this: the antipathy to the partisan in the remark reflects a deception, or self-deception, and jeopardizes rather than enhances education for life and work.

As I have intimated, the background of this antipathy to the partisan is the Enlightenment. Kant declared that movement's ideal of the autonomous individual when he called his readers to thrust off dependence on others for direction. " 'Have courage to use your own reason!'—that," he said, "is the motto of the Enlightenment."[10] With the ensuing shift to the self-governing, or self-defining, individual the meaning of respect for others veered toward non-interference, or even neutrality, with respect to differences of outlook and conviction. The partisan was now bad manners. Conflict was to be domesticated.

The motive was admirable. The Enlightenment grew into full flower on blood-soaked soil. The Thirty Years' War, religion-stoked and staggering in its brutality and senselessness, ended (more or less) in 1648, endowing Europe with a need and a lively desire for peace, or at least respite. Blood-letting had failed to resolve the doctrinal discord from which it sprang. As Stephen

Toulmin writes, circumstances called for a means of determining truth that "was independent of, and neutral between, particular religious loyalties."[11]

The call to thrust off dependence, including dependence on religious authority, displayed the changed conception of rationality that was emerging under the pressure of Europe's agony. Sixteenth century writers such as Montaigne had said that the human condition necessitates uncertainty, ambiguity, and differences of opinion. Descartes, on the other hand, argued that foundations for certainty can be found by *starting* with ideas so clear and distinct to any reflective person as to be (in Toulmin's phrase) "cultural universals."[12] Building from these basic ideas and employing geometrically rigorous forms of argument, a rationality transcending the partisan and available to all humanity could provide entree to universal knowledge. The hope was that by freeing people from the authority (and fanaticism) of particular points of view the Enlightenment could reduce tribal and institutional violence. With persons and communities tolerant of difference and tranquil in diversity, humanity could progress toward the agreement—and peace—inherent in the possibility of universal knowledge.

But the result of Enlightenment conceptions of autonomy and rationality did not conform, and could not conform, to the hope. Consider first personal autonomy, the idea of the individual as self-governing and self-defining, with no need to depend upon others for direction. This idea subverts—indeed, it was *meant* to subvert—accountability to authority, whether religious, familial, or communal. Autonomy was needed, so the thinking went, in order to fend off acquiescence to inherited prejudice and folly. But autonomy also subverts the sustenance needed by the self in order to repel moral illiteracy, rationalization, and weakness of will. This is no mere glitch in the theory, for such moral sustenance is basic. And today, amid alarming and apparently increasing moral ruin, it is more and more preposterous to think otherwise. In truth, the idea of the autonomous self is bound, despite the hopes surrounding it, to enervate morality and to aggravate the discord and strife that attend immorality. Accountability itself may be corrupting, as when the authority behind it, religious or otherwise, is corrupt. But to live without accountability is inescapably corrupting.

The doctrine of personal autonomy was a mistake for another, even more fundamental, reason. It reflected the idea of a universal rationality providing entree to universal knowledge, but such a rationality does not exist. Human languages and the various vernaculars within these languages give particular peoples, each with the particular narratives they have lived and told, the ability to communicate; each language and vernacular bears the freight of stories past and so gives every user an inherited frame of mind. This does not necessarily close off conversation with those whose inheritance is different, but it does mean no neutral vantage point exists from which the self may practice its alleged autonomy. No clear and distinct foundational ideas, universally available, present themselves for autonomous consideration. The direction of others is inherent in every language and touches every language user, making all our thinking, even our most basic thinking, perspectival. In a world of many languages and histories, there can be no universal rationality or universal knowledge. How and what we think at all times reflects a storied past.

The Enlightenment itself is a story lived and told, itself one narrative in the tournament of narratives. The doctrine of peace through personal autonomy and universal knowledge is a perspective, one whose claims, curiously enough, meet with defeat just because of this. Even when the point about perspective goes unacknowledged, the doctrine, with its insistent divinization of the self and denigration of community, evokes disagreement, and to harsh critics appears, indeed, to be a manipulative ideology. The disagreement persists and by persisting underscores the implausibility of the central claims.

The point, it develops, is not *whether* to be partisan but *how*.

Nevertheless, the narrative that shapes the dominant version of higher education continues to be that of the Enlightenment. The debate over "political correctness" sweeping the campus and the wider culture betrays, it is true, growing uneasiness about standard educational assumptions. Still, the curriculum usually comes across as a kind of intellectual bazaar, catering, at least ostensibly, to autonomous selves in the process of forming their being and determining their wants without "direction" (as Kant put it) from others. Students are still said to be learning how to think, not what to think. It is still considered "narrow" and "sectarian" to inculcate a particular point of view.

This holds especially if the point of view involves religious or moral commitment. On these matters in particular, diversity is the prevailing ideal. Every point of view is welcome, but each must be presented as a commodity available to students for their own personal choice.[13] Except in defense of diversity itself, it is bad manners, and bad education, to be partisan.

Just as it is unseemly to instill in students a particular point of view, so it is unseemly to train them in a particular way of life, or discipline, or set of virtues. Despite the fact that learning itself presupposes certain virtues, such as respect and honesty, Jacques Barzun writes that attempting

> to inculcate directly, as a subject of instruction, any set of personal, social, or political virtues is either indoctrination or foolery. In both cases it is something other than schooling.

The "prime object" of education, he declares a few lines later, is "the removal of ignorance."[14]

Other modern educators do, however, connect virtue and learning in the college or university. Ernest Boyer, for example, argues that the overarching purpose of schooling is the training of "informed, critical citizens." He means persons who "are able to judge for themselves and have the courage and confidence to think for themselves."[15] Boyer does not specify further what kind of citizens higher education should produce, but recognizes that the liberal ideal of critical skill is in its own right a feature of the self, a trait of character, a virtue. It is something to be instilled. Education is more than removing ignorance; it is shaping persons.

In the case of Mortimer Kadesh, sympathy for education as shaping persons is more pronounced. His book *Toward an Ethic of Higher Education* explicitly argues that "higher education *is* education for virtue," although it is other things as well.[16] And beyond saying that the college experience should instill "habits of reasonable criticism" and the ability, in a phrase from James Joyce, "'to forge . . . the uncreated conscience'" of the race,[17] Kadesh explores ways in which it may engender other virtues: "compassion," the "absence" of "snobbery," the capacity for "self-expression in relation to others," the "disposition to choose the better over the worse."[18]

But these are virtues Kadesh thinks of as a desired outcome of liberal, or Enlightenment, education. He would still recoil from college teaching configured specifically *for* soldiers, say, or Christians, and meant to train them in their specific way of life. As he puts it, "[R]eligious or military education, however demanding or praiseworthy they may sometimes be, are not in general 'liberal.'"[19]

This is true, but it is not damning. As I have suggested, liberal education is itself a storied point of view, so that "liberal" cannot entail immaculate neutrality or objectivity. Despite this, however, liberal education claims neutrality with respect to certain points of view, especially those involving religious or moral commitment. And it tosses out the gibe "sectarian" (here meaning narrow or bigoted) to describe institutions that openly align themselves with some such point of view.

The deception in all this, or self-deception, is palpable. But antipathy to the partisan jeopardizes education in other ways as well. For one thing, it trivializes differences. When disagreements over faith, politics, morality, and custom flame up in violent strife, as they often do, it is disingenuous to speak, in the customary, bleached-out phraseology, of mere "competing value systems," as though students were consumers meant to pick and choose like shoppers in a marketplace. To be or feign to be impartial is to push the truth away, to keep it at a distance. It is a kind of indifference, and it communicates indifference.

Far from being innocuous, the indifference damages humanity, feeding a kind of ongoing tragedy of the too-open mind. When in matters of faith and morals education must be too open to contain conviction, it can no longer fight off the tendency to spiritual coma that seems in any case to bedevil contemporary culture. Differences trivialized by neutrality feed the trivialization of morality itself—and examples abound: this is an age when ethical judgments can seem repressive at an incest trial, when "standards" at media command posts consist in whatever the market will bear, when lawmakers wring their hands over teen violence and cast their votes for murder weapons. The situation recalls what Yeats, in "The Second Coming," declared of an age without conviction: "Mere anarchy is loosed upon the world, / The blood-dimmed tide is loosed . . . ."

Suspicion of commitment in the classroom does not, of course, produce students with no biases at all; it rather favors their "assimilation," as Patricia Beattie Jung writes, to the "prevailing cultural ethos."[20] The fiction of neutrality tends to baptize the status quo, with its implicit morality or immorality, and to nullify the stark alternatives. Antipathy to the partisan turns out, then, not just to trivialize differences, but also to protect whatever now predominates. Despite the homage paid to criticism, it is fundamentally conservative.

What this entire criticism of liberal education displays is the emerging awareness that the modern era, heralded by Descartes and the Enlightenment, is now passing. The modern outlook, as Kant's Enlightenment motto illustrates, involved a turn away from the authority of tradition and community. The self became the new focus and the new authority. Philosophers at first interpreted the shift optimistically, seeing it, for example, as providing a new and firmer footing for the pursuit of knowledge. Epistemology, indeed, was a dominant concern, but the conversation came in due course to nourish skepticism, too, most famously, perhaps, about knowledge of God but also about knowledge in general. Misgivings about the individual's ability to be, or to find, a foundation for indubitable knowledge sharpened as scholars began to focus on how much a person's outlook is shaped by the history behind it. The realization emerged that outlooks are bequeathed to individuals, not discovered or created by them. How we see and live depends on the background—family, community, history—we each absorb growing up with our particular language and culture. Conversations among persons who see and live differently may occur. They may involve challenges to belief, attempts at justification, adjustments of conviction. But always the beginning point—the "given," as Wittgenstein wrote—must be the community or communities in the background, the already existing "forms of life" that underlie all human action and interaction.[21]

Over the past forty years or so, philosophers have become increasingly alert to the shift from the modern to the "postmodern," as the new awareness is often called. Among its hallmarks, one is the belief, reflected in the criticism so far, that no individual has access to a neutral standpoint from which to learn and know objectively. Even the "foundations" of knowledge, the ideas thought to be the starting point of all our searching, cannot be fully secure, fully beyond question.

Another postmodern hallmark, again reflected in the criticism so far, is recognition of what Nancey Murphy calls "the importance and irreducibility of community."[22] Both the knowledge we have and the skills we practice depend on a legacy bequeathed by, and embraced in, the company of others. Thus the Enlightenment premise of a universal rationality providing entree to universal knowledge collapses. Systems of thought and practice characteristic of particular communities may involve differences too deep to be adjudicated or even understood through conversation alone. With sufficiently different backgrounds, interlocutors may fail to understand each other because they think in different ways, because their forms of rationality conflict.

Even science, in popular imagination the paragon of the knowledge enterprise, is now seen as rooted in tradition and community. As Thomas Kuhn argued in *The Structure of Scientific Revolutions*, what problems are discerned, and how these problems are resolved, reflects a history of investigation and analysis. Along that history, the work of science practitioners reflects the "paradigm" in which they are immersed, the examples, that is, of problem solution (and the related laws, theories, applications and instrumentation) that are standard at their time and place in their field of inquiry. In the daily practice of problem-solving, in other words, a comprehensive view of the subject matter is used, and indeed *assumed*.[23] Although shifts occur over time, with new paradigms replacing old ones, at no point does the individual scientist work from a neutral standpoint or in complete independence of tradition and community.

Does this postmodern shift add up to irrationalism, to the tribalization, as one might say, of knowledge? Does it mean thoughtful conversation across lines of difference can move neither us nor those from whom we differ? Does it leave mere subjectivity in its wake, and make intellectual accountability a pipe dream?

Some say Yes. Nietzsche, who in the nineteenth century anticipated the shift to the postmodern, believed that the ideas we consider true are fixed and binding merely from long usage and endorsement within a particular group. One may employ strategies to promote or subvert a point of view, but it is impossible to adjudicate among contending points of view. So-called "truths" are only fictions to assist the "will to power," conventions whose conventionality has been forgotten.

Postmodernists today understand that the word "true," although used to commend or endorse claims about the world, does not betoken literal correspondence between the claims and the reality that exists in independence of human seeing. Statements accepted as true reflect agreement, or "prejudice," within a social circle; there is no way to provide for their "objective" legitimation. Radical postmodernists proceed from this to outright denial of intellectual accountability across the lines of human difference. Some say we do not need consensus anyway, and should forswear attempts to reach it. Lyotard believes, indeed, that "[w]orking towards consensus is not nice even if you can get it: for it would impose a kind of epistemological 'terror', stifling further experiments of thought."[24]

Others, however, though fully aware of the impossibility of "objective" knowledge, still make vigorous arguments for intellectual accountability. Sheer consent to rival truth claims is not just the embrace of charming or fertile disagreement; it is surrender to injustice and bloodshed, for these are what differences of faith, politics, morality, and custom all too often bring about. Writers such as MacIntyre, McClendon, and Murphy, who will figure prominently in what follows, argue that even though we see the world through our inherited frameworks, no framework must be a prisonhouse. It is possible and important that conversation, both within and across the lines of human difference, should yield new increments of understanding and agreement. The shift to the postmodern does not, in other words, compel anarchy and resignation with respect to human knowledge.

My focus is the idea of the Christian college. I do not say "church-related college" because that phrase is bland and suggests institutions that walk on apologetic tiptoes instead of striding with firm steps. Michael Cartwright dismisses the phrase "Christian college" for its current connotation of "intellectual retreat,"[25] and I acknowledge such retreat as a grave danger in Christian education, though no graver, certainly, than convictional retreat. My point is to suggest the outlines of a postmodern conception of intellectual *accountability* for colleges of explicit Christian *commitment*. How can higher education under the church's auspices contend responsibly—with no retreat of mind or heart—in the human tournament of narratives? How can it nourish post-adolescent minds with its own distinctive vision? How can it be partisan and still hold itself responsible to justify its partisan convictions?

To begin, it must be said unmistakably that the partisanship in question is countercultural. From the biblical narrative this is obvious enough: solidarity with God and God's Messiah means dissent from the wider world. Nevertheless, the lure of respectability within the surrounding, dominant culture has always tantalized the Christian community. As McClendon writes,

> The church's story will not interpret the world to the world's satisfaction. Hence there is a *temptation* (no weaker word will do) for the church to deny her 'counter, original, spare, strange' starting point in Abraham and Jesus and to give instead a self-account or theology that will seem true to the world on the world's own present terms.[26]

What is true for the church is true for its colleges. Here, too, the endurance of distinctively Christian vision must be a matter of deliberate design. In its decisions about personnel, curriculum, and student life, the Christian college must renounce congenial neutrality, what is in any case artifice and self-deception, and embrace without apology its own heritage and discipline. In the tournament of narratives, anything less is a recipe for defeat. Anything less marks capitulation to "the unstoried blandness (and the mortal terrors) of late-twentieth-century liberal individualism."[27]

In the college setting, learning takes place under the leadership of teachers. So if the countercultural, the embrace of distinctive vision, is crucial for responsible Christian partisanship, a corresponding view of the teaching function is also crucial. In the guidance and inspiration of students, intellectual accountability allows, and indeed requires, commitment to a particular point of view.

This means acknowledging the self-deception and emptiness in the platitude about teaching students how to think, not what to

think. The platitude fits neatly with the Enlightenment antago-
nism toward authority and obsession with personal autonomy. It
reflects as well the earlier Socratic form of moral education, which
trained students for criticism of convention without offering a
positive account of the good in human life. The overall impact of
a purely negative approach, as writers of Socrates'sown era realized, was to leave students without reasons for preferring one way
of life to another, and thus without reasons to fend off the blan-
dishments of purely private satisfaction.[28]

Not only in moral training but in all the academic disciplines,
including science, a purely negative procedure yields no depth of
understanding. As Alasdair MacIntyre argues, the effective in-
quirer must first of all have been initiated into a particular community of investigation, into a "particular history of thought and
practice." It is otherwise impossible to know *how* to "rescrutinize"
the theories and arguments that have so far taken hold in that
community, and thus impossible to make new advances in awareness and comprehension.[29] Science illustrates the point convinc-
ingly: any research program reflects to one degree or other some
positive understanding, some "paradigm," of scientific thought
and practice. And any program worth pursuing must hold out
realistic hope of progress toward deeper understanding.[30]

Knowing how to think, then, presupposes knowing what to
think. It presupposes some partisan account of the subject matter,
some positive immersion into a tradition. Being partisan may, it
is true, slump into narrow indoctrination. But it doesn't have to,
and responsible partisanship is in any case fundamental: nothing
positive can happen without it. The road to enlightenment requires advocacy as well as criticism. This holds for moral training,
for science, and for every other discipline.

Responsible partisanship engages the whole person. Yet another respect in which the learning environment at Christian
institutions must swim against the current is in the attention paid
to the total way of life—not just technical, calculating intellect but
also feelings, imagination, habits, and virtues. The mere removal
of ignorance—what Jacques Barzun reveres as the "prime object"
of education—calls for such attention, anyway, since study itself
is a discipline involving virtues. Just paying attention and seeing
clearly—traits important for scholarship as well as moral

growth—require emotional involvement. As Martha Nussbaum argues, interpreting Aristotle, a person may know something as a fact—a connection as father or mother, say, to a child; or the benefit of unearned privilege relative to others in one's society—yet fail to take in the fact "in a full-blooded way," fail to confront or acknowledge what it means and what response it calls for. When a person lacks "the heart's confrontation" with what lies open to view, the deficit narrows vision and foils insight. Perception, to be complete, must involve "emotional and imaginative, as well as intellectual, components."[31]

But as with the bare noticing of facts, so with the emotion and imagination that deepen our perception: they, too, reflect personal experience over time. Emotion and imagination evince stories heard and lived. They reveal communal ways of life. They make manifest the past and present habits, duties and affiliations that constitute the evolving self. All this signals the need for attention to the whole person. Education must concern itself with character, with the total way of life. This matters, indeed, for the mere removal of ignorance; for positive enlightenment, it matters all the more.

McClendon writes about the school in Alexandria where Origen, the great Bible scholar and theologian, first gained fame as a teacher. He told his students no topic or question or opinion was off limits, but at the same time took an unmistakably partisan position. By instruction and example, he sought to instill the theory and practice of Christianity and to model an alliance of piety and scholarship. To him, the school was a training ground; its goal was the formation of lives that would honor and reflect the church's narrative.[32]

The same spirit and goal must infuse the responsible partisanship of Christian colleges today. If all education, to be complete, must engage the whole person, Christian education must do so in a manner appropriate to its own struggle in the tournament of narratives. It must acknowledge conflict, confront conflict, initiate students into conflict. Masking over differences feeds apathy by pushing truth away, whereas the point is to nourish passion and involvement.

In the second volume of his *Systematic Theology* McClendon says that Jesus enrolled his followers "as students in his school, his open air, learn-by-doing, movable, life-changing dialogue." The purpose was "training" for world-changing witness; the method was "costly apprenticeship." Then he alludes to blind Bartimaeus, said by Mark to have received his sight from Jesus and immediately followed him on his dangerous mission to Jerusalem. On the view suggested by the story, declares McClendon, "enlistment and scholarship are integral parts of one whole." Bartimaeus was "the paradigmatic Christian scholar."[33]

MacIntyre, who himself suggests the need for "rival universities," says one task of responsible partisanship is "to enter into controversy with other rival standpoints." This must be done in order to challenge the rival standpoint, but also in order to test one's own account against "the strongest possible objections" against it.[34] The pairing of enlistment and scholarship by no means entails, in other words, a flight from challenges or a refusal to give reasons and make adjustments. Within limits required by the maintenance of basic identity, the Christian college, like a responsibly partisan journal or newspaper, must tolerate—must, indeed, seek out—lively confrontation with other points of view. This can happen, not just in the classroom or library, but through the selection of students or even faculty. Postmodern awareness puts the difficulty of the knowledge enterprise in bold relief, but accountability is still vital. Convictions must still be justified. To be responsible, partisan higher education must provide, or better, be, a context for accountability.

In certain academic disciplines and certain aspects of collegiate bureaucracy, the Christian institution may find itself in virtual consensus with models dominant in the surrounding culture. Consider the natural sciences. Here the Christian setting may evoke a distinctive framework for instruction—it may, for example, lead teachers to discourage the use of scientific knowledge for violent purposes—but the course content will no doubt reflect what broadly respected authorities have had to say. At the points, however, of profound difference—in the human sciences and the humanities; in the administration of student life—the only responsible conduct in the face of challenge is honest conversation. And this means readiness "to amplify, explain, defend, and, if necessary, either modify or abandon" what one believes.[35]

In her book *Theology in the Age of Scientific Reasoning*, Murphy argues that the right method for defending Christian convictions is exactly analogous to the scientific method. She writes from a postmodern point of view and relies on the distinguished philosopher of science, Imre Lakatos. Christian communities, she says, are "experiments" in a "research program." The program has to do with the claims of the Gospel. As in productive science, the convictions central to the Gospel must be held tenaciously. Secondary convictions may be held less tenaciously, but all—the central as well as the secondary—must be willingly subjected to testing. The testing is in the living out of Christian life, and in the meeting of objections to the beliefs and practices associated with that life. The objections are met either by displaying, through words or deeds, their deficiency, or by attempting to make adequate adjustments. Over the long run, evidence accrues that counts for or against the secondary or even the central convictions. The intent and hope, always, is that "new and more consistent models of the Christian theory" may emerge.[36]

A paragraph gives short shrift to the nuance and complexity of Murphy's argument. She means to embrace the postmodern awareness of the limits and uncertainty of human knowledge while arguing for standards of evidential reasoning that defeat "total relativism" and reclaim accountability. Justifications cannot be absolute, even in the natural sciences. In the domain of moral and spiritual conviction, as in the human sciences, the difficulties are even greater. But when challenges are sufficiently understood to cause dismay—a common enough experience—they must be dealt with through honest, open conversation. The attempted justifications, as McClendon writes in his own discussion of these matters, may seem acceptable and effective only in the eyes of the person or community being challenged.[37] But the effort of justification, and the intent of framing new and more consist models of the Christian theory, must be embraced. Otherwise, the partisanship so necessary for growth in knowledge becomes a barrier to growth and ceases to be responsible.

For colleges of explicit Christian commitment, then, intellectual accountability requires a countercultural frame of mind, a deliberate advocacy of the church's distinctive belief and practice and a willing dissent from the wider world. Teachers should be protagonists. They should engage the whole person, intellect and character alike. They should acknowledge and participate in conflict. They should meet challenges with attempted justifications. In these ways colleges that honor and reflect the church's narrative can address the "critical years" of post-adolescence with "life-transforming vision." In these ways, following their particular purpose of education, they can embody and refine the practices of teaching and learning and thus create standards for these activities that assist congregations and eventually the wider world.

The genesis of modernity was, substantially, a hope for peace. But the dream of resolving discord through a universal rationality generating universal knowledge proved elusive. The attempt to realize the dream proved self-deceptive and, all too often, oppressive, not just in its hostility to differentiation but also in its drift toward compelled uniformity. My argument for partisan education is an acknowledgment, as Toulmin puts it, "of the unavoidable complexities of concrete human experience."[38] But as a call for responsible partisanship, it is also an evocation of a humane approach to discord: honest partisanship, involving mind and heart alike, fused with honest conversation and shorn of the need to violently coerce. Here higher education can be a beacon—and especially Christian higher education, whose narrative, in decidedly *un*modern fashion, calls its partisans to peaceable and prayerful regard for those with whom it differs, including its mortal enemies.

The narrative's point is not resignation, it is transformation. In a sometimes winsome but often violent tournament of narratives, colleges embracing such an approach to discord and such a hope of transformation may and must stand tall.

Discipleship: Basing One Life on Another—It's Not What You Know, It's Who You Know

Michael Goldberg

Moses received Torah from Sinai, and he passed it on to Joshua, Joshua to the elders, the elders to the prophets, and the prophets passed it on to the men of the Great Assembly [who] said: 'Raise up many disciples . . .'

Avot 1:1

I want my students to grow up to become just like me . . . each in his or her own way.

James Wm. McClendon, Jr.

Two Rival Versions of Education

From the vantage point of most contemporary institutions of higher learning, the quotation from Avot must seem unbelievably naive while McClendon's quote cannot help but appear incredibly pretentious. From the academy's perspective, we could hardly pick shakier ground than the shifting unpredictability of human life on which to base our claims to knowledge about self and world—let alone about God. As Stephen Toulmin has pointed out, ever since Descartes in 1630, would-be "moderns" have dreamt of a "rational method" so they might rest human knowledge on sure and certain foundations; in quest of their dream, such "foundationalists" have exalted the written over the oral, the universal over the particular, the general over the local, and the timeless over the timely.[1]

Moreover, says Toulmin, this "decontextualized ideal"—a staple of rationalist thought and action until well into the twentieth century—had many offshoots, one of which was Max Weber's view of the "rationalization" of social institutions, a notion which left "little room for cultural or personal idiosyncrasies."[2] Indeed, Weber's 1918 address, "*Wissenschaft als Beruf*," still stands as the statement nonpareil of the present-day academic vocation. In that address, as elsewhere, Weber conceived of the academic's quest for knowledge as an impersonal and solitary undertaking. Thus, for Weber, the phrase "academic community" referred

> not to specific webs of human beings working in close personal relationship to one another, but to such abstract entities as fields of study, scientific disciplines, and forms of rationality.[3]

Strikingly, in a Weberian conceptual world, we can find the term 'discipline' but never the word '*disciple*.' That is, while a student of Weber('s) might speak of being a 'Weberian,' such a one could never, *should* never, speak of being Weber's 'disciple'—at least, not without being arch. Indeed, to use that word in any serious or straightforward way would be immediately to reveal oneself as most definitely *not* following in 'the master's footsteps.' For Weber, mastering a discipline meant being able to follow a certain method in a certain academic field, a method which, as 'scientific,' provided a royal road to the truth independent of any single person or, for that matter, community of persons.

By contrast, arriving at the truth as traditionally understood by Jews and Christians, has hinged not so much on following a method as on *following the lives of other human beings.*[4] So, for instance, as McClendon has made clear, Dietrich Bonhoeffer's conception of Christian discipleship, which Bonhoeffer dubbed "*Nachfolge*"—literally, 'I follow after'—denoted "a communal discipline in which disciples watched over, corrected, and cared for one another."[5] For their part, Judaism's classical sages, the rabbis of the Talmud, believed that *Torah* can have no more fundamental basis for its transmission of the truth of human life than the point of contact where one life touches the next; as the rabbinic source from Avot makes clear, even God's teaching finally rests *in* and *on* human hands. From the classical rabbinic standpoint, any other foundation for teaching Torah spells death not only for Torah, but also for the way of life it seeks to engender.

Rabbinic Discipleship: Basing One Life on Another

For the scholar is like the Torah itself . . . and in its image . . . and as the Holy One, may he be blessed, decreed and gave the Torah to all of Israel, so he gave us the sages, and they are also the essence of Torah.

Rabbi Judah Loew of Prague

Classically, the students of Jewish tradition were called *talmidei chachamim*—'students of the wise'—and *not* students of some disembodied, impersonal 'Wisdom.' Hence, what title or term of address could have better suited that personal relationship of a student to a sage than 'Rabbi'—'*My* Master'? Conversely, how could such a sage's student possibly have been considered anything other than *his* disciple? Ultimately, the rabbis taught Torah not merely by discoursing about it. Instead, they disseminated Torah by *enacting* it. In the last analysis, they imparted Torah by *embodying* it.

The knowledge the rabbis held out to their communities was decidedly not academic, not essentially a knowing *that* but a knowing *how*. In other words, the tradition which the rabbis both created and transmitted was, in Terrence Tilley's felicitous phrase, "overarchingly practical."[6] But as Toulmin notes, from the seventeenth century on, "moderns" have tended to devalue the kind of knowledge that comes through practice. In Toulmin's view, post-1630 we have witnessed

> a historical shift from *practical* philosophy, whose issues arose out of clinical medicine, juridical procedure, moral case analysis, or the rhetorical force of oral reasoning, to a *theoretical* conception of philosophy: the effects of this shift were so deep and long-lasting that the revival of practical philosophy in our own day has taken many people by surprise.[7]

By contrast, the rabbis of the talmudic and medieval periods taught largely through their *practice of making judicial decisions*, whether those decisions were about the amount of damages to be paid in a tort case or about the degree of damage a Torah scroll might suffer and still be 'kosher.' It was just that kind of practical, community-forming knowledge that the rabbis tried to pass on to their disciples—as evidenced by the attention rabbinic sources in the Talmud give to the question of when and where a disciple might act like a master himself by giving practical, authoritative rulings of his own:

> A disciple must not rule [lit.: 'teach'] unless he gains permission from his rabbi. (Sanhedrin 5b)

> Said Rava, "To prevent the commission of a transgression, it is proper [for a disciple to render a ruling] even in his master's presence . . . [Generally, however,][8] in his [i.e., one's master's] presence, it is forbidden [to render a ruling] under the penalty of death; in his absence, it is [likewise] forbidden, but the death penalty is not incurred." (Eruvin 63a)

> Rabbi Joshua ben Korcha says: "From where do we infer that a disciple, sitting in his master's presence and seeing [in a pending case] the merit of the poor and the obligation of the rich, should not keep silent? [From Deut. 1:17] as it is said, 'You shall not fear the face of any man [i.e., even the 'face' (that is, the presence) of your rabbi].'" (Sanhedrin 6b)

What, then, prepared a student to become a rabbinic authority? If we were to base our answer on a contemporary model of 'professional training,' we would typically expect students (including so-called 'divinity students') to attend lectures, read the assigned texts, and take examinations to show they have 'mastered the material.' The rabbis, however, had markedly different expectations regarding mastery; for them, it entailed *service*:

> Even if one has learned Scripture and Mishna, if he has not served rabbinic scholars, he is still an ignoramus. (Berachot 47b)[9]

> Rabbi Joshua ben Levi said, "All manner of work which a servant does for his master a disciple does for his master . . . " (Ketubot 96a)

From the rabbis' standpoint, attending their discourses or judicial proceedings was only part of what discipleship entailed. *Attending to their lives* (in both senses!) was equally or even more important, because the rabbis' knowledge could only be taught *from life to life*.

Consequently, learning to be a rabbi required a practical course of study. For the aspiring rabbi, coming to know the truth of human life involved getting to know *a particular rabbi's way of life*:

> It has been taught: Rabbi Akiva said, "Once I went in after Rabbi Joshua to a toilet, and I learned . . . that it is proper to wipe with the left hand and not with the right." Ben Azzai replied to him, "Did you not act insolently toward your master?" He responded, "It was Torah, and I needed to learn." (Berachot 62a)

As before, we come across a source that must leave members of the academy shaking their heads in disbelief. From their perspective, Rabbi Akiva, no matter how great a sage within Jewish tradition, clearly failed to understand or respect the importance of 'boundaries.' Worse yet, the Talmud reports that Ben Azzai subsequently followed Rabbi Akiva's practical instruction by following *him* into a privy! And yet, that is precisely a key difference between a rabbinic model of learning and a Weberian one. One did not become a disciple with the goal of entering into some guild or elite circle of professional practitioners. On the contrary, *a disciple entered into the rabbis' community of practice with an eye toward extending the rabbis' practice(s) throughout the whole community of Israel.* The rabbis had in principle a specific educational goal: to make every Jew a rabbi. That is, so far as the rabbis were concerned, every Jew—ideally at least—could become an authoritative source about the proper way to put into practice the biblical mandate for the Jewish People to become "a *kingdom of priests* and a holy nation." (Ex. 19:6)[10]

As the rabbis' teaching about life could only be learned from their lives themselves, the relationship between rabbinic master and disciple could have been, and by all rights, should have been *life-shaping*. From the first to last, of central concern to the rabbis was the character of their disciples. More fundamentally, the rabbis and their disciples believed that the *torah* the rabbis taught had the power to *transform* character. Hence, that third-century rabbinic compilation, the Mishna, teaches:

> [If one comes upon] his father's lost property and his rabbi's lost property [and he can only restore the lost property of one of the two to its rightful owner], his rabbi's lost property takes precedence, for his father brought him to this world, but his rabbi brings him to the world to come. (Bava Metzia 2:11)

To speak of the rabbi/disciple relationship as analogous to one between a father and a son is no exaggeration. Typically, a disciple would study with, even live with, one master for several years.[11] During that period, not only would a disciple come to serve his sage devotedly, but a sage was also expected to show devotion to his student:

> There once was an incident with one of Rabbi Akiva's students who fell ill. The sages did not visit him. But when Rabbi Akiva went into [his house] to visit him . . . he became well. [The student] said to him My master, you have revived me! Rabbi Akiva then went outside and expounded, Whoever does not visit the sick is like someone who sheds blood. (Nedarim 40a)[12]

By going outside to make his teaching public, Rabbi Akiva once more revealed the rabbis' education program for what it truly was: a 'practicum' intended for a student population far wider than that of some elite disciple class alone. Rabbi Akiva's act of devotion practiced with regard to his disciple aimed at being a teaching to be put into practice throughout the community as a whole.

Here again, Weberian academics might balk: 'Just who did the rabbis think they were"? A string of rabbinic sources answers that question in no uncertain terms:

> Whoever welcomes his rabbi is like someone who welcomes the *Shechina* [i.e., God's Divine Presence]. (P.T. Eruvin 5a)

> Whoever takes issue with his rabbi is like someone who takes issue with the Shechina. . . . Whoever quarrels with his rabbi is like someone who quarrels with the Shechina. . . . Whoever complains about his rabbi is like someone who complains about the Shechina. . . . Whoever murmurs against his rabbi is like someone who murmurs against the Shechina. (Sanhedrin 110a)

> Reverence for [literally: 'fear of'] your rabbi is like reverence for Heaven. (Pesachim 108a)

Through Torah, the divinely-inspired teaching displayed in their own lives, the rabbis sought to show the Shechina, God's presence, at work in every aspect of life. They meant to extend that sanctifying presence to every corner of their disciples' lives, and ultimately, through "raising up many disciples" who would eventually spread throughout the Diaspora, to the lives of Jewish communities in every corner of the world.

Yeshiva: An Institution for Raising up Disciples

> There is a difference between learning from a book and hearing the words of Torah from a teacher. The book contains words which are unattached to any human spirit; they are like notes of music silently written on a sheet of paper. Teachings from the mouth of the sage have a spirit and a life, so that one who hears them feels immediately tied to the soul of the sage who speaks these words, just as an audience becomes attached to the one who sings the notes of music. . . .
>
> Rabbi Nachman of Bratslav

If traditions are constituted by practices,[13] then as Tilley has reminded us, just as much as traditional practices cannot survive without a community to enact them, they likewise "cannot live without . . . an *enduring institution*" to pass them on throughout the centuries from one community to the next.[14] For the rabbinic practice of raising up disciples, the *yeshiva* has proved to be just such an enduring institution.

In no small measure, the yeshiva has been able to endure as an institution precisely because it has been able to adapt and change through the centuries. Appearing in *Eretz Yisrael* after the destruction of the Second Temple in 70, the yeshiva did not originally exist as an institution separate from a rabbinic court:

> The Jews of Palestine in the first and second centuries CE made no distinction between higher education and judicial activity, and *they had no tradition of academic career training. Study of Jewish law [halacha] was not seen as something that could or should be isolated from its practical applications.*[15]

By the third century, however, during which yeshivot were established in Babylonia, a more distinct didactic function had become recognizable alongside the judicial one. Indeed, the yeshiva, which literally means 'sitting', may have drawn its name from the seating order in the study halls, where more advanced students sat in the front rows while newcomers were seated in the back. The yeshivot of Babylonia expanded their educational orbit further by convening twice each year month-long study sessions attended by thousands of 'lay' Jews. During their approximately eight-hundred-year existence, the Babylonian yeshivot gained wide respect among Jewish communities in the rest of the world by responding to their halachic queries *and* by training students to serve them as rabbis.

With the decline of the Babylonian yeshivot, the institutional mission of the yeshiva changed dramatically. Medieval yeshivot functioned no longer as courts, but as educational institutions exclusively. Moreover, instead of students who were largely beginners coming to learn 'at the feet' of the *rosh yeshiva*, or the 'head of the yeshiva', mature scholars would come to study with him side-by-side as partners. Attended by perhaps only tens of students instead of by the hundreds who flocked to their Babylonia predecessors, these smaller medieval yeshivot fostered study and discussion that grew more and more recondite. Often resorting to tortured explanations, scholars sought to resolve inconsistencies in the Talmud. They developed a new mode of analysis called *pilpul*, which through hairsplitting argumentation attempted to display intellectual virtuosity by reconciling apparent contradictions in earlier texts.

During the last two hundred years, yeshivot have taken institutional elements from different eras of the past and arranged them in a new configuration. Appearing first in Eastern Europe and then, after the Holocaust, in the United States and Israel, these modern yeshivot have followed the ancient Babylonian model by having hundreds of students in attendance, from novices to more accomplished scholars. And yet, they have also modeled themselves after their medieval forerunners by fashioning themselves into purely educational institutions. If anything, their commitment to education surpasses that of their medieval predecessors, for they pride themselves on their almost total devotion to the practice of *[talmud] torah lishma*, 'Torah study for its own sake'— rather than for the sake of, e.g., obtaining rabbinic ordination.

At first glance, the modern yeshiva, stripped of its judicial and rabbinic training functions and clothed only in its commitment to study for its own sake, might seem rather close to the kind of pure academic institution of which Weber might wholeheartedly approve. In reality, however, the modern yeshiva and the modern academy have crucial differences, as William Helmreich, a sociologist and Orthodox Jew himself, has pointed out.[16] Yeshiva students, unlike most university students, do not follow a curriculum consisting of a specific number of courses leading to a degree,[17] nor for that matter do they take formal examinations.[18] Helmreich also calls attention to another significant educational difference between the yeshiva and the university. While a university student generally studies with the same professor a semester or two at most, yeshivah students may remain in the rosh yeshiva's class for five, six, or seven years.[19]

In ancient as well as in medieval times, students were largely drawn to a yeshiva because of the reputation of the rosh yeshiva, and that fact is no less true today. According to another Orthodox Jewish sociologist, Samuel Heilman, many people see the rosh yeshiva as

> the crown of glory of the institution, a living symbol of it. In every sense, he [is] the life of the yeshiva.[20]

Ideally, in the way the rosh yeshiva answers a question or greets a student or chooses his own attire, he instructs students in how he *expects them to behave*.[21] A far cry, it would seem, from current university presidents and the degree of responsibility they are generally willing to take for shaping the character of the students in their institutions. Who among them, after all, would even think of reinstituting the pre-twentieth-century practice of teaching the college's seniors a course in moral philosophy? By contrast, today's rosh yeshiva at his best still fulfills his role as his institutional forebears have for most of the past twenty centuries—that is, as a master practitioner charged with raising up disciples into a shared way of life.

An old rabbinic midrash on Jeremiah 23:29—"'Is not my word like fire?' asks the Lord"—compares Torah to fire; just as fire does not ignite by itself, so, too, words of Torah do not catch fire in one who studies by himself.[22] For close to two millennia, the yeshiva has provided the institutional setting in which the rabbinic masters could enkindle in the minds and hearts of their disciples the spark of talmud torah, which in the midst of an often dark and cold existence, has brought light and warmth to Jewish communities the world over.

It's Not What You Know, It's Who You Know

When rabbis became doctors, Jews became sick.

Irving Greenberg

When I was at the [Jewish Theological] Seminary, the least frequently mentioned word was God.

Art Green

Yeshivot have nourished the Jewish communities around them by developing an internal community of master practitioners, most of whom eventually leave the yeshiva to live and practice on the "outside" what they have learned through their years "inside." Hence, for all its emphasis on the value of studying Torah for its own sake, the learning that takes place in the yeshiva is not, in the last analysis, *academic,* for it aims to transform the life of an entire community. At bottom, that transformative learning practice rests on no other foundation than personal transmission, i.e., on one life *handing over* tradition to another, on one life *receiving* tradition from another—which is exactly what the two classical Hebrew terms for tradition, *masoret* and *kabbala,* respectively denote. If as human beings we have no more basic way of relating the experience of our lives than by rendering it in story form, then not for nothing do so many teachings about rabbinic masters, from the *tannaim of* the first two centuries to the *chasidim* of the last two, come down to us in *stories about their lives.* Referring to a story-framed ethical sermon given by a *maggid,* an itinerant preacher, in one yeshiva, Heilman observes that "character was being formed through the medium of an interpreted narrative."[23] Nor should we view this need for recollection of the story-pieces of a figure's life as some form of sloppy sentimentality, for as Toulmin reminds us *contra* Weber and other foundationalists:

Even at the core of 20th-century physics, idiosyncrasies of persons and cultures cannot be eliminated. The quirks and backgrounds of creative scientists are as relevant to our understanding of their ideas as they are to our understanding of the work of poets or architects. There are things about Einstein's general theory of relativity, for example, that are understood best if we learn that Einstein was a visual rather than a verbal thinker, and things about quantum mechanics that are best explained if we know that Niels Bohr grew up in a household where Kierkegaard's ideas about "complementary" modes of thought were . . . discussed at Sunday dinner.[24]

But what happens when a Jewish educational institution like the yeshiva loses touch with its story, that is, loses touch with the importance of personal contact?

It strikes me (and perhaps the reader, too) as ironic, if not self-defeating, that in this essay on discipleship, on the significance of learning from an individual human life's actual practice rather than from some impersonal, theoretical abstraction, I have thus far taken what might be characterized as an 'academic perspective, the viewpoint of a detached observer whose own life, whose own story, remains out of view. Let me, then, speak a bit from my own life story, as one who, during the mid-1970s, attended the Jewish Theological Seminary in New York, an institution ostensibly committed to the preservation and transmission of tradition within the framework of Conservative Judaism. At the outset, I wish to make clear that what I have to say about the Seminary is by no means necessarily limited to the Seminary alone. It reflects reality, to one degree or another, at other Jewish educational institutions as well, including some that call themselves yeshivot. I speak of the Seminary, though, because it is the only such institution *I know through the experience of my life as a student 'at its gate.'*

As mentioned above, the Seminary saw as the major part of its mission preserving and transmitting tradition. But one wants to ask *which* tradition? Perhaps, in the end, Weber's:

Weber's academics . . . had to renounce, in their callings, spontaneous enjoyment, emotional satisfaction, and communal affections.[25]

[Weber's ideal practitioner] neither inquires about nor finds it necessary to inquire about *the meaning of his actual practice of a vocation within the whole world. . . .*[26]

Indeed, it was a traditional Weberian notion of scholarship and teaching that the Seminary fostered. During my time, there was usually no better way to insult a faculty member than to address him as "Rabbi" instead of "Doctor." Though seemingly trivial, the preferred form of address was extremely revealing. It reflected both the teachers' self-image as well as their image of the institution and of the tradition within which they taught.

I remember a Bible teacher who had spent some lengthy period of time translating a difficult text in Isaiah on the basis of certain parallel cuneiform texts. Barely able to contain himself, he proudly informed us of the text's proper translation. But when we asked him what that *meant*, i.e., *what religious meaning* that prophetic text might have *for us*, he waved his arm as if shooing flies, and said, "That's not my department."

The Bible teacher's answer may well be acceptable within the modern academy. For despite foundationalist quests to decontextualize and depersonalize knowledge, that quest itself *provides a context within which a certain type of personality is produced with a certain set of virtues peculiar to it:* "clarity but not necessarily charity, honesty but not necessarily friendliness, devotion to the [academic] calling but not necessarily loyalty to particular and local communities of learning."[27] But even though the Bible teacher's answer would likely gain acceptance within the academy, it would be, it *must* be, unacceptable in any institution that would lay claim to being heir to what Israel's sages taught. In fact, it remained unclear to me how what the Seminary's teachers taught or what we students learned might be called *Torah*—God's instruction to and for his people. But if talmud torah was not what we did, then into what practice were we being schooled? And what kind of practitioners were we expected to become? Seminary faculty members such as the Bible professor—like many academics everywhere—generally taught their classes and then disappeared. Few shared with students anything at all about their lives, and far fewer shared anything with us at all about *life itself.* The sages believed their distinctive life-embracing practices critical to making God present to their disciples. It can hardly be surprising that at the Seminary, where there were so few true rabbinic masters, God's presence was so largely absent.

But even at the Seminary, some genuine rabbis—and God—could still be found. My rabbi was Jose Faur. He was an anomaly at the Seminary: Sephardic rather than Ashkenazic, a scholar who taught Talmud without Rashi,[28] and someone, who in the midst of a school where students were routinely addressed by their first names—or, more frequently, by no name at all—insisted on addressing me as "Mr. Goldberg," explaining that if "we *talmidei chachamim* fail to treat each other with respect, why should anybody else ever show us respect, either?" During my senior year, Rabbi Faur taught me much about respect for Torah, God, and the Jewish People.

In that year, we seniors were required to take a course entitled "Practical Rabbinics," an odd title in my judgement, for from the standpoint of our rabbinic predecessors, what other kind of rabbinics could there possibly be? In any case, one of the course requirements was that we each give a Sabbath sermon before the Seminary faculty in the Seminary synagogue. Because the services conducted in that synagogue were in essence Orthodox, I, along with another student,[29] objected that there was something highly inappropriate about that assignment's being a precondition of *Conservative* ordination. As an alternative, we offered to deliver our sermons in a Conservative synagogue near the Seminary where some faculty members attended, to no avail. We were threatened that our ordination would be withheld unless we gave our sermons in the prescribed place.

In the days that followed, a variety of people—fellow students, friends, congregational rabbis—gave us 'advice' meant to be helpful: 'Capitulate; why throw away years of hard work?' Revealingly, it was the same kind of counsel, the same kind of 'torah,' one could get from any manager of a K-Mart. We remained undeterred.

Then we received an invitation to come to the office of Rabbi Faur.

It may have been because of Rabbi Faur's generally formal manner that his words when we went to see him had an especially great effect on us: "You are my brothers, and I do not want to see my brothers destroyed." Nevertheless, for all its emotional impact on us, his counsel was essentially still stamped with the K-Mart brand. Then, he added something that made a difference. Rather, he asked us something. He asked why we thought God had given us the Torah in the first place? I forget our answers, but I remember his: "God gave the Torah to create the Jewish People by bringing Jews together." He told us that the ultimatum we had been given was a misuse of Torah, for it put barriers between Jews. But he went on to say that were we to refuse to give our sermons, that is, were we *to refuse to teach Jews Torah,* we would be guilty of the same divisive action. Not chiefly by the words of our sermons, *but by the very act of making ourselves present to those Jews in that setting,* we could show that we were indeed disciples of the sages. Shortly afterwards, we decided to deliver our sermons in the Seminary synagogue.

When I had received·my ordination and it was time to leave the Seminary, I found that I had managed to ingest some information of the sort one gets from lectures, textbooks, and the like.[30] I certainly had no idea of *what to do* with that information, of how to put it into practice, for there was essentially no *community of practice* at the Seminary *from whose life I could learn.* Although I realize that now, I did not understand it then. In fact, at the time, I thought what I needed was a better academic institution to show me how, through studying the philosophy of religion at a doctoral level, I could take the random data the Seminary had given me and turn it into knowledge, or better yet, wisdom.

It was no easy thing to find such an institution, for those with programs in the philosophy of religion were usually hostile to the avowedly religious while those with programs in systematic theology were usually unwelcoming to the declaredly non-Christian. When at last I determined that the Graduate Theological Union in Berkeley might be an institution with programs genuinely open to me in both areas, a Seminary faculty member warned me against going there, saying, "They'll ruin you."

He was right.

Stanley Hauerwas has said that on the flyleaf of Jim McClendon's *Doctrine* should be written: **Warning To Those Schooled in Academic Theology—This Book Could Be Dangerous To Your Career If Taken Seriously.**[31] For me, McClendon's writing was dangerous indeed. It was ruinous to the philosophical confessions and complacencies I had accumulated over the years, not only at the Seminary, but also earlier at Yale. It was Jim's life, however, that made his writing—and his teaching—truly potent. For even throughout the course of my invaluable contact with Rabbi Faur, I had still gone ungrounded, *unpracticed,* in something else: shimmush talmidei chachamim, the practice of personally serving scholars. Jim, of course, is not Jewish, much less a rabbi. But this man, whose background is so unlike mine—a committed Baptist, a courtly Southern gentleman, has taught me more about practicing the ministry of the sacred service between master and disciple than anyone I have ever known.

While my professors at the Seminary typically remained distant, keeping themselves and their lives out of view, Jim, though certainly a private, reserved man, has never tried to hide himself or his life from me. Shortly after I first became one of Jim's students, he and his wife, Marie, separated. After I became aware of that, and because the Seminary had taught me to think of myself as a kind of lay psychotherapist, I asked Jim if there were anything I could do, e.g., offer a shoulder to cry on, an ear to listen, or *a clinical, detached eye* to help Jim get clearer about his "options." But Jim answered, "Yes, pray for me and Marie." I was stunned. Jim had made a thoroughly religious request—about the last thing that anybody at the Seminary—or I—would ever have done. But I did as my teacher asked, serving in the way I had been asked.

A few years later, Jim began work on his planned three-volume baptist systematic theology. He saw it as a project that might well span the rest of his life. And from time to time, Jim has asked for my comments and suggestions on various pieces of the work-in-progress, and I have been truly *honored* by my teacher's requests for this kind of service from me. But at one point, Jim asked something more of me. He requested that, if he were to die before being able to complete the project, I collect his notes and edit them for publication. Once more, I was stunned. The gap between our two traditions seemed at least as large as the gap between Jim's mastery of the material and my own relative unfamiliarity with it. Nevertheless, I agreed. I thank God that the need for serving my master that way has so far not fallen to me, and with thanks in advance to Jim's wife, Nancey, a first-rate Christian theologian in her own right, I am hopeful it never will.

But the opportunities I have had to be of service to Jim pale in comparison to the service, the faithful attentiveness, which Jim has shown me through the years. I am afraid that I am like Rabbi Akiva's sick student. Those who know me know that I am not the most easy-going person in the world, nor has my 'career path' been, shall we say, 'linear.' I am, in short, somebody to whom it is difficult to remain devoted. But virtually no one in my life has shown me the kind of steadfast devotion that Jim, my teacher, has—what the Hebrew Bible calls *chesed*. It is not only that when I have found myself in intellectual straits that Jim has offered me scholarly support. More than that, when I have found myself in psychological straits, Jim has offered me emotional support and when I have found myself in economic straits, he has even offered me financial support. And always, *always*, he has offered *chochma*—God's own wisdom. Jim is, quite simply, the best man I have ever known.

I leave it to the reader to judge whether I have yet mastered the methodological approach Jim has tried to teach me. But in the end, I know that only with a lifetime of practice—and God's help—can I ever hope to master the way of teaching through faithful friendship that Jim has shown me through his life through the years. And I do know this as well. Jim *has* raised me up as *his* disciple . . . in my own way. That way is a *Jewish way* that has grown stronger not in spite of Jim, but *because of* the foundation my master has given me and continues to give me to this day.

CONTRIBUTORS

Elizabeth Barnes is Associate Professor of Theology and Ethics at Baptist Theological Seminary at Richmond. She is the author of *An Affront to the Gospel? The Radical Barth and the Southern Baptist Convention* (Atlanta: Scholars, 1987); and *The Story of Discipleship: Christ, Humanity, and Church in Narrative Perspective* (Nashville: Abingdon, 1994).

David B. Burrell, C.S.C. is Theodore M. Hesburgh Professor of Philosophy and Theology at the University of Notre Dame, and the author of *Freedom and Creation in Three Traditions* (Notre Dame: University of Notre Dame Press, 1993).

Michael Goldberg, an ordained rabbi with a doctorate in philosophy of religion and systematic theology, has held chairs of Jewish Studies and has been a consultant in professional ethics and organizatinal design to the Georgia Supreme Court and various Fortune 500 companies. He is a founder and principal of Vision Design, a consulting group specializing in strategic planning workshops for synagagues and churches.

Stanley Hauerwas is Professor of Theological Ethics at Duke University Divinity School, Durham, North Carolina. His most recent publication is *Dispatches from the Front: Theological Engagements with the Secular* (Durham: Duke University Press, 1994).

Nancey Murphy is Associate Professor of Christian Philosophy at Fuller Theological Seminary. Her first book, *Theology in the Age of Scientific Reasoning* (Ithaca: Cornell University Press, 1990) won the American Academy of Religion award for excellence. Other works include *Reasoning and Rhetoric in Religion* (Philadelphia: Trinity Press International, 1994).

Ched Myers lives in Los Angeles and works as a regional program director for the American Friends Service Committee. He is the author of *Binding the Strong Man: A Political Reading of Mark's Story* *of Jesus* (Maryknoll: Orbis, 1988) and *Who Will Roll Away the Stone? Discipleship Queries for First World Christians* (Orbis, 1994)

Mark Nation is a doctoral candidate in Christian Ethics at Fuller Theological Seminary, working with James McClendon, and pastor of Ladera Church of the Brethren in Los Angeles. He has published articles on Dietrich Bonhoeffer and Reinhold Niebuhr. He has also done extensive work on the writings of John H. Yoder.

Charles Scriven was James McClendon's doctoral student at the Graduate Theological Union between 1978 and 1983. He is the author of *The Transformation of Culture: Christian Social Ethics After H. Richard Niebuhr* (Scottdale: Herald, 1988). He currently serves as President of Columbia Union College.

James M. Smith began his teaching career at the University of Illinois, but he has spent most of his career at California State University, Fresno. He has published several articles in ethics and social philosophy. With James McClendon he co-authored several articles in the philosophy of religion as well as *Understanding Religious Convictions* (Notre Dame: University of Notre Dame Press, 1975).

Theophus Smith is Professor of Religion at Emory University. He is the author of *Conjuring Culture: Biblical Foundations of Black America* (New York: Oxford University Press, 1994).

Glen H. Stassen is Professor of Christian Ethics at Southern Baptist Theological Seminary, and author of *Just Peacemaking: Transforming Initiatives for Justice and Peace* (Louisville: Westminster/John Knox, 1992). He is also the author, with John Howard Yoder and Diane Yeager, of *Authentic Transformation: A New Vision of Christ and Culture* (Nashville: Abingdon, 1994).

Richard Steele is a United Methodist Pastor, and teaches at the Milwaukee Theological Institute.

Terrence W. Tilley is Professor of Religion at Florida State University. His most recent book is *The Evils of Theodicy* (Washington: Georgetown University Press, 1991).

John H. Yoder is Professor of Theology in the Department of Theology of the University of Notre Dame. His best-known writings are *The Politics of Jesus*, 2nd ed.(Grand Rapids: Eerdmans, 1994) and *The Priestly Kingdom* (Notre Dame: The University of Notre Dame Press, 1984).

Introduction

1. For additional details, see Jeffrey Stout, *The Flight from Authority* (Notre Dame: University of Notre Dame Press, 1981), pp. 3–5; Ronald Thiemann, *Revelation and Theology* (Notre Dame: University of Notre Dame Press, 1984), pp. 44–46; Richard Rorty, *Philosophy and the Mirror of Nature* (Princeton: Princeton University Press, 1979), pp. 157–63.

2. *Discourse on Method* (1637), second part.

3. *Cosmopolis: The Hidden Agenda of Modernity* (New York: Macmillan, 1990), ch. 1.

4. Third *Meditation*.

5. See Wallace Matson, *A New History of Philosophy*, vol. II (San Diego: Harcourt Brace Jovanovich, 1987), p. 280.

6. *The Logic of Scientific Discovery* (New York: Harper, 1965); translation by Popper, et al., of *Logik der Forschung* (Vienna, 1935), p. 111.

7. "Two Dogmas of Empiricism," in *From a Logical Point of View* (Oxford: Oxford University Press, 1953), pp. 42–43. Originally published in 1951.

8. "Falsification and the Methodology of Scientific Research Programmes," in *The Methodology of Scientific Research Programmes: Philosophical Papers, Volume 1*, ed. John Worrall and Gregory Currie (Cambridge: Cambridge University Press, 1978), pp. 8–101. Originally published in *Criticism and the Growth of Knowledge*, ed. Imre Lakatos and Alan Musgrave (Cambridge: Cambridge University Press, 1970), pp. 91–196.

9. See *Whose Justice? Which Rationality?* (Notre Dame: University of Notre Dame Press, 1988); and *Three Rival Versions of Moral Enquiry: Encyclopaedia, Genealogy, and Tradition* (Notre Dame: University of Notre Dame Press, 1990).

10. See Murphy's essay in this collection for further details.

11. See Thiemann, *Revelation and Theology*, for an account of the damage done by pressing a doctrine of revelation into the service of foundationalist epistemology.

12. *The Flight from Authority*, p. 147.

13. One notable exception is Barth, who, not surprisingly, has been an important influence in Hauerwas's work.

14. It may be of interest to the ethicists among our readers to know that despite the fact that much of the work on this *Festschrift* was done in McClendon's own study, I only had to lie twice to keep the project a secret.

15. First edition, Notre Dame: University of Notre Dame Press, 1975; second edition, titled *Convictions: Defusing Religious Relativism*, Valley Forge: Trinity Press International, 1995.

16. Cf. Hume's claim that his *Treatise* fell still-born from the press.

17. "Ad Hoc Apologetics," *The Journal of Religion* 66 (July, 1986), pp. 282–301.

18. First edition, Nashville: Abingdon, 1974; second edition, Philadelphia: Trinity Press International, 1990.

19. Cf. MacIntyre's claim that a moral tradition cannot be understood apart from a sociological account of the society that puts it into practice. *After Virtue*, 2nd ed. (Notre Dame: University of Notre Dame Press, 1984), ch. 3.

20. Nashville: Abingdon, 1981.

21. For a further development of this issue, see the essay herein by James M. Smith.

22. All published by Abingdon Press.

23. In particular, see Hans Frei, *The Eclipse of Biblical Narrative* (New Haven: Yale University Press, 1974).

24. In "God and Human Attitudes," in *Divine Commands and Morality*, ed. Paul Helm (Oxford: Oxford University Press, 1981), pp. 34–48.

25. See *Understanding Religious Convictions*, p. vii.

26. If this is the case, then so as not to mix metaphors, we should speak instead of "sub-ethical" discussions, but this does not have so lofty a sound to it.

27. See *Ethics*, pp. 98–102.

Chapter 1: Worship and Autonomy
James M. Smith

1. James Wm. McClendon, Jr. and James M. Smith, *Understanding Religious Convictions* (Notre Dame: University of Notre Dame Press, 1975).

2. J. L. Austin, *How to Do Things with Words* (Oxford: Clarendon Press, 1962).

3. John Searle, *Speech Acts* (Cambridge: Cambridge University Press, 1969).

4. McClendon and Smith, *Understanding Religious Convictions*, p. 7.

5. James Rachels, "God and Human Attitudes," in *Divine Commands and Morality*, ed. Paul Helm (Oxford: Oxford University Press, 1981), pp. 34–48.

6. Ibid., p. 41.

7. Ibid, pp. 43–44.

8. Ibid., p. 45.

9. cf. Santayana on fanaticism: "Redoubling our efforts having forgotten the goal."

10. McClendon and Smith, *Understanding Religious Convictions*, p. 7.

11. Ibid., p. 44.

12. Ibid.

13. Ibid.

Chapter 2: Convictions and Operative Warrant
David B. Burrell, C.S.C.

1. For "retrospective justification," see my "Religious Belief and Rationality" in *Rationality and Religious Belief*, ed. C. F. Delaney (Notre Dame: University of Notre Dame Press, 1979), and Nicholas Lash's Introduction to the University of Notre Dame Press edition of J. H. Newman's *Grammar of Assent* (1979), where his recapitulation of Newman's mode of argument coheres nicely with the lines of "retrospective justification."

2. See Newman's *Grammar* (note 1) and *Faith and Rationality: Reason and Belief in God*, ed. Alvin Plantinga and Nicholas Wolterstorff (Notre Dame: University of Notre Dame Press, 1983).

3. Initially in *Whose Justice? Which Rationality?* (Notre Dame: University of Notre Dame Press, 1988), followed by *Three Rival Versions of Moral Enquiry* (Notre Dame: University of Notre Dame Press, 1980).

4. *Faith and Belief* (Princeton: Princeton University Press, 1979).

5. *The Nature of Doctrine* (Philadelphia: Westminster, 1984).

6. The reference here is more directly to Kierkegaard's "Socrates" in *Concluding Unscientific Postscript* than to Plato's dialogues, though the parentage of S.K.'s figure is clear.

7. Bernard J. F. Lonergan, *Insight* (London: Longmans, 1957), ch. 9: "Judgment."

8. For a positioning of Lonergan within modern philosophical currents, see Michael McCarthy, *The Crisis of Philosophy* (Albany: State University of New York Press, 1991).

Chapter 3: In Favor of a 'Practical Theory of Religion': Montaigne and Pascal
Terrence W. Tilley

1. James Wm. McClendon, Jr., *Doctrine: Systematic Theology II* (Nashville: Abingdon, 1994), p. 421.

2. Ibid., p. 28; compare Alasdair MacIntyre, *After Virtue* (Notre Dame: University of Notre Dame Press, 1981).

3. See, for instance, Terence Penelhum, *God and Skepticism: A Study in Skepticism and Fideism* (Boston: Reidel, 1981), *passim*.

4. William A. Clebsch, *Christianity in European History* (New York: Oxford University Press, 1979), p. 246.

5. The evident exception is D. Z. Phillips who has bucked the mainstream in philosophy of religion by espousing a Wittgensteinian approach which makes the religious form of life central. But Phillips's approach leaves no room to ask whether anyone *ought* to participate in a religious form of life or in which religious form of life one should participate, which is just what is at issue in the tradition of Montaigne and Pascal (to be discussed below) and in the present. As the reign of modernity has waned, philosophers of religion have begun to take new paths in understanding religion, including cross-cultural comparative philosophy of religion (e.g., John Hick, *An Interpretation of Religion*; New Haven: Yale University Press, 1989) and studies of the coherence of traditional theological doctrines (e.g., Thomas Morris, *The Logic of God Incarnate*; Ithaca: Cornell University Press, 1986).

6. The evident exception is William P. Alston (see his *Perceiving God: The Epistemology of Religious Experience*; Ithaca: Cornell University Press, 1991), some of whose accomplishments I note below. However, Alston does not adequately recognize the variety of religious practices and I do not see how his predominantly externalist epistemological stance can deal with issues raised by Code, Jaggar and others (discussed below), and their significance for religious practice (brought out in the "postlude" below).

7. See Terrence W. Tilley, "Reformed Epistemology in a Jamesian Perspective," *Horizons* 16, no. 1 (Spring, 1992), pp. 84–98.

8. I have sketched this situation in a slightly later period as a problem of many authorities in *The Evils of Theodicy* (Washington: Georgetown University Press, 1991), pp. 221–25. Stephen Toulmin, *Cosmopolis: The Hidden Agenda of Modernity* (New York: Free Press, 1992), has discussed the social history of France in the late sixteenth and early seventeenth century and shown how the arguments about religion were not leisurely notional arguments, but urgent practical ones.

9. For example, see William P. Alston, "Religious Experience and Religious Belief," *Nous* 16, no. 1 (1982), pp. 3–12.

10. I use *phronesis* here rather than "prudence" because "prudence" has become associated in much modern philosophy not with the practical wisdom Aristotle described, but with cost-benefit or risk-benefit calculations, often self-serving ones. In general, I will use terms like "wisdom" or "practical wisdom" as English equivalents for *phronesis*. For an example of this approach, see Terrence W. Tilley, "The Prudence of Religious Commitment" *Horizons* 16, No. 1 (Spring, 1989), pp. 84–98.

11. 'Epistemologists' is in 'scare quotes' to note the fact that there is an ongoing dispute about the possibility of a feminist epistemology. See

Lorraine Code, *What Can She Know? Feminist Theory and the Construction of Knowledge* (Ithaca: Cornell University Press, 1991), pp. 314–24, for a discussion of this issue.

12. Code, p. 267.

13. Alison M. Jaggar, "Love and Knowledge: Emotion in Feminist Epistemology," in *Gender/Body/Knowledge: Feminist Reconstructions of Being and Knowing*, ed. Alison M. Jaggar and Susan R. Bordo (New Brunswick: Rutgers University Press, 1989), p. 154.

14. Ibid., pp. 154–55.

15. Ibid., p. 156. For discussions of issues in "naturalized epistemology," see Hilary Kornblith, editor, *Naturalizing Epistemology* (Cambridge: MIT Press, 1985).

16. Michel de Montaigne, *The Complete Essays of Montaigne*, tran. Donald M. Frame (Stanford: Stanford University Press, 1965), p. 121.

17. This usage should not be conflated with "internalism" and "externalism" in epistemology. The epistemic externalist finds that a believer may have a justified or warranted belief without being aware of how or being able to show that that belief is justified or warranted. The epistemic internalist includes such awareness in some way as a necessary condition for knowing, warrant or justification.

18. Ibid., p. 160.

19. For a discussion of this point, see Terrence W. Tilley, *Talking of God: An Introduction to Philosophical Analysis of Religious Language* (New York: Paulist, 1978), pp. 12–18.

20. Montaigne, pp. 704–705.

21. Tilley, "Prudence of Religious Commitment."

22. Penelhum, *God and Skepticism*, p. 71.

23. Ibid.

24. Thomas V. Morris, "Pascalian Wagering," in *Contemporary Perspectives on Religious Epistemology*, ed. R. Douglas Geivett and Brendan Sweetman (New York: Oxford University Press, 1992), p. 261.

25. Ibid., p. 267. Philosophical commentary on the Wager argument has usually taken the issue Pascal addresses to be theoretical, not practical. James wrongly presumes that one must antecedently have faith in the practice to undertake it: " . . . a faith in masses and holy water adopted wilfully after such a mechanical calculation would lack the inner soul of faith's reality. . . ." (William James, "The Will to Believe," *The Will to Believe and Other Essays in Popular Philosophy*; New York: Dover, 1956; reprint of the 1987 edition, p. 6). Morris's criticism is on target, but James is correct in one thing: he takes the problem of "many *practices*" (which I develop below) seriously, while Morris in his mature work on Pascal (*Making Sense of It All: Pascal and the Meaning of Life*; Grand Rapids: Eerdmans, 1992), working out of a committed Christian perspective,

ignores this possibility. One *cannot* have faith in masses and holy water antecedent to participating in the practice; one participates and *develops* faith in and love of God *through* participating seriously in the practices. The real issue, then, is practical: which practices, which set of practices, should be ours when more than one is open to us? So far as I know, Morris has not followed Pascal into Catholic practices, and seems not even to have considered the question of intra-Christian pluralism seriously.

26. Penelhum, *God and Skepticism*, pp. 73–74.

27. William G. Lycan and George N. Schlesinger, "You Bet Your Life: Pascal's Wager Defended," in *Contemporary Perspectives on Religious Epistemology*, pp. 275–78.

28. Penelhum, *God and Skepticism*, p. 63.

29. Blaise Pascal, *Pensées*, translated by W. F. Trotter (New York: Dutton, 1958) § 233.

30. Ibid., § 609.

31. Ibid.

32. Jonathan Wilson, in correspondence, suggested that this approach may lead to a liberal, pluralistic account construing each religion as a particular and partial response to a transcendent One. But what makes soteriocentric pluralism an attractive option is that it is an 'improvement' over inclusivist and exclusivist views of salvation. The present approach is not soteriocentric and does not address, much less start with, problems of salvation. I don't think one can theoretically resolve the problems of who is saved and whether all religions are different responses to the One. Nor do I think response to the Greatest or the One is a foundation for religious belief. This Anselmian twist on Pascal is a negative filter: it merely rules out some practices and some traditions as embodying wise religious commitment. It is merely a coarse criterion developed from *Pensées*, not a foundation.

33. Pascal, § 618.

34. Jaggar, p. 154.

35. See Philip C. Almond, "The Buddha of Christendom: A Review of the Legend of Barlaam and Josaphat," *Religious Studies* 23 (1987), pp. 391–406.

Chapter 4: Walk and Word: The Alternatives to Methodologism
John H. Yoder

1. Karl Barth complained that the young Germans in his Colloquium "return again and again to the question . . . as to what the characteristic 'thought form' of the *Dogmatics* is. They feel that if they knew that, they could then decide whether or not to get on the train which is apparently travelling inexorably from its specific starting point to its

destination." Eberhard Busch, *Karl Barth : His Life from Letters and Auto-biographical Texts* (Philadelphia: Fortress, 1976), p. 403, December 1954.

2. That methodological assumption showed through, although not self-consciously, in the outline for a multi-author collection of essays in the light of which this text was first drafted. The editors of that collection assured me that such a presupposition was not self-conscious on their part; that seems to me to confirm my point, namely that what I am describing is a tacitly assumed axiom ratherthan a stated postulate. I thank those editors for their aututhorization to use the text in the present *Festschrift*. That collection is tentatively titled *Christian Theism and Moral Philosophy*, edited by Michael Beaty, Carlton Fisher, and Mark T. Nelson.

3. *Encheiridion* LI. To the standard translations by Carter, Long, and Oldfather, Sisela Bok adds a version of her own in *Lying* (New York, Random House, 1978), p. 11. Ancient philosophers did not claim originality; Epictetus may well not have invented the saying.

4. Although my concern arose on other grounds, it could be said that the present paper also supports Epictetus' next comment: "We spend all our time on the third topic, employing all our diligence about it, and neglect the first. At the same time that we go on lying, we study to show how its wrongness can be demonstrated."

5. Most of the titles of the papers in the book referred to in note 2 above provide answers on this third "justificatory" level.

6. The term "foundationalism" is one of those current slogan-terms so widely and loosely used that no common definition can be counted on. The "lexicon" in Jeffrey Stout's *Ethics After Babel* (Boston: Beacon, 1988; pp. 293ff.) does not list the "ism" but does define "foundational moral criterion" as "that from which all non-foundational [a redundancy; he means all other] moral knowledge is derived." Thus we may define "foundationalism" as the claim that such a deeper and surer, more general level is both accessible and imperative, so that moral discourse can start from scratch before attending to any concrete moral judgments. In Stout's own text the term is frequent; the "failure of foundationalism" is his theme on pp. 198f, 209, 213f. I agree with his argument there; but it should be noted that to make rejecting foundationalism a *basic* defining statement is itself a foundationalist move.

7. All the manuals recognize that some carefully specified kinds of lies may in fact be held to be socially useful.

8. Or, to say the same thing in reverse, it may arise but "mother told me" answers it automatically and univocally.

9. With these increasingly complex justifications the complexity of choices grows as well. If "harm to others" is the criterion, one can, as I said above, begin to look for loophole cases where a lie would do no harm or might even do someone some good.

10. It is also the theme of the other articles in the book cited above. I do not doubt the pertinence of those debates; I merely challenge their priority and their claim to be foundational.

11. Were Epictetus writing in our day he would have to ask a fourth question: "which community?" The world then was not homogeneous, but a Stoic could get away with talking as if it were. Today he could not. Thus the methodologism rises to a higher power: "On what grounds do you justify the choice of which community to get your signals from?"

12. I state some such arguments below pp. 86ff; but they must be evaluated "according to the setting." Some settings are corrective, some are missionary, some are catechetical; each needs its own language.

13. One thinks of needing to correct for rigid legalism, or of settings where guilt matters more than empowerment.

14. One thinks of catechesis, the making of academic encyclopaediae and summae.

15. I Cor. 12:4ff.; cf. "The Hermeneutics of Peoplehood" in my *The Priestly Kingdom* (Notre Dame: Notre Dame University Press, 1985), esp. pp. 28–34, and *The Fullness of Christ* (Elgin: Brethren Press, 1987).

16. I Cor. 14:14, 26–33; cf. also my "Sacrament as Social Ethic" in *Theology Today* XLVII, no.1 (Spring 1991), pp. 33ff., esp. p. 35.

17. "'All things are lawful for me', but I will not be enslaved by anything." (I Cor. 6:12); "'All things are lawful,' but not all things build up,"(10:23).

18. I John 4:1; the criterion for that testing is the historic humanity of Jesus (*i.e.* his having "come in the flesh").

19. Cf. the passage "This land is our land" in my *Priestly Kingdom*, pp. 59ff.

20. Albert R. Jonsen and Stephen Toulmin, *The Abuse of Casuistry: A History of Moral Reasoning* (Berkeley: University of California Press, 1988). The authors do indicate that they found themselves and others agreeing about a set of problems in the realm of medical ethics, but they do not commend those shared conclusions to their readers, nor do they display with convincing contemporary specimens how the discipline whose misuse they admit, whose abuse they deplore, whose rehabilitation they advocate, and whose logic they sketchily summarize, can now provide solid guidance.

21. Stout, *Ethics After Babel*. Cf. the "Review Symposium" in *Theology Today* XLVI, no. 1 (April 1989), pp. 55-73. Stout's best example of a moral certainty is one that seems to have been chosen on the ground that no reader will disagree, namely the wrongness of slavery. He wrestles little with what that intrinsic wrongness means for the moral status of the many people who without that knowledge practiced slavery, but does grant that "saying that slavery is wrong is not the same as imputing blame

for practicing it" (31). This opens up a new ambivalent evaluation, "justified [or excusable] but wrong." The other hard category, to which he does not attend, would be slavery-like arrangements, like immigrant laborers in Pennsylvania coal mines a century ago, unable to get out of their debt to the company for their food and housing.

22. Alasdair MacIntyre, *After Virtue* (Notre Dame: University of Notre Dame Press, 1981); *Whose Justice? Which Rationality?* (Notre Dame: University of Notre Dame Press, 1988); *Three Rival Versions of Moral Enquiry: Encyclopaedia, Genealogy, and Tradition* (Notre Dame: University of Notre Dame Press, 1990). This observation is not meant as any challenge to the great pedagogical helpfulness of MacIntyre's surveys, as they contribute to deconstructing prior commonplaces and as a thick description of a few of the the diverse settings of moral discourse, demonstrating both the strengths and the limits of using overarching types to make sense of our debates.

23. In his vol. II (Chicago: Univerity of Chicago Press, 1984) he discusses marriage, suicide, population, and biomedical research funding. His analyses are thoroughly documented and insightful.

24. E.g. Leslie Griffin, "The Problem of Dirty Hands", *Journal of Religious Ethics* 17, no. 1 (Spring 1989), pp. 36f. Griffin however recognizes that I would not accept her characterisation as accurate, and that my view is not true after all to the "clean hands" ideal type she is interested in describing.

25. E.g. Bruce Birch and Larry Rasmussen *Bible & Ethics in the Christian Life* (Minneapolis: Augsburg, 1976. The second edition of this book (1989) shifts its description of me, citing more affirmatively my comments on some other themes. In other cases, the fact that my argument about politics can be taken as representing a standard style option can be used as grounds to set it aside politely, respectfully, but without further attention; cf. James Gustafson, *Ethics from a Theocentric Perspective* 1:74. Gustafson says complimentary things about my stance but does not converse with its critique.

26. Killing in war does differ from the other kinds of moral test in that the infringement on the Gospel imperative has been institutionalized as the others have not. There is no venerable "just prevarication tradition" or "just adultery tradition", as there is a "just war tradition". There are, it is true, casuistic systems which do work carefully at the hard cases concerning all of the basic imperatives (cf. e.g. note 20 above); but the scale and the legal legitimacy with which killing in war has been not only justified as a borderline case, but made imperative as an institutional obligation, finds no parallel in other moral areas. In some settings brothels have been legitimized, but service in them has not been made a civic duty. Today abortion is widely legitimized, but not made an obligation.

Lying for the sake of the interest of one's own group may be pressed upon a person as an ingroup duty, but always with the awareness that it wrongs someone, and that it will cease to work once it becomes the rule.

27. Cf. Leslie Griffin, "The Problem of Dirty Hands," p. 36. The same juxtaposition of principled rigor about lying with proportional flexibility about killing characterizes the article "War" in *The Catholic Encyclopedia* (New York: Universal Knowledge Foundation, 1912), 15:546.

28. James warns that there should not be many teachers because language is unruly (3:1-8). Timothy is warned against "disputing about words (II Tim. 2:14). Cf. my *Priestly Kingdom* p. 32.

29. This is the point of the criticism of "commensuration" in John Finnis, "The Consistent Ethic—A Philosophical Critique," in *Joseph Cardinal Bernardin; A Consistent Ethic of Life*, ed. Thomas Fuechtmann (New York: Sheed and Ward, 1988), pp. 140–81, especially pp. 150ff.

30. The terms "decisionism" and "quandarism" are sometimes used to characterize mental strategies which inappropriately narrow the moral agenda. I subsume those insights within my preference for the term "punctualism," as describing the concentration on decision and act as punctual in one time and place, without depth (components like character), breadth (relations to other persons) or length (past covenants and future intentions).

31. The moral development theories of Kohlberg are a prime example of mixing in one system claims to have observed developmental patterns, philosophical assumptions about the different values of different ways to think morally, and prior yet less-examined cultural biases.

32. An earlier description of the methodological pluralism which I find at work in the Bible, and which I advocate as the right way to do moral reasoning today, was offered in my "Hermeneutics of Peoplehood," in *The Priestly Kingdom*, p.37.

33. Cf. note 2 above.

34. I have in fact never set out to make the case for "doing ethics from the Bible" as the methodologically right approach. When I have been asked to discuss such a question (as did happen twice within the context of the American Academy of Religion) it was because others ascribed to my expositions of the ethical witness of the New Testament (e.g. *The Politics of Jesus*, Grand Rapids, Eerdmans, 1972—not a field in which I have written much since then) a methodological prejudgement much like what I am here concerned to disavow.

35. Cf. my "The Authority of Tradition" in *The Priestly Kingdom* pp. 63–79, for an exposition of the way in which movements of reformation affirm tradition by the very act of critiquing it. They thereby both affirm and relativise the past more fundamentally than do those "high church" institutions which, because they claim unique authority to interpret the

deposit (as if there were just one) normatively, in fact cut themselves loose from concrete accountability. In this connection cf. the shared witness which Jim McClendon and I formulated on "Christian Identity in Ecumenical Perspective" in the *Journal of Ecumenical Studies* 27 (Summer 1990), pp. 561–80.

36. Cf. my paper on "The Authority of the Canon" in *Essays on Biblical Interpretation: Anabaptist-Mennonite Perspectives*, ed. Willard M. Swartley (Elkhart: Institute of Mennonite Studies, 1984), pp. 265–90, for a review of how scholasticism mortgaged the possibility of wholesome recourse to scripture. From my perspective, what that scholasticism did then was the equivalent of what the several philosophical disjunctions I am challenging do today, even when they think they are transcending it; it subsumed divine freedom under a humanly dictated definition of rational necessity.

37. To take one major institutional exmple; the World Council of Churches, which has invested enormous dialogical effort in matters of church order (episcopacy etc.) and forms of worship (baptism, eucharist, ministry), has never planned a serious study of the moral acceptability of war as a confession-dividing issue. The one very thin exception was a very small exploratory meeting held in May-June 1968, whose recommendations for follow-up were not implemented: cf. Donald Durnbaugh, ed., *On Earth Peace* (Elgin: Brethren Press, 1978), p. 307.

Chapter 5: 'I Will Ask *You* a Question': Interrogatory Theology
Ched Myers

1 "Towards an Indigenous Theology of the Cross," *Interpretation* 30, p. 162.

2. Ched Myers, *Binding the Strong Man: A Political Reading of Mark's Story of Jesus* (Maryknoll: Orbis, 1988), pp. 306f.

3. Nancey Murphy and James Wm. McClendon, Jr., "Distinguishing Modern and Postmodern Theologies," *Modern Theology* 5, no. 3 (April 1989), pp. 191ff.

4. See Herbert Marcuse, *One Dimensional Man: Studies in the Ideology of Advanced Industrial Society* (Boston: Beacon, 1964).

5. Christopher Lasch, *The True and Only Heaven: Progress and Its Critics* (New York: Norton, 1991).

6. William Appleman Williams, *Empire as a Way of Life* (New York: Oxford University Press, 1980).

7. *No Life Without Roots: Culture and Development* (London: Zed, 1990), p. 52.

8. Quoted in Matthew Lamb, "The Challenge of Critical Theory," in *Sociology and Human Destiny*, ed. G. Baum (New York: Seabury, 1980), p. 188.

9. *Ethics: Systematic Theology*, Volume I (Nashville: Abingdon, 1986), pp. 36ff.

10. On this initiative see *Baptist Peacemaker* XIII, no. 2 (Summer 1993), p. 1.

11. See Robert McAffee Brown, ed., *Kairos: Three Prophetic Challenges to the Church* (Grand Rapids: Eerdmans, 1990).

12. Bill Wylie Kellermann, *Seasons of Faith and Conscience: Kairos, Confession, Liturgy* (Maryknoll: Orbis, 1991), p. 36.

13. John Howard Yoder, *Karl Barth and the Problem of War* (New York: Abingdon, 1970), p. 133.

14. Brown, *Kairos*, pp. 143ff.

15. See Ignacio Castuera, ed., *Dreams on Fire, Embers of Hope: From the Pulpits of Los Angeles After the Riots* (St Louis: Chalice, 1992), pp. 101ff.

16. John Howard Yoder, *When War is Unjust: Being Honest in Just-War Thinking* (Minneapolis: Augsburg, 1984), pp. 74ff.

17. "Towards an Indigenous Theology of the Cross," *Interpretation* 30 (April, 1976), p. 162.

18. Minneapolis: Augsburg, 1989, p. 36

19. Paulo Friere, "The Adult Literacy Process as Cultural Action for Freedom," in *World Development: An Introductory Reader*, ed. H. Castel (NY: Macmillan, 1971), p. 264.

20. Myers, *Binding the Strong Man*, pp. 297ff.

21. Ibid., pp. 241ff.

22. The Greek terms *dogma / dogmatizoō* appear only a few times in the New Testament, and refer to imperial decrees (Luke 2:1; Acts 17:7) or legal doctrines (Eph. 2:15; Col 2:14,20) that must be overcome by the gospel. Only once are they used to refer to Christian discourse—the resolution of social conflicts proposed by the Jerusalem apostolic council in Acts 16:4 (Gerhard Kittel, Theological Dictionary of the New Testament, trans. Geoffrey W. Bromiley; Grand Rapids: Eerdmans, 1964, 2:230). For a reconstructive look at the practice of teaching Christian doctrine see the Prologue to McClendon's *Doctrine: Systematic Theology*, Volume II (Nashville: Abingdon, 1994).

23. "The Challenge of Critical Theory," p. 186; cf. *Solidarity with Victims: Toward a Theology of Social Transformation* (New York: Crossroads, 1982).

24. "'To Brush History Against the Grain': The Eschatology of the Frankfurt School and Ernst Bloch," *Journal of the American Academy of Religion* 51, no. 4 (December 1983), p. 631.

25. Lamb, "The Challenge of Critical Theory," p. 186.

26. Ibid., p. 190.

27. Ibid., p. 191.

28. Ibid.

29. Ibid., p. 202.

30. Herbert Marcuse, *One Dimensional Man*, p. xvi.

31. Jürgen Moltmann, "An Open Letter to Jose Miguez Bonino." Christianity and Crisis (March 29, 1976), pp. 57ff; Anna Abayasekera, et al., "Faith and Ideologies," *SE/84* 11, no. 4 (1975), pp. 1ff.

32. Herbert Richardson, ed., *Religion and Political Society* (New York: Harper & Row, 1974), p. 1.

33. Juan Luis Segundo, "Capitalism Versus Socialism: *Crux Theologica.*" In *Frontiers of Theology in Latin America*, ed. R. Gibellini (Maryknoll: Orbis, 1979), pp. 246f.

34. Terry Eagleton, *Walter Benjamin: Or Towards a Revolutionary Criticism* (London: Verso, 1981), p. 141.

35. See e.g. Roland Barthes, *Mythologies*, tran. A. Lavers (New York: Hill & Wang, 1972).

36. Raymond Williams, *Marxism and Literature* (London: Oxford University Press, 1977), p. 168.

37. Terry Eagleton, *Literary Theory: An Introduction* (Minneapolis: University of Minnesota Press, 1983), p. 142. Deconstructionism is currently ascendant in the professional guild of North American theologians and biblical scholars. For many the preoccupation with discourse shrugs off the matter of practice (except, of course, "discursive practice"). While such attitudes no doubt reflect the social location of the university, I agree with Robert Weimann's warning about the "refusal of the latest avant-garde to serve in any re-presentative function":

> There is no point in ignoring the disruption suffered by the liberal imagination and the forlorn stand of the traditional humanistic education vis-a-vis the anonymity of the powers that be (not to mention the threats to the survival of human life, which are, literally, unspeakable). The urgency of the issues raised by the antirepresentationalist directions of post-structuralist thought must not be underestimated, especially when so many forms of interpretation and representation (including their political correlative) can be shown to constitute "a technique of power," a form of "reduction, repression, obliteration of fact" (*Structure and Society in Literary History: Studies in the History and Theory of Historical Criticism* (Baltimore: Johns Hopkins University Press, 1984), pp. 291f.

38. See Jack Nelson-Pallmeyer, *War Against the Poor: Low-Intensity Conflict and Christian Faith* (Maryknoll: Orbis, 1989), and *Brave New World Order: Must We Pledge Allegiance?* (Maryknoll: Orbis, 1992)

39. Jon Sobrino, *Christology at the Crossroad: A Latin American Approach*, tran. J. Drury (Maryknoll: Orbis, 1978), p. 222.

40. Lamb, "The Challenge of Critical Theory," p. 187.

41. Mendes-Flohr, "'To Brush History Against the Grain'," p. 635.

42. Carl Braaten, *Christ and Counter-Christ: Apocalyptic Themes in Theology and Culture* (Philadelphia: Fortress, 1972), p. 10.

43. See Ched Myers, *Who Will Roll Away the Stone? Discipleship Queries for First World Christians* (Maryknoll: Orbis, 1994), ch. 12.

44. Gary Smith, ed., *Benjamin: Philosophy, History, Aesthetics* (Chicago: University of Chicago Press, 1989).

45. *One Dimensional Man*, pp. xiiif.

46. Herbert Marcuse, *An Essay on Liberation* (Boston: Beacon, 1969), p. 6.

47. Edward Abbey, *One Life at a Time, Please* (New York: Henry Holt & Co., 1988), p. 168.

48. Owen Chadwick, *The Reformation* (London: Penguin, 1964), pp. 59ff.

49. "The Nature of the Anabaptist Protest," *Mennonite Quarterly Review* 45, no. 4 (October 1971), pp. 291ff; "The Anabaptist Critique of Constantinian Christendom," *Mennonite Quarterly Review* 55, no. 3 (July 1981), pp. 218ff.

50. *Ethics*, p. 20.

51. The Friends (under the influence of John 15:15) began as a non-conformist movement founded by George Fox (1624–91) in Stuart England during the mid and late 17th century. It quickly spread to North America, where William Penn attempted to found a colony on Quaker socio-political ideals; Elbert Russell, *The History of Quakerism* (Richmond, Friends United Press, 1979).

"Unprogrammed" Friends refer to their silent worship services as "meetings," and their polity is organized by local monthly meetings and regional yearly meetings. Today they are outnumbered by "programmed" Friends, whose churches and theology tend to resemble conservative baptist-type traditions.

52. Leonard Kenworthy, *Quaker Quotations on Faith and Practice*, Pamphlet (Kennett Square, PA: Quaker Publications, 1981), xxx:71.

53. "Testimonies, Queries and Advices in Historical Perspective," in *Friends Consultation on Testimonies, Queries and Advices*, Proceedings of conference held December 8–11, 1988 (Richmond, IN: Quaker Hill Conference Center, 1988), pp. 1–15.

54. Ibid., p. 9.

55. Ibid., p. 2.

56. Ibid., p. 1.

57. Douglas Steere, ed., *Quaker Spirituality: Selected Writings*, Classics of Western Spirituality (New York: Paulist Press, 1984), pp. 22f.

58. Kenworthy, *Quaker Quotations on Faith and Practice*, xxx:72.

59. Herb Lape, "Friends Testimonies, Queries and Advices in Revising Quaker Faith and Practice." in *Friends Consultation on Testimonies, Queries and Advices*, p. 29.

60. *The Journal and Major Essays of John Woolman*, ed. P. Moulton (Richmond, IN: Friends United Press, 1989), pp. 3f.

61. Harold Loukes, *The Uncomfortable Queries*, Study in Fellowship no. 30. (London: Friends Home Service Committee; 1968), pp. 1ff.

62 *Faith and Practice of Pacific Yearly Meeting of the Religious Society of Friends: A Quaker Quide to Christian Doctrine* (San Francisco: Pacific Yearly Meeting, 1985), pp. 12-13.

63. Mainstream Christian reliance on the traditional just war ethic has rarely functioned to empower church members to *critique*, much less *noncooperate*, with authority when the demands of war violate the limits of principle (Yoder, *When War is Unjust*). I have already noted how many U.S. Catholics discovered that they did not know how to *implement* their bishops' 1983 Peace Pastoral at the parish or parochial school level, since there were few institutional precedents for moral formation on political issues.

64. Peter Brock, *Pioneers of the Peaceable Kingdom: The Quaker Peace Testimony from the Colonial Era to the First World War* (Princeton: Princeton University Press, 1968).

65 *Faith and Practice of Pacific Yearly Meeting*, p. 25.

66. Brock, *Pioneers of the Peaceable Kingdom*, pp. 122ff

67. William Durland, *People Pay for Peace: A Military Tax Refusal Guide for Radical Religious Pacifists and People of Conscience* (Colorado Springs: Center Peace Publishers, 1982).

68. Jones, "Testimonies, Queries and Advices in Historical Perspective," pp. 9f.

69 *Christian Faith and Practice in the Experience of the Society of Friends* (London: London Yearly Meeting).

70. Lape, "Friends Testimonies, Queries and Advices in Revising Quaker Faith and Practice," p. 24.

71. Michael Sheehan, *Beyond Majority Rule: Voteless Decisions in the Religious Society of Friends* (Westchester, PA: Philadelphia Yearly Meeting, 1983).

72. Stanley Hauerwas, *A Community of Character: Toward a Constructive Christian Social Ethic* (Notre Dame: University of Notre Dame Press, 1981), pp.

73 *Faith and Practice of Philadelphia Yearly Meeting of the Religious Society of Friends: A Book of Christian Discipline* (Philadelphia: Phliadelphia Yearly Meeting, 1972).

74. Janet Clayton, "Cornel West: Seeking to Expand America's 'Public'Conversation," *Los Angeles Times* (May 9, 1993), p. M3.

75. P. 17.

Chapter 6: Ethnography-as-Theology: Inscribing the African American Sacred Story
Theophus Smith

1. *The Nature of Doctrine: Religion and Theology in a Postliberal Age* (Philadelphia: Westminster, 1984), p. 115.

2. James Clifford and George E. Marcus, eds., *Writing Culture: The Poetics and Politics of Ethnography* (Berkeley: University of California Press, 1986).

3. *Mimesis: The Representation of Reality in Western Literature*, (Garden City: Doubleday/Anchor Books, 1952), pp. 14–15. Cf. Auerbach, "Figura," in *Scenes from the Drama of European Literature*, ed. Wald Godzich and Jochen Schulte-Sasse (Minneapolis: University of Minnesota Press, 1984), pp. 11–76.

4. Paul Tillich, *Systematic Theology*, Volume 1 (Chicago: University of Chicago Press, 1951), p. 36. Cf. Paul Tillich, *Theology of Culture* (London: Oxford University Press, 1959).

5. Robert J. Schreiter, *Constructing Local Theologies* (Maryknoll: Orbis, 1985), pp. 13, 62, 80–93.

6. See Stanley Hauerwas, with Richard Bondi and David B. Burrell, *Truthfulness and Tragedy: Further Investigations in Christian Ethics* (Notre Dame: University of Notre Dame Press, 1977).

7. "Post-Modern Ethnography: From Document of the Occult to Occult Document," in Clifford and Marcus, eds., *Writing Culture*, p. 127.

8. James Wm. McClendon, Jr., *Biography as Theology: How Life Stories Can Remake Today's Theology* (Nashville: Abingdon, 1974), pp. 90, 93. The Exodus figure has informed Afro-American political projects from the post-Reconstruction period to the recent civil rights movement, in which a premier instance is Martin Luther King's leadership of the freedom movement. The figural dimension of King's leadership has been nicely articulated by historian Lerone Bennett, Jr. as consisting of two foci: "his original choice of himself as a symbolic being . . . and the further fact that the movement was already based on the solid rock of Negro religious tradition." That tradition was biblical and typological, which explains both King's aptitude for, and success in, representing himself as a type of Moses.

9. Auerbach, "Figura," p. 58.

10. Werner Sollors, *Beyond Ethnicity: Consent and Descent in American Culture* (New York: Oxford University Press, 1986), pp. 50, 57.

11. "Mother wit is a popular term in black speech referring to common sense. Mother wit is the kind of good sense not necessarily learned from books or in school. Mother wit [bears the] connotation of collective wisdom acquired by the experience of living and from generations past

[and] is often expressed in folklore." Alan Dundes, *Mother-Wit From the Laughing Barrel* (New York: Garland, 1981), p. xiv.

12. Diedre L. Badejo, "The Yoruba and Afro-American Trickster: A Contextual Comparison." *Présence Africaine* 147, no. 3 (1988), pp. 10, 15.

13. Albert J. Raboteau, *Slave Religion: The Invisible Institution in the Antebellum South* (New York: Oxford University Press, 1980), p. 251. Raboteau cites the Harding comment as follows: Vincent Harding, "The Uses of the Afro-American Past," *The Religious Situation*, 1969, edited by Donald R. Cutter (Boston: Beacon Press, 1969), pp. 829–40. On Afro-American "symbolic reversals" see Lucius T. Outlaw, "Language and Consciousness: Towards a Hermeneutic of Black Culture," *Cultural Hermeneutics* 1 (1974), pp. 403f.

14. James M. Glass, "The Philosopher and the Shaman: The Political Vision as Incantation," *Political Theory* 2:2 (May 1974):186.

15. Charles Shelby Rooks, "Toward the Promised Land: An Analysis of the Religious Experience of Black America" *The Black Church* II, no. I (September 1973), p. 8.

16. Harold Dean Trulear, "The Lord Will Make a Way Somehow: Black Worship and the Afro-American Story," *The Journal of the Interdenominational Theological Center* XIII, no. 1 (1985), p. 101.

17. See René Girard, *Things Hidden Since the Foundation of the World*, with J.-M. Ourgoulian and G. Lefort (Stanford: Stanford University Press, 1987).

18. Albert J. Raboteau, *Slave Religion*, p. 313.

19. Adela Yarbro Collins, *Crisis and Catharsis: The Power of the Apocalypse* (Philadelphia: Westminster, 1984), pp. 152–53.

20. "As far as we know, the book of Revelation was written to avoid violence rather than to encourage it. The faithful are called upon to endure, not to take up arms. The violent imagery was apparently intended to release aggressive feelings in a harmless way. Nevertheless, what is cathartic for one person may be inflammatory for another. . . . Norman Cohn's book *The Pusuit of the Millennium* has shown that apocalyptic imagery has been linked historically to violence under certain conditions." However, Collin's hypothesis of cathartic release is unconvincing in the terms she employs. "The projection," she offers in explanation, "of the conflict onto a cosmic screen [of good vs. evil], as it were, is cathartic in the sense that it clarifies and objectifies the conflict. Fearful feelings are vented by the very act of expressing them, especially in this larger-than-life and exaggerated way." But it is obvious with a moment's reflection that intensification can just as easily lead to the reinforcement— and to the reactionary and aggressive escalation—of such feelings rather than to their purgation.

Indeed, in a more critical mode Collins admits as much. She admits that "the long-term effectiveness of the Apocalypse's means of reducing tension . . . is questionable because of the use of violent imagery, its ambiguous effect, and the ambiguity of violence itself." Ibid, pp. 170–71. Lacking a more developed theory of catharsis—or an analytic treatment of violence and religion such as Girardian theory provides—Collins is unable to derive a principle for differentiating between the violent and the nonviolent potentials in apocalyptic imagery.

21. In all four of the gospels, René Girard maintains, apocalyptic violence is ascribed to human beings principally, and not to a vengeful God. Contrary to conventional apocalyptic sensibilities, a non-sacrificial gospel reading locates the nemesis of our species internally rather than projecting it onto 'the sacred':

> We must realize that the apocalytic violence predicted by the Gospels is not divine in origin. In the Gospels, this violence is always brought home to men, and not to God. What makes the reader think that this is still the Old Testament wrath of God is the fact that most features of the Apocalypse, the great images in the picture, are drawn from Old Testament texts.
>
> These images remain relevant because they describe the mimetic and sacrificial crisis . . . but this time there is no longer a god to cut short the violence, or indeed to inflict it in the first place. So we have a lengthy decomposition of the city of man . . . In the last days, we are told, 'most men's love will grow cold'. As a result, the combat between [mimetic] doubles will be in evidence everywhere. Meaningless conflict will be worldwide . . . " Girard, *Things Hidden*, p. 188.

Here Girard's analysis provides a principle, missing in Collin's analysis, for differentiating between violent (sacrificial) *and* nonviolent (nonsacrificial) appropriations of the cardinal text of Christian apocalyptic. It is, moreover, a priniciple that can supplement her and complete her cathartic hypothesis. Nonviolent readings attribute apocalyptic phenomena to human agency and failure rather than to the active will or menace of a vengeful God. The principle of violence, on the contrary, operates in a sacrificial matrix which identifies "violence and the sacred." In that matrix God or the gods provide the ultimate sanction for humanity's intraspecies production of victims. Therein 'the sacred' is constituted as the sanction for our collective, primordial recourse to victimization. When human beings instead acknowledge responsibility for violence as our own social production, we require no such divine sanction. We thus dissolve the identification of violence with the sacred and therefore demystify our own violence. The question of practice remains, however: What do we do with this acknowledged self-generation of violence?

22. Cf. Scott Heller, "Worldwide 'Diaspora' of Peoples Poses New Challenges for Scholars," *The Chronicle of Higher Education* XXXVIII, no. 39 (June 3, 1992), pp. A7–9.

23. Martin Luther King, Jr., *Strength to Love*, in *A Testament of Hope: The Essential Writings of Martin Luther King, Jr.*, ed. James M. Washington (New York: HarperCollins, 1991), pp. 621–29.

24. David H. Kelsey, *The Uses of Scripture in Recent Theology* (Philadelphia: Fortress, 1975), p. 163. I quote Kelsey here because my use of the term 'pharmacopeia' conforms precisely to his description of a theological project that is imaginatively informed by a "single metaphorical judgment." However, Kelsey's comment also orients the trajectory of such a judgment toward the church and its activities. In this regard the pertinence of the current study to ecclesiology, practical theology and church life, may be insufficiently articulated. It is evident that my initial efforts to elaborate the metaphorical utility of 'pharmacopeia' more readily comprise a cultural rather than an ecclesial theology. As already acknowledged, the major influence on my efforts in this regard is Paul Tillich's program of a "theology of culture," which he presented as a newly developing contemporary source of systematic theology. Of course, this initial influence in no way precludes ecclesially oriented developments of this study in the future.

25. See Robert Farris Thompson, *Flash of the Spirit: African and Afro-American Art and Philosophy* (New York, Vintage, 1984), p. 107.

26. Timothy L. Smith, "Slavery and Theology: The Emergence of Black Christian Consciousness in 19th Century America," *Church History* 41 (1972), p. 498.

27. Ibid., pp. 497–512.

28. Archie Smith, Jr., *The Relational Self: Ethics and Therapy from a Black Church Perspective* (Nashville: Abingdon, 1982), p. 76.

29. Lindbeck, *The Nature of Doctrine*, p. 114.

30. Here I complete the postliberal trajectory of Lindbeck's endeavor by correcting his liberal retreat from proclamation with Barth's kerygmatic insistence, while at the same time balancing Barth's counter-liberal neo-orthodoxy with Lindbeck's attention to religion as discursive practices in addition to beliefs and experiences.

31. Jacques Derrida, *Dissemination*, trans. Barbara Johnson (Chicago: University of Chicago Press, 1981).

32. See Amanda Porterfield, "Shamanism: A Psychosocial Definition," *Journal of the American Academy of Religion* LV, no. 4 (Winter 1987): 725–26. As Porterfield argues, shamanism is personally *embodied* symbol production for the purpose of psychological and social *conflict resolution*.

33. King, *Strength to Love*, p. 617.

34. Erica Sherover-Marcuse, *Emancipation and Consciousness: Dogmatic and Dialectical Perspectives in the Early Marx* (New York: Basil Blackwell, 1986), pp. 141–42.

Chapter 7: The Church's One Foundation is Jesus Christ Her Lord; Or, In a World Without Foundations: All We Have is the Church
Stanley Hauerwas

1. James Wm. McClendon, Jr. and James M. Smith, *Understanding Religious Convictions* (Notre Dame: University of Notre Dame Press, 1975). McClendon's and Smith's account of convictions has never been exploited sufficiently in recent theology. In particular if their account of justification were followed the way theological convictions could interact with other convictions communities would be enriched. Nancey Murphy's *Theology in the Age of Scientific Reasoning* (Ithaca: Cornell University Press, 1990) is an example of the kind of work McClendon's and Smith's analysis should encourage.

2. For McClendon's account of that tradition see his *Ethics: Systematic Theology*, Volume I (Nashville: Abingdon, 1986), pp. 27–35. In my "Reading McClendon Takes Practice," (unpublished manuscript) I raise the question of whether a baptist can be, as McClendon's claiming of Dorothy Day might suggest, a Catholic. Of course McClendon claims her as part of the baptist tradition.

3. I confess I find the "humility" of much of current Christian theology and practice humiliating. In a time like ours the Church's task is to celebrate the triumph of our Lord. God is providing the Church with that possibility by freeing us from our secular power. Our new found weakness can become a source of renewed power. As John Milbank observes, "the pathos of modern theology is its false humility" (*Theology and Social Theory: Beyond Secular Reason*; Cambridge: Basil Blackwell, 1990, p. 1). Milbank counters the totalizing narratives of modernity with what he takes to be the totalizing narrative of the Church. I have no doubt that we Christians, particularly when confronted by liberalism, cannot help but appear imperialistic, but I am not sure our story is well told if we try to replace the totalizing narratives of modernity. Christians must live by witness.

4. My frequent claim that the first task of the church is not to make the world just, but to make the world the world must be understood in this light. There is no world unless there is a church nor can the world have a history without the church. That is the reason that the church knows the world better than the world can know itself.

5. Though McClendon develops the notion of practice in the section of the *Ethics* dealing with the social strand he certainly does not restrict practices to that strand. See *Ethics*, pp. 162–84.

6. McClendon, *Ethics*, p. 66.

7. Methodist clergy do not belong to the local churches they serve. They are members of their respective annual conferences.

8. James Wm. McClendon, *Doctrine: Systematic Theology*, Volume II (Nashville: Abingdon, 1994), Part II.

9. For a more extended reflection on Broadway United Methodist Church see the chapter "The Ministry of a Congregation: Rethinking Christian Ethics for a Church-Centered Seminary," in my *Christian Existence Today: Essays on Church, World, and Living In Between* (Durham: Labyrinth, 1988), pp. 111–32.

10. David and Barbara Koehler joined Broadway at the same time I was received. David wrote the letter that appears in "Ministry of a Congregation" in my *Christian Existence Today*.

11. This is a paraphrase of Cardinal Suhard's wonderful suggestion, "To be a witness does not consist in engaging in propaganda, nor even in stirring people up, but in being a living mystery. It means to live in such a way that one's life would not make sense if God did not exist." I do not know where Cardinal Suhard said or wrote this. I have it on Reverend Michael Baxter's, C.S.C. ordination announcement.

12. The Reverend John Smith was the pastor at Broadway from 1974–1984. He labored for years to help us see the importance of the eucharist for the constitution of our common life. I tell the story in the "Ministry of a Congregation."

13. Sarah Webb-Phillips became the minister to Broadway two years after John Smith. She was wonderfully diligent about those, like me, who had moved but had not transferred our membership.

14. Gary Camp was mildly mentally handicapped. He attended with his mother for many years. At his mother's death, Gary, who was in his late twenties, was devastated. But the church remained his home.

15. James W. McClendon, Jr. *Biography as Theology*, 2nd ed. (Philadelphia: Trinity Press International, 1990). The first edition was published in 1974.

16. The first four lives are those that shape McClendon's account in *Biography*, the latter three are the heart of the *Ethics*.

Chapter 8: Narrative Theology and the Religious Affections
Richard Steele

1. George Lindbeck, *The Nature of Doctrine: Religion and Theology in a Postliberal Age* (Philadelphia: Westminster, 1984), pp. 16–21, 30–32, and *passim*.

2. On James McClendon's use of Edwards, see *Ethics: Systematic Theology*, Volume I (Nashville: Abingdon, 1986), pp. 110–55; and *Doctrine: Systematic Theology*, Volume II (Nashville: Abingdon, 1994), chs. 1, 3, 6, and 9. On his use of various analytic philosophers, see "Baptism as a Performative Sign," *Theology Today* 23, no. 3 (October 1966), pp. 403–416; "How Is Religious Talk Justifiable," in *American Philosophy and the Future*,

ed. Michael Novak (New York: Scribner's, 1968), pp. 324–46; "Can There Be Talk About God-and-the-World?," *Harvard Theological Review* 62, no. 1 (January 1969), pp. 33–49; and James Wm. McClendon, Jr. and James M. Smith, *Understanding Religious Convictions* (Notre Dame: University of Notre Dame Press, 1975), pp. 49–83.

3. The following account of feelings and emotions draws heavily upon the following sources: Errol Bedford, "Emotions," in *The Philosophy of Mind*, ed. V. C. Chappell (Englewood Cliffs: Prentice-Hall, 1962), pp. 110–26; Robert M. Gordon, "The Aboutness of Emotions," *American Philosophical Quarterly* 11, no. 1 (January 1974), pp. 27–36; Paul L. Holmer, *Making Christian Sense* (Philadelphia: Westminster, 1984), pp. 36–60; Anthony Kenny, *Action, Emotion and Will* (New York: Humanities, 1963); G. D. Marshall, "On Being Affected," *Mind* 77 (April 1968), pp. 243–59; Robert C. Roberts, *Spirituality and Human Emotions* (Grand Rapids: Eerdmans, 1982), pp. 12–24; Gilbert Ryle, "Feelings," *The Philosophical Quarterly* 1, no. 3 (April 1951), pp. 193–205; *idem., The Concept of Mind* (New York: Barnes & Noble, 1949); and Robert C. Solomon, *The Passions: The Myth and Nature of Human Emotion* (New York: Anchor/Doubleday, 1976; reprint ed., Notre Dame: University of Notre Dame Press, 1983).

4. Space limitations prohibit me from analyzing the equally distinctive languages of sentiments, moods, attitudes, and passions. The reader is referred to the literature cited in the previous note, and especially to the works by Holmer, Kenny, Roberts, and Ryle, for just such an analysis.

5. Let me make two caveats here: First, although I will try to show that all emotions entail judgments, I do not hold that all judgments entail emotions. For we can make judgments about objects in which we have little or no interest, and therefore about which we have little or no emotion. Nor do I mean to reduce emotions to judgments, as if emotions were purely cognitive and not also conative. Second, here and elsewhere I use the term "object" in the formal, grammatical sense, e.g., in the sense that a preposition takes one. (And as we shall see, emotions are often modified by prepositional phrases.) But the specific object of an emotion might be a person, a thing, an event, or a situation. In particular, I want to emphasize that for someone to make someone else the "object" of his emotions (e.g., love or envy) does not mean that the former is thereby treating the latter as a dehumanized "thing." Cf. the following definition of "object relations" given in *A Psychiatric Glossary*, 3rd ed. (Washington, D.C.: American Psychiatric Association, 1969), p. 65: "the emotional bonds that exist between an individual and another person."

6. The conditions under which emotions are irrational or "go wrong" are explained by Solomon, 381–88.

7. Of course, we can sometimes say of someone that "his judgment was clouded by emotion," which seems quite the reverse of saying that

his emotions were disordered by faulty judgments. But there is no contradiction here, for the psychological insight that our emotions effect our judgments does not touch the epistemological fact that we cannot even have emotions without making judgments about their objects. If I am known to resent another scholar for getting a fat research grant denied to me, and later write a scathing review of his ensuing book, one might suspect that my judgment of his *work* was clouded by my emotions toward *him*. But it would also be true to say that my emotions toward him were clouded by my judgment that *I* deserved that grant.

8. Cf. Stanley Hauerwas, *The Peaceable Kingdom: A Primer in Christian Ethics* (Notre Dame: University of Notre Dame Press, 1983), pp. 121–30; and McClendon, *Ethics*, pp. 47–75.

9. On "moral beauty," see Jonathan Edwards, *The Nature of True Virtue* in *The Works of Jonathan Edwards*, Vol. 8, *Ethical Writings*, ed. Paul Ramsey (New Haven: Yale University Press, 1989), pp. 537–627.

10. This is one of the key arguments in Solomon's magisterial study cited above. On p. 25 he writes: "Against the alleged passivity of the passions, I shall defend the theory that our passions are our own *doings*, and thus our own responsibility. And in place of that familiar lack of discrimination which takes all passions to be of equal value, I shall attempt to identify those passions with which I believe people can live *best*, in the light of reflection, and with the unhesitating acceptance of responsibility for the world we are thereby creating for ourselves." I agree with Solomon *that* we are responsible for our passions, but as an Augustinian Christian, I dispute his Existentialist views as to *which* ones enable people to "live best."

11. Pain, however, is one feeling that sometimes *is* fraught with moral significance, as the whole field of medical ethics shows. But its significance resides not in the physiological experience itself (for it is sometimes medically necessary and morally justifiable to *inflict* pain on someone), but in the fact that everything else in one's life can be thrown out of joint when pain is intense, constant, and irremediable.

12. See especially the following works by McClendon: *Biography as Theology: How Life Stories Can Remake Today's Theology*, new ed. (Philadelphia: Trinity Press International, 1990); "Three Strands of Christian Ethics," *Journal of Religious Ethics* 6, no. 1 (Spring 1978), pp. 54–80; *Ethics*, pp. 328–56; and "Narrative Ethics and Christian Ethics," *Faith and Philosophy* 3, no. 4 (October 1986), pp. 383–96. Terrence W. Tilley offers a splendid overview of the literature (and makes some important contributions of his own) in *Story Theology* (Collegeville: The Liturgical Press, 1985).

13. David Hume, *The Natural History of Religion*, ed. H. E. Root (Stanford, CA: Stanford University Press, 1956), pp. 52f. (slightly amended).

14. See J. B. Bury, *A History of Greece*, 2nd ed. (New York: The Modern Library, Random House, 1913), pp. 427–36, for an admiring portrait. Bury's chief source is Thucydides, *The Peloponnesian War*, Bks. 4 and 5.

15. Herodotus, *The Histories*, Bk. VII, Paras. 172–239.

16. Thucydides, *The Peloponnesian War*, Bk. V, Para. 9. The full story of the Battle of Amphipolis occupies Paragraphs 6–11. Actually, the Peloponnesian army under Brasidas was about equal in number, although inferior in battle experience, to the crack Athenian troops under Cleon. But Brasidas outwitted Cleon by leading a small force against the center of the Athenian line, while his lieutenant brought the rest of the Peloponnesians against the Athenian right flank. Brasidas was mortally wounded in the battle, but lived to see the victory that he had engineered. The city of Amphipolis, originally an Athenian colony, passed, apparently quite happily, into the hands of the Peloponnesian League, named Brasidas as its new founder, and began offering sacrifices and celebrating athletic competitions in his honor.

17. Jerald C. Brauer, ed., *The Westminster Dictionary of Church History* (Philadelphia: Westminster, 1971), s.v. "Bellarmine, Robert"; and Kenneth Scott Latourette, *A History of Christianity*, rev. ed., 2 vols. (New York: Harper & Row, Publishers, 1975), 2:848f.

18. Justo L. González, *A History of Christian Thought*, rev. ed., Volume 3, *From the Protestant Reformation to the Twentieth Century* (Nashville, Abingdon, 1987), p. 206.

19. Brauer, ed., *The Westminster Dictionary of Church History*, p. 101.

20. Gonzalez, *A History of Christian Thought*, 3:206.

21. Owen Chadwick, *The Reformation*, rev. ed., *The Penguin History of The Church*, Volume 3 (London: Penguin, 1972), p. 369.

22. It may be worth noting that Bellarmine was trained by the founder of the Society of Jesus himself, Ignatius Loyola. The *Spiritual Exercises* of Ignatius, which constitute the basis of Jesuit spiritual formation, include an important section titled, "To Have the True Sentiment Which We Ought to Have in the Church Militant." A modern interpreter of the *Exercises* claims that the rules set down in this section "are meant to be helpful in developing a true and loving sensitivity to the ways of thinking, feeling, and acting as a Catholic in our present-day Church." See David L. Fleming, S.J., *The Spiritual Exercises of St. Ignatius: A Literal Translation and a Contemporary Reading* (St. Louis: The Institute of Jesuit Sources, 1978), pp. 230ff.

23. This is why the advocates of modern liberal society seem to assume that nothing could be more intellectually or morally confining than "sectarianism." See Stanley M. Hauerwas, *Christian Existence Today: Essays on Church, World and Living In Between* (Durham: Labyrinth, 1988), pp. 1–21. To the "sectarian," however, liberalism may seem intellectually

and morally bankrupt precisely because, in its repudiation of any authoritative narratives which might unite the welter of sub-groups and counter-cultures that exist in modern society, it is unable to tell us who our heroes and saints should be. This fact is reflected in our public iconography. Those old portraits of Washington and Lincoln, solemn and venerable, have been removed from most schoolroom walls because, as a people, we are no longer sure that the national story in which they played such major roles is intelligible. How can those who willingly subordinated private interest to the public good serve as moral exemplars for children learning to be competitive producers and acquisitive consumers in the marketplace? The *patres patriae* have thus been replaced with colorful pictures of Bert and Ernie, who typify the only ideal we have left, namely, that people who have virtually nothing in common and are unwilling to make any extreme demands on each other can nevertheless get along happily.

24. Cf. McClendon's pithy phrase, "tournament of narratives," *Ethics*, p. 143, discussed in chapter 14 of this volume by Charles Scriven. Cf. also Alasdair MacIntyre, *After Virtue* (Notre Dame: University of Notre Dame Press, 1981). MacIntyre's objective, as stated on p. iii, is to show how, in the modern world, "various rival and heterogeneous moral schemes . . . compete for our allegiance."

25. It should be apparent that while I *do* want to align myself with those Christian thinkers who have emphasized "the religion of the heart," such as Augustine, Calvin, Edwards, Wesley, Pascal, and Kierkegaard, I certainly do *not* want to imply that "religion is a private matter," as many Americans appear to believe. For a penetrating analysis of the popular American notion that religion, like everything else, is a matter of private opinion and personal choice, see Robert N. Bellah, Richard Madsen, William M. Sullivan, Ann Swidler, and Steven M. Tipton, *Habits of the Heart: Individualism and Commitment in American Life* (Berkeley: University of California Press, 1985), pp. 219–49; and *idem, The Good Society* (New York: Vintage/Random House, 1991), pp. 179–219.

26. Romans 12:9-19, NEB (selected verses).

27. An exhaustive catalog of these emotions and a wonderful discussion of four biblical characters (David, Paul, John, and Jesus) who exhibited them are to be found in Jonathan Edwards, *A Treatise Concerning Religious Affections*, ed. John Smith, vol. 1 of *The Works of Jonathan Edwards* (New Haven: Yale University Press, 1959), pp. 93–124.

28. This is the hallmark of McClendon's baptist hermeneutic. See *Ethics*, pp. 17–46.

29. Cf. Jonathan Edwards, *The Distinguishing Marks of a Work of the Spirit of God* in *The Great Awakening*, ed. C. C. Goen, vol. 4 of *The Works of Jonathan Edwards* (New Haven: Yale University Press, 1972), 213–288.

Edwards's text is I John 4:1, "Beloved, believe not every spirit, but try the spirits whether they are of God. . . ."

30. *Ethics*, p. 143.

31. Lindbeck, *The Nature of Doctrine*, p. 21.

32. Lindbeck does not include James on his list of representative experiential-expressivists, but the following discussion of his position should indicate why he belongs there.

33. *The Varieties of Religious Experience* (New York: Mentor, 1958), p. 42.

34. Lindbeck, *The Nature of Doctrine*, p. 40. For a charming and subtle discussion of how the differing philosophical and religious ideals of Christianity and Buddhism, as well as Stoicism and Deism, affect their differing attitudes toward human emotion, see Kosuke Koyama, *Water-buffalo Theology* (Maryknoll: Orbis, 1974), pp. 95–105, 115–25, and 133–60 (Koyama makes no reference here to the ideology of the French revolution, but elsewhere in the book he shows a keen understanding of Marxism and Maoism).

35. I am indebted to Professor Lindbeck for taking the time to discuss some of the ideas included in this section with me. He was sympathetic with my suggestion that experiential-expressivism and foundationalism are kindred spirits, but observed that the former cannot properly be regarded as a species of the latter unless its theory of religious experience is linked, á la Karl Rahner, with a transcendentalist epistemology.

Chapter 9: Community, Narrative, and an Ecological Doctrine of Creation: Creation and Ecology Beyond Modern Atheism
Elizabeth Barnes

1. San Francisco: HarperCollins, 1992.

2. Boston: Beacon, 1989.

3. Nashville: Abingdon, 1974.

4. *Ethics: Systematic Theology*, Volume I (Nashville: Abingdon, 1986).

5. *Doctrine: Systematic Theology*, Volume II (Nashville: Abingdon, 1994).

6. Ibid., p. 148

7. Ibid., p. 149

8. Ibid.

9. Ibid.

10. *Ethics*, p. 33.

11. *Doctrine*, p. 161.

12. Ibid.

13. Ibid., p. 162.

14. Ibid., p. 165.

15. Ibid.

16. Ibid.
17. Ibid., p. 166.
18. Ibid.
19. Ibid.
20. Ibid., p. 167.
21. Ibid., p. 169.
22. Ibid.
23. Ibid., pp. 176-77.
24. Ibid., p. 177.
25. Ibid., p. 189
26. Ruether, *Gaia and God: An Ecofeminist Theology of Earth Healing,* p. 2.
27. Ibid., p. 4.
28. Ibid., p. 206.
29. Ibid., p. 207.
30. Ibid., p. 171.
31. Ibid., pp. 249–51.
32. Ibid., p. 252.
33. Ibid.
34. Ibid., pp. 254–55.
35. Ibid., p. 258.
36. Ibid., p. 270.
37. Daly and Cobb, Jr., *For The Common Good: Redirecting the Economy Toward Community,* p. 20.
38. Ibid.
39. Ibid., p. 375.
40. Ibid., p. 397.
41. Ibid., pp. 397–98.
42. Chapter 7.
43. Ibid., p. 307.
44. Ibid, p. 309.
45. Ibid, p. 314.
46. Ibid, p. 309
47. Ibid., p. 189 (emphasis added)

Chapter 10: Narrative Justice as Reiteration
Glen H. Stassen

1. James Wm. McClendon, Jr., *Biography as Theology: How Life Stories Can Remake Today's Theology* (Nashville: Abingdon, 1974), pp. 82–83. I have translated this early writing into gender-inclusive language, in keeping with McClendon's own style and spirit.
2. Ibid., p. 93.
3. Ibid., pp. 114–15.

4. James Wm. McClendon, Jr., *Ethics: Systematic Theology*, Volume I (Nashville: Abingdon, 1986), p. 191.

5. Ibid., p. 194.

6. Ibid., p. 280.

7. McClendon, *Doctrine: Systematic Theology*, Volume II (Nashville: Abingdon, 1994), p. 306.

8. A story well told by Jerry Gentry, "Narrative Ethics and Economic Justice: Toward an Ethics of Inclusion" (unpublished Ph.D. dissertation, Southern Baptist Theological Seminary, 1989). Gentry's work is the best exception to the judgment I have just expressed. He deserves much thanks as an inspiration for what I write here.

9. Since at least my dissertation on "The Sovereignty of God in the Theological Ethics of H. Richard Niebuhr," (Duke University, 1967), and in various writings since then.

10. McClendon, *Biography as Theology*, pp. 14ff.

11. H. R. Niebuhr, "The Grace of Doing Nothing," *The Christian Century*, 44 (March 23, 1932), pp. 378–80; Reinhold Niebuhr, "Must We Do Nothing?" ibid. (March 30, 1932), pp. 415–17; H.R. Niebuhr, "The Only Way Into the Kingdom of God," ibid. (April 6, 1932), p. 447. Hans Frei interprets the debate, and Reinhold's misunderstanding, in his "H. Richard Niebuhr on History, Church, and Nation," in *The Legacy of H. Richard Niebuhr*, ed. Ronald F. Thiemann (Minneapolis: Fortress, 1991), pp. 15ff.

12. In his unpublished manuscript written for the Hazen Foundation, "Reinhold Niebuhr's Understanding of History" (summer, 1949), H. Richard focuses his criticisms on this point—God's active involvement in history, in Jesus' history and our history. It is symbolic that he did not publish the manuscript, and that few people even know of it. I have never seen it cited. I owe thanks to Waldo Beach for my copy.

13. McClendon, *Biography as Theology*, p. 32.

14. McClendon, *Ethics*, pp. 64ff. and *passim*.

15. Public Lecture, Spalding University, November 5, 1993.

16. Mikael Broadway concludes that Walzer's Aristotelian and narrative attention to communal habits of thought contrasts with other thinkers who are individualistic, heavily abstract and ahistorical ("Paying Attention: Michael Walzer and Theology of the Political," unpublished paper presented to the Religion and Social Sciences Section of the American Academy of Religion, 1991, pp. 1, 5–6, 14). Elizabeth Bounds writes that Walzer "seems to combine the best of . . . a liberal insistence on the equal worth of all human beings and a rich communitarian account of historically-grounded communal moral life," while discarding "the problematic features, such as the liberal abstract self and the communitarian avoidance of questions of equality" (Elizabeth Bounds, "'At Home in the Community': The Communal Discourse of Michael Walzer," paper

presented at the Religion and Social Science Section of the American Academy of Religion (1991), p. 1, and forthcoming in the *Journal of Religious Ethics*). L. Gregory Jones concludes, with Jeffrey Stout, that "Michael Walzer's vision of . . . justice is more useful" than John Rawls's; it "does not rest on a conception of rationality but is rooted in and warranted by social complexity" ("Should Christians affirm Rawls' Justice as Fairness? A Response to Professor Beckley," *Journal of Religious Ethics* 16, no. 2 (Summer, 1988), pp. 259 and 262). Georgia Warnke praises his understanding of justice for being socially and historically situated rather than abstract and detached ("Social Interpretation and Political Theory: Walzer and His Critics," in *Hermeneutics and Critical Theory in Ethics and Politics*, ed. Michael Kelly (Cambridge, Mass.: MIT Press, 1990), p. 219). William Galston notices the same virtues in his "Community, Democracy, Philosophy: The Political Thought of Michael Walzer," *Political Theory* 17, no. 1: (1989), p. 119. James Turner Johnson concludes that "his taking religion seriously . . . makes Walzer's work of special interest for the religious ethicist; in many ways they are engaged in the same, or convergent, critical tasks" ("Michael Walzer and Religious Ethics," *Religious Studies Review* 16, no. 3 (1990), p. 202).

17. Young, *Justice and the Politics of Difference* (Princeton: Princeton University Press, 1990), pp. 6f., 17f., 72, 81, 91, 105, 210, 216, 217).

18. Susan Moller Okin, *Justice, Gender and the Family* (New York: Basic, 1989), pp. 9, 62, 111–12.

19. *The Company of Critics* (New York: Basic, 1988), pp. 67f.

20. Walzer, "A Particularism of My Own," *Religious Studies Review* 16, no. 3 (1990), pp. 195–6.

21. Walzer, *Obligations: Essays on Disobedience, War, and Citizenship* (New York: Simon and Schuster, 1970), p. 22.

22. *Company of Critics*, pp. 149–51.

23. Ibid., p. 207.

24. Ibid., p. 203.

25. Ibid., p. 236.

26. Seyla Benhabib, *Situating the Self: Gender, Community and Postmodernism in Contemporary Ethics* (New York: Routledge, 1992), pp. 70ff.

27. *Exodus and Revolution*, pp. ix-x.

28. Ibid., p. 149.

29. *Spheres of Justice*, pp. xiii-xiv and 17.

30. Walzer, *Spheres of Justice*, p. 18.

31. I have taken up this issue in my essay, "Michael Walzer's Situated Justice," *Journal of Religious Ethics* (forthcoming Fall, 1994).

32. *Spheres of Justice*, pp. 44–45, 47, 203, 207, 209.

33. Ibid., p. 47.

34. Ibid., pp. 314 and 320.

35. Fritz Stern, *The Politics of Cultural Despair: A Study in the Rise of the Germanic Ideology* (Garden City: Doubleday, 1965), pp. 1–3, 10, 16f., 337.

36. Okin, *Justice, Gender, and the Family*, pp. 46, 51, 53, 61, and 71.

37. David Hollenbach, *Claims in Conflict: Retrieving and Renewing the Catholic Human Rights Tradition* (New York: Paulist, 1979; and *Justice, Peace and Human Rights: American Catholic Social Ethics in a Pluralistic World* (New York: Crossroad, 1988).

38. In a forthcoming work entitled *The Character of Our Communities* (Nashville: Abingdon, 1995).

39. I have tried to tell the story in my *Just Peacemaking: Transforming Initiatives for Justice and Peace* (Louisville: Westminster/John Knox, 1992), chapter six.

40. McClendon, *Ethics*, pp. 65–66. I have brought together McClendon's words into what is mostly quotation and part paraphrase.

41. McClendon, "Three Strands of Christian Ethics," in *Journal of Religious Ethics* 6, no. 1 (Spring, 1978), pp. 54–80.

42. *Ethics*, p. 67.

43. *Political Action* (Chicago: Quadrangle, 1971); *Radical Principles* (New York: Basic, 1980).

44. *Ethics*, p. 31.

45. Stassen, *Just Peacemaking* (Louisville: Westminster/John Knox, 1992), pp. 39ff., 71ff., and chapter 6. Jürgen Moltmann and Glen Stassen, *Justice Creates Peace* (Louisville: Baptist Peacemaker International Spirituality Series, 1988).

46. Stephen Charles Mott, *Biblical Ethics and Social Change* (New York: Oxford University Press, 1982), chapters 2, 4, and 5. Bruce C. Birch, *Let Justice Roll Down: The Old Testament, Ethics, and Christian Life* (Louisville: Westminster/John Knox, 1991).

Chapter 11: Living in Another World as One Response to Relativism
Mark Nation

1. Quoted in Clifford Geertz, *The Interpretation of Cultures* (New York: Basic, 1973), p. 87.

2. James Wm. McClendon, Jr., *Biography As Theology*, 2nd ed. (Philadelphia: Trinity Press International 1990), p. 23.

3. Among others, Jacques Ellul and Paul Johnson, in various writings, have challenged these overstatements.

4. Though I will below add some refinement to my discussion of relativism and absolutism or objectivism, I am not, in this paper, concerned with the various uses of the terms. For some of that discussion see, *inter alia*, Richard J. Bernstein, *Beyond Objectivism and Relativism* (Philadelphia: University of Pennsylvania Press, 1983); Michael Krausz and Jack

W. Meiland, eds., *Relativism: Cognitive and Moral* (Notre Dame: University of Notre Dame Press, 1982); and Michael Krausz, ed., *Relativism: Interpretation and Confrontation* (Notre Dame: University of Notre Dame Press, 1989).

5. Peter L. Berger, *The Heretical Imperative* (Garden City: Doubleday, 1979), p. 10. Kenneth J. Gergen in *The Saturated Self* (New York: Basic, 1991) ascribes the "vertigo of relativity" more to what he would describe as a postmodern world. But both Berger and Gergen are referring to much the same phenomenon.

6. Krausz and Meiland, eds., *Relativism*, p. 6; see also Alasdair MacIntyre, "Relativism, Power, and Philosophy," in *After Philosophy: End or Transformation?*, ed. Kenneth Baynes, James Bohman, and Thomas McCarthy (Cambridge: MIT Press, 1987), p. 386.

7. Patrick Gardiner, "German Philosophy and the Rise of Relativism," *The Monist* 64 (April 1981), pp. 138–53.

8. Ibid., p. 146.

9. Ibid.

10. Ibid., p. 142: cf. John Milbank, *Theology and Social Theory: Beyond Secular Reason* (Cambridge, Mass.: Basil Blackwell, 1990), pp. 148–54.

11. The chief book that articulates his basic approach to the sociology of knowledge is the one he coauthored with Thomas Luckmann, *The Social Construction of Reality* (New York: Anchor, 1967). It is interesting to note that they give as the chief intellectual antecedents for the sociology of knowledge Marx, Nietzsche, and historicism (p. 5).

12. Peter L. Berger, *The Heretical Imperative* (Garden City: Anchor, 1979), p. 11; what follows is taken from chapter 1.

13. For a brief discussion of plausibility structures see Peter L. Berger, *A Rumor of Angels: Modern Society and the Rediscovery of the Supernatural* (Garden City: Anchor, 1970), 34ff.

14. The passion with which many in our society speak of the overriding value of individual choice also illustrates the American traditions rooted in individualism and, especially, individual liberty.

15. Berger, *The Heretical Imperative*, p. 28.

16. Ibid., p .10.

17. Gergen, *The Saturated Self*, p. 49.

18. Ibid., p. 86.

19. Allan Bloom, *The Closing of the American Mind* (New York: Simon & Schuster, 1987), p. 25.

20. Ibid., p. 26.

21. This point is made by many people. See, e.g., Bernard Williams, *Morality: An Introduction to Ethics* (New York: Harper & Row, 1972), pp. 20–26. See also Peter Berger's fine chapter, "The Perspective of Sociology: Relativizing the Relativizers," in *A Rumor of Angels*, pp. 28–48.

22. Stanley Fish, *Is There a Text in This Class?: The Authority of Interpretive Communities* (Cambridge: Harvard University Press, 1980), p. 319, emphasis his.

23. Richard Rorty, "Solidarity or Objectivity?" in Krausz, ed., *Relativism*, pp. 40–41.

24. Friedrich Nietzsche, "On Truth and Lie in an Extra-Moral Sense," in *The Portable Nietzsche*, ed. Walter Kaufmann (New York: Penguin, 1968), pp. 46–47.

25. Rorty, "Solidarity or Objectivity?", p. 37.

26. Although I hope it will be clear that my proposal is connected to the philosophical agenda of Alasdair MacIntyre as described, e.g., in *After Virtue*, rev. ed. (Notre Dame: University of Notre Dame Press, 1984).

27. Stanley Hauerwas, "Why the Truth Demands Truthfulness: An Imperious Engagement with Hartt," in Stanley Hauerwas and L. Gregory Jones, eds., *Why Narrative? Readings in Narrative Theology* (Grand Rapids: Eerdmans, 1989), pp. 303–310. What is needed is also set forth in James William McClendon, Jr., *Ethics: Systematic Theology*, Volume I (Nashville: Abingdon, 1986), esp. pp. 348–56.

28. John Howard Yoder, *The Priestly Kingdom: Social Ethics as Gospel* (Notre Dame: University of Notre Dame Press, 1984), p. 11.

29. Stanley Hauerwas, *After Christendom?: How the Church Is to Behave If Freedom, Justice, and a Christian Nation Are Bad Ideas* (Nashville: Abingdon, 1991), p. 97.

30. After first reading Peter Berger and reflecting on socialization within the church, I had questions about deliberately socializing within the church. Through a combination of my residual adherence to foundationalist assumptions and lingering Feuerbachian doubts I thought that any such felt *need* must be rooted in atheism. For God doesn't need our help to convince people to believe in him. But on further reflection I realized that was nonsense. Any group that believes in what they do—families or the military, e.g.—socialize their members. Intentional socializing, in itself, speaks neither for nor against the truth claims being made by the socializers. And, besides, was it not God who first created socializing structures for the people who would serve him?

31. On one model of disciplining see Marlin Jeschke, *Disciplining in the Church: Recovering a Ministry of the Gospel*, 3rd ed. (Scottdale: Herald, 1988).

32. Working out the details of this for specific congregations is far from simple. It has to be done with wisdom, attentiveness to the needs of the congregation involved, a mind for practicalities, and a sensitivity to the theological commitments of the church.

33. For one argument for the centrality of nonviolence for Christian convictions see Stanley Hauerwas, *The Peaceable Kingdom: A Primer in*

Christian Ethics (Notre Dame: University of Notre Dame Press, 1983). For the implications of this claim for interfaith dialogue see John H. Yoder, "The Disavowal of Constantine: An Alternative Perspective on Interfaith Dialogue," *Tantur Year Book 1975/76*, pp. 47–68, reprinted in John H. Yoder, *The Royal Priesthood*, ed. Michael G. Cartwright (Grand Rapids: Eerdmans, 1994).

34. On this point see John H. Yoder, *The Original Revolution*, rev. ed. (Scottdale: Herald, 1977), esp. chapter 3; and John Howard Yoder, *The Politics of Jesus*, rev. ed. (Grand Rapids: Eerdmans, 1994).

35. The following account is taken from Philip P. Hallie, *Lest Innocent Blood Be Shed* (New York: Harper & Row, 1979).

36. Ibid., p. 34.

37. Ibid., p. 203.

38. Others have estimated that the number of Jews saved by the Chambonnais is closer to 5,000. See, e.g., Gay Block and Malka Drucker, *Rescuers: Portraits of Moral Courage in the Holocaust* (NY: Holmes & Meier Pub. Inc., 1992), p. 113.

39. If one does not believe the integrity of lives matter for how correlative convictions are perceived one ought to, on the one hand, be present at a conference where Dietrich Bonhoeffer is a primary focus or, on the other hand, listen carefully when a televangelist is caught in a scandal.

40. Richard Rorty, *Philosophy and the Mirror of Nature*, (Princeton: Princeton University Press, 1979), p. 4.

Chapter 12: Textual Relativism, Philosophy of Language, and the baptist Vision
Nancey Murphy

1. Notre Dame: University of Notre Dame Press, 1975.

2. *An Essay Concerning Human Understanding* (1690), III, ii, 2.

3. *Essay*, III, iv, 17.

4. *Language, Truth and Logic* (New York: Dover, n.d.), p. 107. Originally published in 1936.

5. *The Christian Faith*, ed. H.R. Mackintosh, J.S Stewart (Edinburgh: T. & T. Clark, 1960). First German edition, 1821/22.

6. See George Lindbeck's critique of both propositional and experiential-expressivist accounts of doctrine in *The Nature of Doctrine* (Philadelphia: Westminster, 1984). For an example of the misunderstandings created by different theories of language, see Margo Houts, "Language, Gender, and God: How Traditionalists and Feminists Play the Inclusive Language Game," Fuller Theological Seminary dissertation, 1993. Houts makes it clear that much of the heat generated by discussions of 'inclusive' language for God comes from the fact that feminist theologians

generally employ an expressivist theory of religious language; tradition-alists, a representational theory.

7. Ludwig Wittgenstein, in his later work, made a similar move. He focused on the use of language to make moves in a "language game." See especially *Philosophical Investigations*, trans. G.E.M. Anscombe (New York: Macmillan, 1953).

8. For Austin's account, see *How To Do Things with Words* (Cambridge, MA: Harvard University Press, 1962).

9. See *The Nature of Doctrine*.

10. See *Revelation and Theology* (Notre Dame: University of Notre Dame Press, 1985).

11. *Signs of the Times: Deconstruction and the Fall of Paul de Man* (New York: Poseidon, 1992), p. 41. However, notice the modern assumptions implicit in Lehman's comment: language *describes* experience or communicates (expresses?) ideas.

12. Christopher Norris, *Deconstruction: Theory and Practice* (London and New York: Methuen, 1982), p. 22.

13. David Lehman, *Signs of the Times*, pp. 41–42.

14. Quoted without citation by John Passmore, *Recent Philosophers* (La Salle, IL: Open Court, 1985), p. 27.

15. Quoted without citation by Lehman, *Signs of the Times*, p. 129. It strikes me as odd to have two footnotes in a row indicating that an author is named by another but the source is not given. In an account of deconstructionism it would be much more appropriate to cite the text without naming the author!

16. "Reader Response Theories," in *Contemporary Literary Theory: A Christian Appraisal*, eds. Clarence Walhout and Leland Rykern (Grand Rapids: Eerdmans, 1991), p. 125–48.

17. "Literature in the Reader: Affective Stylistics," in Jane P. Tompkins, ed., *Reader-Response Criticism: From Formalism to Post-Structuralism* (Baltimore and London: Johns Hopkins University Press, 1980), pp. 70–100; quotation from pp. 77–78. First published in 1970.

18. "Literature and the Reader," p. 71.

19. In *Is There a Text in This Class?* (Cambridge: Harvard University Press, 1980), pp. 303–321.

20. "Is There a Text in This Class?," p. 305.

21. See *The Aims of Interpretation* (Chicago: University of Chicago Press, 1978).

22. In *The Eclipse of Biblical Narrative* (New Haven: Yale University Press, 1974).

23. See especially the works of Anthony Thiselton: "The Parables as Language-Event: Some Comments on Fuchs's Hermeneutics in the Light of Linguistic Philosophy," *Scottish Journal of Theology* 23 (1970), pp. 437–

68; *The Two Horizons: New Testament Hermeneutics and Philosophical Description* (Grand Rapids: Eerdmans, 1980); and *New Horizons in Hermeneutics: The Theory and Practice of Transforming Biblical Reading* (Grand Rapids: Zondervan, 1992).

24. For a parallel Wittgensteinian critique, see Thiselton, *New Horizons*, pp. 126–28.

25. Thiselton points out that Schleiermacher was the first to raise transcendental questions about the possibility of hermeneutics; ibid., p. 205.

26. "Indeed, constant copying and circulation could almost be described as a prerequisite to final inclusion in the New Testament, for books not found generally useful, and hence not copied and circulated, would not have found their way into the canon." Norman Perrin and Dennis Duling, *The New Testament: An Introduction* (New York: Harcourt Brace Jovanovich, 1982), p. 450.

27. As it is for Fish: "If everyone is continually executing interpretive strategies and in that act constituting texts, intentions, speakers, and authors, how can any one of us know whether or not he is a member of the same interpretive community as any other of us? The answer is that he can't, since any evidence brought forward to support the claim would itself be an interpretation (especially if the "other" were an author long dead). The only "proof" of membership is fellowship, the nod of recognition from someone in the same community, someone who says to you what neither of us could ever prove to a third party: 'we know.'" "Interpreting the Variorum," in *Is There a Text in This Class?*, pp. 164–84; quotation pp. 183–84. First published in 1976.

28. Dennis M. Patterson has made the same point: "What Fish's Account leaves out is the constitutive role of action in the constitution of meaning. Meanings do not spring from interpretations but from action— ways of *using* signs, linguistic and otherwise." "The Poverty of Interpretive Universalism and the Reconstruction of Legal Theory," 72 *Texas Law Review* 1 (November, 1993), pp. 1-56; quotation, p. 49.

29. See *Philosophical Investigations*, op. cit., esp sections 269 and 275.

30. *The Identity of Jesus Christ: The Hermeneutical Bases of Dogmatic Theology* (Philadelphia: Fortress, 1975).

31. "Interpreting the Variorum," p. 182.

32. *Ethics: Systematic Theology*, Volume I (Nashville: Abingdon, 1986); *Doctrine: Systematic Theology*, Volume II (1994); and *Vision: Systematic Theology*, Volume III (projected).

33. *Ethics*, pp. 27–28.

34. Ibid., p. 31.

35. Davie Napier, "Prophet, Prophetism," in *The Interpreter's Diction-ary of the Bible*, ed. George A. Buttrick, 4 vols., (Nashville: Abingdon, 1962), p. 906. Quoted by McClendon, *Ethics*, p. 33.

36. "The Church's Mission to a Postmodern Culture," in Frederic Burnham, ed., *Postmodern Theology: Christian Faith in a Pluralistic World* (New York: Harper and Row, 1989), pp. 37–55.

37. Postmodern (holist) theologians may find it interesting that phi-losophy of language can be shown to have consequences not only for hermeneutics but also for ecclesiology.

38. See Ronald Thiemann's *Revelation and Theology* on the perils of trying to adapt a doctrine of revelation to do service for a foundationalist epistemology.

39. See especially Alasdair MacIntyre, *Whose Justice? Which Rational-ity?* (Notre Dame: University of Notre Dame Press, 1988). In philosophy of science, see the writings of Imre Lakatos, in *The Methodology of Scientific Research Programmes: Philosophical Papers*, Volume 1, eds. John Worrall and Gregory Currie (Cambridge: Cambridge University Press, 1978).

40. This conclusion is consistent with MacIntyre's notion of tradi-tion-based enquiry: a prerequisite for the rational development of a tradition is the formation of people with the moral character that enables them to understand and appropriate the tradition's formative texts. See *Three Rival Versions of Moral Enquiry: Encyclopaedia, Genealogy and Tradi-tion* (Notre Dame: University of Notre Dame Press, 1990).

Chapter 13: Schooling for the Tournament of Narratives: Post-modernism and the Idea of the Christian College
Charles Scriven

1. James William, McClendon, Jr., *Ethics: Systematic Theology*, Vol-ume I (Nashville: Abingdon, 1986), p. 143.

2. Sharon Parks, *The Critical Years* (San Francisco: Harper and Row, 1986), p. 96.

3. Parker Palmer, *To Know As We Are Known* (San Francisco: Harper and Row, 1983), p. 17.

4. James Tunstead Burtchaell, "The Alienation of Christian Higher Education in America: Diagnosis and Prognosis," in Stanley Hauerwas and John Westerhoff, eds., *Schooling Christians* (Grand Rapids: Eerdmans, 1992), p. 154.

5. Ibid., p. 133.

6. Quoted in Jaroslav Pelikan, *The Idea of the University: A Reexami-nation* (New Haven: Yale University Press, 1992), p. 39.

7. Burtchaell, "The Alienation of Christian Higher Education," p. 132.

8. Mortimer Kadesh, *Toward an Ethic of Higher Education* (Stanford: Stanford University Press, 1991), pp. 73, 79.

9. Quoted by Courtney Leatherman in "Southern Baptist College Enters Carefully Into Women's Studies," *The Chronicle of Higher Education*, July 14, 1993, p. A13.

10. Quoted in James C. Livingston, *Modern Christian Thought* (New York: Macmillan, 1971), p. 1.

11. Stephen Toulmin, *Cosmopolis: The Hidden Agenda of Modernity* (New York: Free Press, 1990), p. 70.

12. Ibid., p. 189.

13. See Michael G. Cartwright, "Looking Both Ways: A 'Holy Experiement' in American Higher Education," in Hauerwas and Westerhoff, eds., *Schooling Christians*, p. 209.

14. Jacques Barzun, *Begin Here* (Chicago: University of Chicago Press, 1991), pp. 53, 54.

15. Quoted in Nicholas Wolterstorff, "The Schools We Deserve," in Hauerwas and Westerhoff, eds., *Schooling Christians*, p. 5.

16. Kadesh, *Higher Education*, p. 175, italics his.

17. Ibid., pp. 73, 163.

18. Ibid., pp. 164–69.

19. Ibid., p. 82.

20. Patricia Beattie Jung, "A Call for Reform Schools," in Hauerwas and Westerhof, eds., *Schooling Christians*, p. 117.

21. Wittgenstein, *Philosophical Investigations* 226e.

22. Nancey Murphy, *Theology in the Age of Scientific Reasoning* (Ithaca: Cornell University Press, 1990), p. 201.

23. My summary relies on Murphy, ibid., pp. 56, 57.

24. Quoted in David E. Cooper, "Postmodernism and 'The End of Philosophy'," *Journal of Philosophical Studies*, I (1993), 54.

25. Cartwright, "Looking Both Ways," p. 213.

26. McClendon, *Ethics*, p. 17.

27. Ibid., pp. 71, 72.

28. See Martha Nussbaum, "Aristophanes and Socrates on Learning Practical Wisdom," in Jeffrey Henderson, ed., *Yale Classical Studies* 26 (Cambridge: Cambridge University Press, 1980), pp. 43–97.

29. Alasdair MacIntyre, *Three Rival Versions of Moral Enquiry* (Notre Dame: University of Notre Dame Press, 1990), p. 201.

30. See Murphy, *Theology in the Age of Scientific Reasoning*, pp. 59, 60.

31. Martha Nussbaum, *Love's Knowledge* (New York: Oxford University Press, 1990), pp. 79–81.

32. McClendon, *Ethics*, pp. 42–44.

33. James William McClendon, Jr., *Doctrine: Systematic Theology*, Volume II (Nashville: Abingdon, 1994), p. 32.

34. MacIntyre, *Three Rival Versions of Moral Enquiry*, p. 231.

35. Ibid., p. 201.

36. Murphy, *Theology in the Age of Scientific Reasoning*, p. 196.

37. James William McClendon, Jr., and James M. Smith, *Understanding Religious Convictions* (Notre Dame: University of Notre Dame Press, 1975), p. 182.

38. Toulmin, *Cosmopolis*, p. 201.

Chapter 14: Discipleship: Basing One Life on Another—It's Not What You Know, It's Who You Know
Michael Goldberg

1. Stephen Toulmin, *Cosmopolis: The Hidden Agenda of Modernity* (Chicago: The University of Chicago Press, 1990), pp. 30ff, 104, 174.

2. Ibid., p. 200.

3. Mark R. Schwehn, "The Academic Vocation: 'Specialists without Spirit, Sensualists without Heart'?" *Cross Currents*, Summer 1992, p. 193. Cf. Max Weber, "Science as a Vocation," in *From Max Weber: Essays in Sociology*, trans. and eds. H. H. Gerth and C. Wright Mills (New York: Oxford University Press, 1977), pp. 129–56. See also Max Weber, *The Protestant Work Ethic and the Spirit of Capitalism*, trans. Talcott Parsons (New York: Scribner's, 1958), pp. 106–108.

4. In what follows, I am not arguing against the importance of method or, for that matter, of rational discourse and argument, with which, after all, rabbinic Judaism is replete. However, I am saying that more fundamental and more *authoritative* than any methodological approach for Jews (or Christians) is the person or group of persons who created and transmitted it.

5. James Wm. McClendon, Jr., *Ethics: Systematic Theology*, Volume I (Nashville: Abingdon, 1986), p. 196.

6. "In Favor of a 'Practical Theory of Religion': Montaigne and Pascal," p. 50 above.

7. Toulmin, *Cosmopolis*, p. 34.

8. This insertion may be an unwarranted attempt on my part to harmonize Rava's conflicting, even contradictory, views here. In any case, however, the main point remains the same: it was no small or simple matter deciding under what circumstances a disciple could himself become a rabbi exercising practical judgment affecting the community.

9. The phrase *shimmesh talmidei chachamim* is well-known in rabbinic literature, denoting disciples' attending upon, ministering to, i.e., *serving* their rabbinic teachers. The medieval exegete, Rashi (i.e., **Ra**bbi **Sh**lomo Itzchaki, [1040–1106]) makes a comment here that further illuminates this passage. He explains this text as referring to someone who, though having studied Mishna along with Bible, has failed to study Gemara, the

massive rabbinic commentary on these two. At the time of this text's composition, the Gemara was still an 'oral' document, in the process of being formed out of the 'give and take' between sages. Hence learning Gemara, like serving sages, was something that could only be accomplished by *coming in personal contact with them*. Cf. also Yoma 86a.

10. I say "in principle" and "ideally" to indicate that the rabbis were well aware of the intellectual limitations of some and the moral limitations of others (see the next paragraph in the text). They would also, admittedly, have barred women from the rabbinate. I believe, however, that the logical and moral force of the rabbis' own educational program would have eventually forced them to change women's status in this respect much as the moral logical force of the political program of the Founding Fathers - many of whom were slaveholders - eventually forced America to change the status of blacks from slaves to citizens. Cf. Garry Wills, *Lincoln at Gettysburg* (New York: Simon and Schuster, 1992).

11. Cf., e.g., Eruvin 53a and Avoda Zara 19a-b.

12. See also Makkot 10a.

13. Cf. James Wm. McClendon, Jr., *Doctrine: Systematic Theology*, Volume II (Nashville: Abingdon, 1994), chap. 10.

14. Terrence Tilley, "Institutions, Communities, and Remembering Signs: A Catholic's Response to McClendon, *Doctrine*, Part III," paper delivered at Congress on Systematic Christian Theology in America Today, Fuller Theological Seminary, Pasadena, California, 22 May 1993.

15. Italics mine; for much of what follows here, see *The Encyclopedia of Religion*, s.v. "Yeshivah," by Shaul Stampfer and *Encyclopedia Judaica*, s.v. "Academies in Babylonia and Ere[t]z Yisrael," by Moshe Beer.

16. At times, Helmreich's own religious commitment, like those of another Orthodox Jewish sociologist, Samuel Heilman (see infra), tend to make him not so much a sympathetic observer as a romantic apologist. Nevertheless, Helmreich's observations, like Heilman's, are, in broad outline, reliable.

I am very grateful to Rabbi Marc Wilson for his invaluable insights on the modern Orthodox yeshiva based on his personal experience. For my experiential insights on a contemporary Conservative yeshiva, see Section IV, below.

17. William B. Helmreich, *The World of the Yeshiva: An Intimate Portrait of Orthodox Jewry* (New York: Free Press, 1982), p. xii.

18. Ibid., p. 7.

19. Ibid., p. 71. In maintaining this practice, the institution of the modern yeshiva continues a pattern of discipleship established long ago. Cf., e.g., Eruvin 53a: "The Judeans who learned from one master retained their learning, but the Galileans who did not learn from one master did not retain their learning."

20. Cf. Samuel Heilman, *Defenders of the Faith: Inside Ultra-Orthodox Jewry* (New York: Schocken, 1992), p. 260.

21. Helmreich, *The World of the Yeshiva*, p. 71.

22. Ta'anit 7a.

23. Heilman, *Defenders of the Faith*, p. 247.

24. Toulmin, *Cosmopolis*, p. 201.

25. Schwehn, "The Academic Vocation," p. 192.

26. Max Weber, *Economy and Society: Essays in Sociology*, eds. and trans. Guenther Roth and Claus Wittich (New York: Bedminster, 1967), p. 548, quoted in Schwehn, p. 191; italics mine.

27. Schwehn, "The Academic Vocation," p. 195.

28. Rashi's classic commentary on the Talmud still stands as the primary text studied alongside of the text of the Gemara itself.

29. My steadfast friend to this day, Rabbi Sheldon Pennes.

30. Of course, even sacred religious texts like the Talmud—and perhaps especially sacred texts—can be taught and learned like textbooks. Those who study and learn that way need to remember that there is always a difference between a recipe for a cake and the cake itself.

31. Stanley Hauerwas, "Reading McClendon Takes Practice: Lessons in the Craft of Theology," paper presented at a Congress on Systematic Christian Theology in America Today, Fuller Theological Seminary, Pasadena, California, 21 May 1993.